D0719445

Presented to:

my beloved Jane

From:

Kay with love and gratitude
Philemon 4-7

September 6, 2001

Precious One,

Do You Know....
God Loves You?

KAY ARTHUR

COUNTRYMAN ®

PREFACE

So many times when life becomes difficult, when we struggle, hurt or are tempted, or when we temporarily veer from that straight narrow road God has put us on, we need to know, to be reassured just how much God loves us, how precious we are to God.

And that, Beloved, is why the heavenly Father in His sovereignty has put this book into your hands.

He wants you to know that you are loved with an everlasting love. No matter what is transpiring in your life, you are not alone. Not abandoned. Not forsaken. He is there and He is God. He has not left His throne. Whatever your situation, you can rest assured that it is not more than you can bear. Your Father has provided His way of escape—and that is through His unchangeable precepts and promises.

It is my prayer, Beloved, that God will use this book in your life, in the lives of those you love and care about and in the lives of those who for whatever reason need a touch from God. How I pray that these unchanging truths from God's infallible Word will draw you close to His all-sufficient breast and there each one will be comforted with the comfort, which God alone can give.

KAY ARTHUR

AND THE ANGEL
OF THE LORD SAID,

"For you are [precious;]
so give heed to the message and gain understanding.

"Oh man of [preciousness,] do not be afraid.
Peace be with you; take courage and be courageous!"

Now as soon as he spoke to me, I received strength and said,
"May my lord speak, for you have strengthened me."

DANIEL 9:23, 10:19

6

PRECIOUS

Do you know, do you really know how very much God loves you? It's so interesting that the first time the word *love* is used in the Bible it is connected with sacrifice—the sacrifice of a son by a father. And in that account lays a picture of the breadth and length and height and depth of God's unfathomable love—the love He holds for you, right where you are, wherever you are.

Come, Beloved of God, and explore the passage with me. Let's see how the Creator of the heavens and the earth and all that it contains introduces the subject of love into His book, the Holy Bible.

In the first twenty-one chapters of Genesis, we are introduced to our Creator, our Covenant God—a God who is grieved to the heart by the rebellion, the independence, the sinfulness of those He created in His image. We stand amazed, dumb-

struck in wonderment that the One who brought the world into existence by the very power of His Word and who has not only the ability but the right to destroy those who have marred His image would be constrained by His very

nature that makes Him God.

In Genesis 22, God speaks to Abraham, the one with whom He made a covenant promising Him that he would be the father of many nations and that in him all the nations of the earth would be blessed.

"Take now your son, your only son, whom you love, Isaac, and go to the land of Moriah; and offer him there as a burnt offering on one of the mountains of which I will tell you."

Isaac, in God's eyes was Abraham's only son—the son of God's covenant promise, the progenitor, the line through which the Son of God would some-day come—born from the womb of Mary, a daughter of the great Patriarch, Abraham and the great King, David. Isaac was the fulfillment of a twenty-five-year old promise, born miraculously from an impotent man of one hun-dred and the dead womb of Sarah, his ninety-year old wife. Now he is to be put to death? His only son? His son whom he loves more than life itself? His son of covenant?

Why? Why?!? Because from the very beginning God wanted us to have a picture of the great love with which He has loved us. A love that would sacrifice His only begotten Son for us when we were sinners, helpless, without hope— enemies of God.

Think about it, Beloved . . . ask God to give you a glimpse of "the breadth and length and height and depth and to know the love of Christ which surpasses knowledge, that you may be filled up to all the fullness of God" (Ephesians 3:18–19).

Precious ONE,

Come back with me to Abraham as he ascends the mount of Moriah with his son Isaac. There is yet more for us to learn about the love of God in this divinely designed portrait of love. Isaac was to be a burnt offering. A burnt offering, as later explained in the book of Leviticus, is a voluntary offering . . . but one that makes atonement, one that covers over, that pacifies the holiness of God. The sacrifice was to be an offering from the flock, the herd—male and without defect.

Now, skip over the millenniums and come to about the year A. D. 29, to the land of Moriah, to the city of Jerusalem and look at the Lamb of God nailed on Calvary's tree. His name is Jesus, which means God our Savior. A male taken from among mankind—made for a little while lower than the angels, made flesh and blood yet born of a virgin, born of God's seed, born without sin that He might taste death for every man and that through death He might render powerless him who had the power of death, that is, the devil (Hebrews 2:9, 14).

This is the One "foreknown before the foundation of the world, but [who] has appeared in these last times for the sake of you." This is the One who will redeem you from sin, from death, from the lake of fire where the worm dies not and the fire is not quenched. You will not be redeemed "with perishable things like silver or gold from your futile way of life . . . but with precious blood, as of a lamb unblemished and spotless, the blood of Christ" (1 Peter 1:20, 18, 19).

Isaac, Abraham's only son whom he loved, was to be a burnt offering to God—a priceless ancient portrait of the great love with which God has loved you. Now, are you beginning to understand why I call you precious?

PRECIOUS

Stand with me, gaze once again at this magnificent portrait of love for I don't want to miss a single holy detail.

Abraham rose early in the morning of the next day, saddled his donkey, took two of his young men with him and his son, Isaac. Abraham, himself, split the wood for  his son, the burnt offering and went to the place which God had told him. He arrived on the third day. Turning to the two young men, he said, "Stay here with the donkey and I and the lad will go yonder ; and we will worship and return to you."

You didn't miss Abraham's words did you, Beloved? "We will go—worship—return." Both would go. Both would worship. Both would return! What Abraham and Isaac were about to do was an act of worship. To worship someone is to look at that individual's worth and honor that person accordingly. God had given the command—offer your son, your only son whom you love, as a burnt offering. God was God. God was to be obeyed.

And God would be obeyed without question, without argument. There is no record here of anything but submission to the will of God. God was Abraham's covenant God—a God who would never break a covenant, a solemn binding agreement made by passing through pieces of flesh. And this is what God alone had done on the day He made a covenant with Abraham (Genesis 15).

God would be obeyed. Yet Abraham was convinced that somehow he and Isaac would return. If he put Isaac to death as God commanded then God would simply have to raise Isaac from the dead because God had made a promise. He had told

Abraham, "Sarah your wife shall bear you a son, and you shall call his name Isaac; and I will establish my covenant with him for an everlasting covenant for his descendants after him" (Genesis 17:19).

What faith! What trust! What confidence! This is true worship—to worship God in spirit and in truth (John 4:23).

But could God be trusted? Would you have trusted Him in such circumstances?

Precious ONE,

I left you with the question, "Can God be trusted?" What was your answer? Do you really believe that we can trust Him totally, fully, completely—without reservation, without hesitation? I think your answer would depend on how secure you are in His love and in His character.

Abraham seems to have been totally secure in both—for without question or hesitation he climbed that mountain designated by God to the place of sacrifice.

Love obeyed. Faith trusted in what it could not see—they both would return.

Now, take a closer look at this picture for there is so much more to be seen.

Who carried the wood for the altar and the offering? "And Abraham took the wood of the burnt offering and laid it on Isaac his son, and he took in his hand the fire and the knife. So the two of them on the shoulders of Jesus Christ? Roman soldiers or God? It was God, Beloved. The cross was God's invention. The Roman soldiers and the Jews were but His instruments. And who would take the life of Jesus? Only God.

Before there were ever more than two human beings on the face of the earth, when God turned to the Serpent of Old, the devil, Satan, in the Garden of Eden, He uttered the first prophecy—the first promise of the gospel: the death of His Son that would triumph over the Serpent's power. Listen to His words:

And the Lord God said to the serpent . . . "And I will

walked on together" (Genesis 22:6).

The son would carry the wood, the father would carry the instruments of death.

And what of Calvary? Who was it that laid the cross

put enmity between
you and the woman,
and between your
seed and her seed;
He shall bruise
you on the head
and you shall
bruise him on
the heel."

Do you know that
Crucifixion is the only form
of death that bruises the
heel? From the very beginning God knew how His Son
would die. The wood of a
cross would be laid on his
shoulders, the wood to
which He would be nailed in
the process of crucifixion.
"And it was the third hour
when they crucified Him."
"There they crucified Him,
and with Him two other
men, one on either side, and
Jesus in between."

"I am poured out like
water, and all my bones are
out of joint; My
heart is like wax; it is
melted within me. My
strength is dried up like a
potsherd, and my tongue
cleaves to my jaws; and You
lay me in the dust of death.
For dogs have surrounded
me; a band of evildoers has
encompassed me; they
pierced my hands and my
feet. I can count all my
bones. They look, they stare
at me; they divide my gar-
ments among them, and for
my clothing they cast lots"
(Mark 15:25, John 19:18,

Psalm 22:14–18).

The serpent would bruise the Christ, the promised One, the seed of the woman, on the heel—but it would not be a mortal wound! Remember, Abraham believed Isaac would be raised from the dead; he would return with Abraham to the two men waiting at the foot of the mount. But how?

PRECIOUS *One,*

You can know with an absolute certainty that God loves you because He is a covenant keeping God. When you believe in Jesus Christ then you enter into all the promises of the New Covenant. This is the covenant promised in Jeremiah 31:31–34 but not inaugurated by Jesus Christ until the night in which He was betrayed. The night where in the Upper Room, He took the bread and broke it, gave it to the disciples, and said, "Take eat; this is My body. And when He had taken a cup and given thanks, He gave it to them, saying, 'Drink from it, all of you; for this is my blood of the covenant, which is poured out for many for forgiveness of sins.'"

This is the covenant that gives you, me, every believer "the promise of Spirit through faith" (Galatians 3:14).

Abraham trusted God to be true to His covenant…and so did Isaac. Isaac was not a little boy; rather he was in the strength of new manhood. He could have run, fought his father— but he didn't. It was not a matter of his will—but of his father's, and to that Isaac would submit. Isaac would be obedient unto death—death on an altar. Listen carefully to their conversation and you will see it all played out before your eyes.

Isaac spoke to Abraham his father and said, "My father!" And he said, "Here I am, my son." And he said, "Behold, the fire and the wood, but where is the lamb for the burnt offering?"

And Abraham said, "God will provide for Himself the lamb for the burnt offering, my son." So the two of them walked on together.

Then they came to the place of which God had told him; and Abraham built the altar there, and arranged the wood, and bound his son Isaac, and laid him on the altar on top of the wood (Genesis 22:7–9).

Isaac utters not a word. He allows himself

to be bound by his father and then raised in his arms and laid upon the altar. Think about it, Beloved. Picture it in your mind's eye. Abraham builds the altar, arranges the wood—and then binds his son. And His son lets him because he believes his father. Isaac trusts Abraham. One can only imagine the pain of it all. Even knowing of the promise it could not have been easy for either father or son. In fact it must have been hell—tearing at their gut—storming their eyes. But they did what God said to do—without question.

That is faith—and God saw it and honored it.

O'Beloved, we are going to talk about difficult situations— trials—testings— temptations that would cause you to doubt God's love and forgiveness, where He is, if He cares, and why, if He is God, that He allows such things. When you do— remember the faith of this father and son.

PRECIOUS

Do you realize that without faith, you cannot please God? When you and I don't believe God then we are saying that He is untrustworthy—or unable to do what He promised—or unwilling to keep His promises. When we refuse to believe we show disrespect for Him. There is no fear of God before our eyes—no respect or trust.

Genesis 22:1 tells us that God was testing Abraham when He told him to offer up Isaac as a burnt offering. Would Abraham walk in obedience, would He trust God to be God—would he fear God? Let's continue with our story.

When "Abraham stretched out his hand, and took the knife to slay his son" God saw the genuineness of Abraham's faith. Hebrews eleven, that great chapter on faith, tells us that

"by faith, Abraham, when he was tested, offered up Isaac, and he who had received the promises was offering up his only begotten son; it was he to whom it was said, 'in Isaac your descendants [seed] shall be called.' He considered that God is able to raise men even from the dead, from which he also received him back as a type [figuratively speaking]" (Hebrews 11:17–19).

Abraham believed God. He so believed God that nothing—even the love and loss of his son—would keep  him from walking in faith's obedience. In his heart of hearts Abraham was convinced that God would raise Isaac from the dead. God had to because of the covenant He had made and affirmed twenty-four years earlier at the announcement of Isaac's long awaited birth!

Seeing Abraham's faith, "the angel of the LORD called to him from heaven, and said, 'Abraham, Abraham!'

And he said, 'Here I am.'

And he said, "Do not stretch out your hand against the lad, and do nothing to him; for now I know that you fear God, since you have not withheld your son, your only son, from Me.'"

Then Abraham raised his eyes and looked, and behold, behind him a ram caught in the thicket by his horns; and Abraham went and took the ram, and offered him up for a burnt offering in the place of his son.

And Abraham called the name of that place The LORD Will Provide, as it is said to this day, 'In the mount of the LORD it will be provided'" (Genesis 22:11–14).

And what is the substance we see in shadow form in this ancient portrait of the love of God? It is the fulfillment of Abraham's promise to his son when Isaac asked where the sacrifice was. Abraham told Isaac that God would provide—Himself—the sacrifice.

The substitute for you, me, mankind would not be a ram as it was for Isaac; rather it would be the very Son of God, Jesus Christ, provided for us on the mount of the Lord. Jesus our Jehovah Jireh, would be the One through whose death and resurrection God would provide all our needs according to His riches in glory. In the mount of the Lord it would be seen—the testimony of God's inexplicable love for mankind as God made Jesus who knew no sin to be sin for us so that you and I could have His righteousness (2 Corinthians 5:21) and thereby live with God forever. For without righteousness no man shall see God.

Now will you believe, Precious One, that God loves you and whatever happens you can trust Him?

Precious ONE,

What then shall we say to the things we have learned . . . or simply reviewed as we looked at the first mention of the word love in the Bible?

Do you realize that if God is for you, Precious One, who can really be against you?

"He who did not spare His own Son, but delivered Him over for us all, how will He not also with Him freely give us all things? Who will bring a charge against God's elect? God is the one who justifies; who is the one who condemns? Christ Jesus is He who died, yes, rather who was raised, who is at the right hand of God, who also intercedes for us.

Who will separate us from the love of Christ? Will tribulation, or distress, or persecution, or famine, or nakedness, or peril, or sword?

Just as it is written, 'For Your sake we are being put to death all day long; we were considered as sheep to be slaughtered.'

But in all these things we overwhelmingly con-quer through Him who loved us.

For I am convinced that neither death, nor life, nor angels, nor principalities, nor things present, nor things to come, nor powers, nor height, nor depth, nor any other created thing, shall be able to separate us from the love of God, which is in Christ Jesus our Lord" (Romans 8:32–39).

Are you convinced?

PRECIOUS *One,*

Now can you understand that what concerns you is of the utmost concern to God? It matters not how great or how small the problem or need. If you belong to the Lord Jesus Christ, every need, every trial, every temptation that touches you touches God, because you are His child. Bone of His bone, flesh of His flesh. You are part of a family, a community. Jesus is not only your Savior, your Lord, your elder brother—He is the head of the body, the family of believers called the church. Isaiah tells us that Jesus is your "Wonderful Counselor, Mighty God, Eternal Father, Prince of Peace" and the government of your life rests on His shoulders (Isaiah 9:6).

This is why God tells you, His child, to quit struggling, to stop being anxious. Instead you are to humble yourself by casting every single care, every last thing that makes you anxious, worried, or upset upon Him (1 Peter 5:7). You belong to Jesus, and Jesus belongs to you. He is your shepherd. You are His sheep. God uses this metaphor for several reasons, but one of them is because of the nature of sheep. Sheep are helpless animals whose welfare depends on the care given them by their shepherd. Sheep are not burden-bearing animals. So Precious One, join me as we learn to cast all our cares on Him, knowing that what concerns you and me is of the utmost concern to Him.

Why don't you simply take a moment now to tell the Lord that you want to roll the weight off your shoulders onto His. Then, Beloved, in your mind's eye picture Him reaching down and lifting that burden off your shoulders onto His. Did you see Him smile because of your simple act of trust?

Precious ONE,

Remember the words at the beginning of this book? Let me write them out for you again.

"For you are [precious;] so give heed to the message and gain understanding....

"Oh man of [preciousness,] do not be afraid.

Peace be with you; take courage and be courageous!"

Now as soon as he spoke to me, I received strength and said, "May my lord speak, for you have strengthened me" (Daniel 9:23; 10:19).

How I want you to understand that as God called Daniel "precious," a man of high esteem, that you, too, are precious to God. In His eyes, your life has worth, value, purpose.

When you forget how precious you are to your Father God, when you think that God doesn't care or that He won't or can't care because of something you've done or because of who you are, then dear one, you are losing a battle with the enemy of your soul.

This is why it is critical

that you not only under- stand but also believe what Jesus tells us in John 8:44  about the devil. Jesus tells us in no uncertain words that Satan is a liar and has been a murderer from the begin- ning. He is our archenemy who does not abide in the truth. Rather he is the father of lies and you must not believe him.

If you are afraid to commit yourself to God, to roll your burden over to His shoulders and leave it there, as I urged you earlier, then you need to get into the Word of God, the Bible, so you have a proper under- standing of God, of His character and of His sover- eignty. Then, Beloved, you will know the freedom, the power that comes from knowing and believing the truth.

God is able to care for you right down to the smallest need, the minutest detail because He is God and there is none, absolutely none greater than Him.

May I suggest, Beloved, that you simply put this book down, close your eyes, shut out everything around you and simply tell God that you want truth—nothing more, nothing less. Then ask Him to expose every lie that you have embraced or are in danger of believing.

Ask and He will answer because you are precious to Him and what concerns you is of the utmost concern to Him.

Precious ONE,

Did you know that John 15:16 says you have been chosen by God. Peter writes in his first epistle that you are part of a chosen race, a royal priesthood, a holy nation, a people for God's own possession.

As you stand firm in God's grace—no matter the trial, no matter the battle, no matter the suffering—

glory will follow (1 Peter 5:10–12). How do I know? I know because God's Word says so, and God does not lie! He cannot lie—it goes against His nature. And if, my friend, you are wondering if you can believe this, then remember who the liar is! It is the devil (John 8:44), and his ambition is to devour you (1 Peter 5:8–9).

The only way to have victory over the enemy is by believing and obeying God no matter what you think, no matter how you feel. Victory is for those who "resist the devil, firm in their faith." You may

ture in Christ Jesus and that old things passed away and all things became new (2 Corinthians 5:17).

So resist the lies and condemnation of the evil one, Beloved! God's grace is there. Stand firm in it! Victory is assured for 1 John 5:4 tells us whoever is born of God overcomes the world!

resist him once and he may flee instantly, or you may have to resist him a hundred times in a hundred seconds, a hundred minutes. I know. I've had to do it when I battled memories of the immoral lifestyle that was mine before I became God's child.

But not any more! My shield of faith eventually quenched all the firey darts of the enemy for I continued to believe my God— that my sins are forgiven, that I became a new crea-

Ask God to expose the lies that you have embraced so that you can replace them with the truths of God's Word . . . truths that will set you free.

PRECIOUS *One,*

I want to say this as gently as possible because it is something you may want to think about. If deep down you are dissatisfied with life in general or maybe even downright miserable, maybe it's because your focus is on you rather than on God.

Misery comes when we are the focus of our lives. However, when God is the focus rather than self, everything else takes second place to His will for our lives. In essence, nothing else really matters. God is the only One we have to please. He is the only One to whom we are truly and rightly answerable. When we are set free from the bondage of pleasing man—of currying man's favor and man's approval—man will not be able to make us miserable or dissatisfied, for only what pleases God will please us.

How I love Paul's words in Galatians 1:10. They are so freeing. In fact you may want to memorize them. This can be done easily by simply writing them on a card and reading them aloud three times every morning, afternoon, and evening. Listen, Beloved. Believe and be liberated from having to have the approbation of man.

"For am I now seeking the favor of men, or of God? Or am I striving to please men? If I were still trying to please men, I would not be a bond-servant of Christ."

Precious ONE,

Have you ever stopped to consider: What is my worth to God? Why was I born? What is the purpose of my existence?

As I sat in my big, old chair in our parlor where I have my quiet time, I was thinking of the magnificence and power of our Father in creating the world and in forming man from the dust of the earth. Then I thought of Ephesians 1:4–5: "He chose us in Him before the foundation of the world. In love He predestined us to adoption, . . . through Jesus Christ to Himself, according to the kind intention of His will!"

Do you know how absolutely precious you are to God? Do you realize the significance of your life? It has a purpose! A specific purpose! You are not an accident. You are planned! You are not useless. You are not worthless. You are not unredeemable. Your worth and your purpose in life do not depend on who you are, on what you have done, or on what has been done to you. It does not depend on where you have been, even if you have been to the very precipice of hell. Your worth and purpose depend on God and God alone—His will, His calling, His choosing, His love!

If this is hard to grasp, Precious One, then take a moment and ask God to root these truths deep in the soil of your heart, to anchor them in your mind. Read Psalm 139 and mark every occurrence of "I, me, my." Then knowing that this Psalm was written for you, bask in what you learn about you . . . and about God.

PRECIOUS *One,*

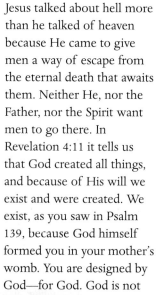

Let's take a few moments and consider how the death, burial, and resurrection of Jesus Christ substantiates the value God puts upon you—upon mankind in general.

All mankind was born in sin. Sin entered into the world through Adam and consequently as Romans 5:12 tells us it was passed to all men, therefore all are condemned to die. "The wages of sin is death." " The soul that sins surely dies." The death that God speaks of is not only physical death, it is spiritual death—hell and eventually the Lake of Fire.

But this is not what God wants! In fact,

Jesus talked about hell more than he talked of heaven because He came to give men a way of escape from the eternal death that awaits them. Neither He, nor the Father, nor the Spirit want men to go there. In Revelation 4:11 it tells us that God created all things, and because of His will we exist and were created. We exist, as you saw in Psalm 139, because God himself formed you in your mother's womb. You are designed by God—for God. God is not willing that any should perish and that, Beloved, is why He caused His Son to be born of a

virgin and then thirty three years later crucified Him on a cross. Then three days later God raised Him from the dead, never to die again.

Catch the love of God: "But God, being rich in mercy, because of His great love with which He loved us, even when we were dead in our transgressions, made us alive together with Christ (by grace you have been saved) and raised us up with Him, and seated us with Him in the heavenly places in Christ Jesus so that in the ages to come He might show the surpassing riches of His grace in kindness toward us in Christ Jesus" (Ephesians 2:4–7).

God so loved the world, He so loved you, Precious One, "that He gave His only begotten Son so that whoever believes in Him would not perish but have eternal life" (John 3:16).

God provided a way for us, for all mankind to miss hell, to escape "eternal punishment," the "eternal fire which has been prepared for the devil and his angels" (Matthew 25:46, 41).

We escape by believing in Jesus Christ. By believing that Jesus is the Christ (the Messiah, the One promised by God), the Son of God, One with the Father, the Way, the Truth, the Life, the only means by which a person can pass from death to life and receive absolute forgiveness of sins.

The belief that God talks about is not a mere intellectual exercise, rather it includes a commitment of one's self to that belief, a trust that once embraced impacts the life of the believer.

However, if a man or woman refuses to believe, then according to God's Word, that person will experience the wrath of God. Listen with a hearing heart to Jesus' words recorded for us at the end of the third chapter of John: "He who believes in the Son has eternal life, but he who does not obey [or believe] the Son shall not see life, but the wrath of God abides on him" (John 3:36).

I have waited to ask you this question, but now, out of love, I must ask it. Have you believed, Beloved? Really believed? If you haven't, then according to His Word God's wrath is abiding on you—even though He loved you enough to crucify His Son for you.

God has done all that He will, all that He can to secure your future—now, from the human perspective, you must believe. Let me ask again, have you believed, Beloved? And if not, will you? Will you do it now? Will you tell God the Father that you will receive His Son as your Lord, your God, your Savior? John 1:12 tells us that "as many as received Him, to them He gave the right to become children of God, even to those who believe in His name."

If you will believe, receive Jesus Christ who was with God from the beginning and who is God (John 1:1), you can know that instantly you will pass from death to life, from the power of Satan to the kingdom of God, and you will receive forgiveness of sins (Acts 26:18; Colossians 1:13-14; Ephesians 2:5). You will become His child, you will belong to His forever family.

So, Precious One, why don't you simply pause where you are and talk to God aloud. Either thank Him for already saving you or tell Him that you want to be saved—that you will believe. Or if neither of these options suits you, then tell God why you don't want to receive Jesus Christ now. It will be good to verbalize it.

Precious ONE,

Have you ever opened a Christmas present, taken out the gift, and unknowingly missed part of it—the part wrapped carefully in tissue paper, hidden in the corner of the box? The box is thrown away and, with it, part of the gift.

What a sense of loss it brings both to the receiver and to the giver when the giver asks about it and discovers his treasured gift was inadvertently discarded.

Because of this, as we talk of salvation, I want to make sure you understand what is tucked in with that priceless gift. Jesus was not born simply to pay for your sins. He was born to save you from sin, from trans-gressing, from going over the line of what is right—day by day, moment by moment, temptation by temptation.

Jesus came to override your natural desire, to break the habits of a lifetime, to put the old you, "the old man," the "old self" to death and to make you into a new person. He came to set you free, to grant you victory.

Tucked into the gift of salvation through believing in the Lord Jesus Christ is not only the forgiveness of all your sins, but the power, the ability, to be saved from the compulsion of doing what you know you shouldn't do! That's why the angel said to Joseph, "You shall call His name Jesus, for He will save His people from their sins" (Matthew 1:21).

PRECIOUS

Have you ever seriously read or studied the book of Romans? If not you ought to because it is the constitution of our faith. In chapters 1–3:20 God shows us that both Jews and Gentiles "are all under sin" (3:9). Then in chapters 3:21–5 He tells us how we are justified only through faith, not by the Law or by circumcision. In Romans 5 after explaining that whereas we became sinners through the transgression of one man, Adam, we are now made righteous through "the obedience of the One"—the last Adam so to speak— the Lord Jesus Christ. Having dealt with our salvation, God then deals with our sanctification as He explains in Romans 6 why it

is impossible for a believer to continue in habitual sin.

This is one of those treasures tucked in the package of salvation that I don't want you to miss. A believer is no longer able to continue to habitually, continually sin, as he or she once did before believing in Jesus Christ. Why? Because when we were baptized ("identified," "united with" is what this transliterated word *baptized* means) we were united into Jesus' death and

buried
with Him
"though baptism
into death, in
order that as Christ
was raised from the dead

through the glory of the Father, so we too might walk in newness of life" (Romans 6:4).

Did you see that—newness of life! Newness of life because "our old self [man] was crucified with Him, that our body of sin [our body as an instrument of sin] might be done away with, that we should no longer be slaves to sin; for he who has died is freed from sin" (Romans 6:6–7).

Rejoice, Precious One, rejoice! The love of God has brought to you the power of God, which sets you free from slavery to sin, and from the power of sin. You no longer have to sin— you can refuse sin's desire to "reign in your mortal body that you should obey its lusts." You can choose to present the members of your body "as instruments of righteousness to God. For sin shall not be master over you, for you are not under law, but under grace" (Romans 6:12–14).

O, Freed One, loved and saved by God, why don't you spend some time in prayer. What I have written is heavy stuff—heavy but essential, worth its spiritual weight in gold. Ask God to make it clear to you, very clear. Then take every member of your body, starting at the top of your head with your mind, your eyes, ears, mouth . . . and yield them to God one by one until you come right down to your toes.

As you do, if any member seems enslaved to a particular sin—such as your mind thinking immoral thoughts or caught in pornography, first thank God that you have been freed through the death of your "old man" to those thoughts—to that sin whatever it is. Then aloud renounce that sin and all that goes with it, including the lies and strongholds of the enemy. Then ask God to fill every cell of your mind with the Holy Spirit.

He will, Precious One—He will. Nothing would please Him more because He sees your heart, your desire to be all that you should be, to walk in the power of His Spirit.

PRECIOUS *One,*

If you ever wonder how you can know with an absolute certainty that you have truly been born again, born from above, and therefore possess eternal life, then the short epistle of First John is the book for you to read and mark.

The New Inductive Study Bible has excellent instructions for studying and marking this book (as it does for all sixty-six books). It also has a chart where after marking every occurrence of the word "know" you can list what you know and how you know it.

One of the "know's"

you mark would tell you that one reason was "in order that you might know that you have eternal life." In 1 John 3:5, John assures us that Jesus Christ appeared "in order to take away sins; and in Him there is no sin. No one who abides in Him sins; no one who sins has seen Him or knows Him" (1 John 3:5–6).

As you read these verses it's really helpful to know the Greek tenses used for the verb "sins" in the last sentence. Sins is in the present tense, a tense that indicates continuous or habitual action. When you understand this, it is obvious that God is not saying that a Christian does not commit singular acts of sin. Rather He is saying that the Christian does not sin continuously as he did before he was saved.

First John 2:1–2 says " if anyone sins [aorist tense, which indicates an action; however not continuous] we have an Advocate with the Father, Jesus Christ the righteous;" Who is "the propitiation [the satisfactory payment] for our sins and not for ours only but also for those of the whole world." In other words we see from these verses that Christians will sin but it won't be the habitual practice of their lives.

Why can't a true believer habitually sin? Because " His seed (God's son Jesus Christ) abides in him (or her, God is speaking generically of believers regardless of sex), and he cannot sin (present tense, therefore habitually) because he is born of God."

Now then, listen to the bottom line of it all: "By this the children of God and the children of the devil are obvious; anyone who does not practice [once again present tense] righteousness is not of God, nor the one who does not love [present tense] his brother" (1 John 3:10).

Isn't it awesome, Precious One, to delve into the Word of God and see truth?

That is the only reason I write any book; to introduce you, my beloved reader, to truth—truth that dispels darkness, counteracts lies, and liberates us.

The love of God not only paid for your past sins, present sins, and future sins—through the death, burial and resurrection of God's Son—it liberated you from sin's power the moment you embraced God's gift of love in faith. This, Beloved, is one of the ways you know with an absolute certainty that you are His child forever.

Precious ONE,

Ephesians is such a rich treasure for it teaches us what it means to be "in Christ"—to belong to Him. It begins with a eulogy of praise to God because He has "blessed us with every spiritual blessing in the heavenly places in Christ" (Ephesians 1:3).

Writing under the inspiration of the Holy Spirit, Paul then goes on to tell us in verse four that God chose us in Christ "before the foundation of the world so that we would be holy and

without blame." Without blame! Without blame literally means without any spots or blemishes. It's a phrase used to describe the requirements placed on any animals, which were to be sacrificed to God. Isn't is awesome, Beloved to realize that He saved you so He could take away your shame— everything that marred and disfigured you whether you did it to yourself or others did it to you!

Now God's goal is for

Sanctification is a process. A process that begins the minute you and I believe and consequently receive the gift of the Holy Spirit. Ephesians 1:13–14 tells us, "In Him, you also, after listening to the message of truth, the gospel of your salvation—having also believed, you were sealed in Him with the Holy Spirit of promise, who is given as a pledge of our inheritance, with a view to the redemption of God's own possession, to the praise of His glory."

you to live a life totally set apart for Himself. That is holiness—or what the Bible sometimes calls "sanctification." When God tells us to "be holy even as I am holy", it involves a choice. The choice in every situation to be what He would have you be, to you do what He would have you do.

Does that sound impossible? Improbable maybe, but not impossible. Yet as probable as you choose to make it.

The Holy Spirit is the sanctifier.

And how does sanctification happen?

It happens day by day,

moment by moment, incident by incident, choice by choice. In every situation of life you have a choice—a choice to believe God and to walk in His ways under the power of the Spirit or to yield to your flesh and allow the world to squeeze you into its mold.

But why would a believer ever choose to yield to the flesh? Why would we ever allow the world to squeeze us into its mold? You know, don't you! Because, although we now belong to God and are indwelt by the Spirit of God (Eph. 1:14; 2 Cor. 6:19–20), we still live in a body of flesh—and the flesh likes to have its way. "The flesh sets its desire against the Spirit and the Spirit against the flesh; for these are in opposition to one another, so that you may not do the things that you please" (Galatians 5:17).

We're also tempted to yield to the flesh

because the pressure of the world is so strong.

So where does that leave us, Beloved? It leaves us in the position of learning a whole new lifestyle, adopting a whole new worldview—being transformed by the renewing of

our minds so that we can put to the test "what the will of God is—that which is good and acceptable (well pleasing) and perfect."

And why would you and I want this? Accept this? Choose this? Because, Precious One, we fear our God. By that I mean, we are to respect Him, trust Him, and honor Him for Who He is.

Someday we are going to stand before Him at the judgment seat of Christ and give an answer for the deeds done in these bodies whether they be good or bad. "Therefore also we have as our ambition . . . to be pleasing to Him" (2 Corinthians 5:9–10).

Also if we are thinking people we will realize that its because we know we're loved by our Father God who desires our highest good. The love of Christ will constrain us—control us (2 Corinthians 5:14).

PRECIOUS One,

More than anything else when I was growing up, I wanted to be accepted. Accepted by my peers. I wanted to be loved. I wanted to be admired. But if I couldn't have the admiration—at least I wanted acceptance. When you tallied up the schools I went to as I grew up they almost added up to the number of years I was in school. We moved a lot—and breaking into a new neighborhood, a new class where the kids had their old friends, was not easy.

When I came to know Jesus Christ at the age of twenty-nine,

you cannot imagine the joy I felt when I picked up a Bible in the King James version and saw verses five and six of Ephesians one. As I write them out for you, you need to realize that Ephesians one is practically one long sentence in the original Greek so I am jumping into the midst of this awesome eulogy that gives Paul no time to stop and put in a period. Listen with your eyes and your heart, Beloved: . . . "in love, having predestined us to adoption as sons by Jesus Christ to Himself, according to the good pleasure of His will to the praise of the glory of His grace by which He made us accepted in the Beloved."

Predestine is the word *proorizo* in the Greek which means to mark out beforehand. Which takes us to the

beginning of the eulogy of Ephesians one where we learn that God chose us in Christ Jesus before the foundation of the world. Incredible isn't it? Incomprehensible, except by faith! You were chosen by

God. I was chosen by God. Every child of God was chosen by God. Before the foundation of the world! Talk about being loved! Being special! We were not only chosen, we were marked out beforehand for adoption into the very family of God! And all because it was the good pleasure of His will! Stop and just think about that for a moment or two. You and I are His because that is what God wanted, what brought Him pleasure.

God made me what I always wanted to be—accepted! But listen to this: accepted where? Accepted in the one and only place acceptance counts and lasts for eternity—in Jesus Christ!

People may reject you and me—but God never will once we believe and receive Jesus Christ! Precious One, you are accepted in the Beloved.

Precious ONE,

Do you know that you are God's workmanship? Whether raised in your natural family or adopted, born legitimate or illegitimate— God formed you in your mother's womb. Moment by moment He breathes into you the breath of life so that you may live all the days He has numbered before there was yet one of them. No person can shorten them or lengthen them. Revelation one tells us Jesus has the keys to hell and death and no one can open what He shuts or shut what He opens. You are in God's hands!

The Almighty God has gifted you and placed you in His body just as He desired. You are His "according to the kind attention of His will," "according to the riches of His grace," "according to His kind intention which He purposed in Him" (Ephesians 1:5, 7, 9).

Feel it or not, believe it or not, Precious One, you are linked to the big eternal plan of God. You have an inheritance predestined "according to His purpose who works all things after the counsel of His will" (Ephesians 1:11).

The question is, do you know that you have such significant purpose in God's plan? Do you understand the value of your life? O Beloved, ask God to give you a sense of destiny! Be God's woman, God's man in this hour. Seize the moment the Lord gives to you and live it in His power to the fullest. It's His hour and yours!

PRECIOUS *One,*

Have you begun to comprehend the breadth, length, height, and depth of Christ's love for you—a love that surpasses knowledge? Or are you walking around, lost in the maze of the enemy's lies? Are you blocked at every turn by thoughts and feelings that lead you down dead-end paths? Are you confused not knowing where to go, where to turn, or what to do because you are walking by your emotions, your feelings, your suppositions? Are you living by the evaluations, the opinions, the counsel of others rather than by the absolute truth of God's inerrant Word?

More and more it seems that my eyes are being opened to see that our peace, our happiness, our sanity, our well-being, our soundness of mind, and our effectiveness all go back to what we believe and in Whom we believe. Will we believe God and His Word regardless of anything? Or will we believe someone or something else?

Don't miss life. Don't miss that loving relationship with God. Choose to believe God no matter what. This is my prayer for you: "That you being rooted and grounded in love, may be able to comprehend with all the saints what is the width and length and depth and height—to know the love of Christ which passes knowledge."

Precious ONE,

If you feel incapacitated and unable to go forward in your relationships or get on with your life—to really know success—then maybe it is because you are living under the power of a lie sown in your life through another person or experience. If that is true, I don't know what it is, and maybe you don't know either, but God does. And God wants you to be set free. Truth will do that.

So may I suggest that you set apart some time to be totally alone before God. As you do, ask Him to take you back in your memory to the incident that introduced that lie. When God brings that to your mind, then ask God to show you what He thinks about what was done to you, what was said to you. He will show you,

Beloved, because He came to destroy the works of the devil. He will remind you of the truth of His Word—and what He says about such lies, such destructive behavior. And when He does, then simply thank Him  for hearing your prayer and tell Him that you will walk in the healing power of His Word.

Let your prayer be, "Search me, O God, and know my heart; try me and know my anxious thoughts; and see if there be any hurtful way in me, and lead me in the everlasting way" (Psalm 139:23–24).

PRECIOUS *in His Sight*

Where will you put your faith? Will it be in the character of God, in the Word of God, or in what you feel, what you think, what others say or believe? You alone, Beloved, can decide that, for this is the choice God gives you. No one can decide for you. Just know that Jesus said, "Be it done to you according to your faith" (Matthew 9:29).

You may say, "But my faith in God and in His Word is too small, too unstable, too unsteady, too weak—and everything else overrides it." If that is really so, then you can and must change it. You must spend time with God in His Word.

There is no other way. An intimate relationship with God is the primary need of your life.

And how does one gain such intimacy?

First, set aside time for your heavenly Father to communicate with you through His Word and through His Spirit. Find a place in your home that will be your "God spot." For me, it's a big old chair in my parlor in the winter and a swing in my yard in the summer. When I sit down in either place, the first words that come almost involuntarily from my lips are, "Oh thank you, Father." I know we are going to be together in a quiet and uninterrupted way, for this is our time.

Second, open the Word

of God, preferably where you left off, and begin to read. Read and mark the text. (If you don't know how, then contact us. That is why God raised up Precept Ministries International). Pause and think about what you have seen—what you have learned about God, about His ways, His commandments, His promises. Ask Him to show you how you measure up to the truth that you have read, what He would have you to learn, to remember, to do—and to pray.

If you journal, journal. Because I write so much, I don't journal. I must have started over a dozen. However the wide margins of my New Inductive Study Bible are my journal where I record the lessons for life, the insights I gain about God, the cross-references He brings to my mind. The markings in the text—the key words, the geographical locations, the time phrases—my obser-vations are all there to remind me of what I have learned from God.

Finally, now that your heart is awakened and in tune with His, spend time communicating with Him in prayer. Lay it all at His feet—pour out your heart—persist in prayer. And with it all, you will find yourself truly worshipping God, sitting at His feet and learning of Him—something which He promises will never be taken away from you (Luke 10:38–42).

PRECIOUS *Grace*

Galatians 5:22–23 says, "The fruit of the Spirit is love, joy, peace, patience, kindness, goodness, faithfulness, gentleness, self-control." Did you notice that the first of the nine-fold fruit of the Spirit is love? When you are filled with the Spirit, controlled by the Spirit, love will be manifested in your life. Agape love—unconditional love—is God's love. Believers are the ones who possess this love. Nonbelievers don't know this kind of love. They don't possess it because God is not in them, and God is love (agape).

Oh, they can experience the eros kind of love—the sexual, sensual love. They can have *störge* love, the natural love of a mother, father, or one human being for another.

They can have *phileo* love, a love based on finding something pleasing in another person. But the only wellspring from which unconditional agape love is drawn is God's spring, the blessed Holy Spirit.

Let me say it another way—

repeat it so you don't miss it. If you are a child of God, then agape love is in you because God is in you and "God is love." (1 John 4:8) Thus, no true child of God can legitimately say to another, "I'm sorry but I don't love you," or "I can't love you any more."

Love is the distinguishing mark of believers. That is why God can command us to love one another even as our Lord Jesus loved us (John 13:34). He loved us sacrificially, unconditionally, when we were sinners—helpless, without hope, ungodly. When we were enemies of God (Romans 5:6–10).

Awesome isn't it? Now let's love not only those in the body but those in the world so they will long to know our God. Why don't you ask God today, whom He would have you love—and how.

PRECIOUS One,

Are you going through a difficult situation, a trial?

Do you realize that whatever the situation—whatever the stress—it is designed to *make* you, not to destroy you. In biblical terms it is a test—a test permitted by God to mold you into the image of His Son rather than disfigure you for life. It is a test you can pass, a trial you can endure, a temptation you can survive. If it weren't, Beloved, your sovereign God would not have allowed it. God never tests us to see if we'll fail—but to show us how strong we are. How far we have come. A test is a faith builder, and He wants you to score a hundred on the exam!

In 1 Corinthians 10:13, God assures us that He will not permit us to be tried or tested or tempted beyond what we can bear. No matter what happens to you, God has totally and completely and absolutely equipped and prepared you for it. Otherwise He would not have allowed it to come at this time, at this stage in your Christian experience.

So rest, Precious One. These words of His were recorded and preserved for you: Come to Me, all who are weary and heavy-laden, and I will give you rest (Matthew 11:28).

You are not to fight the afflictions, the trials and disappointments, the oppressions, the humbling situations. Instead, Romans 5 tells us that you are to exult in them. And exult you can because your Sovereign Father is in total control. In His perfect design He permitted this situation to strengthen you, not to weaken you. You're in  training—your faith is being exercised.

Sing, beloved. Sing as you "work out" —sing His praises. Recall and rehearse His promises. Walk in faith's obedience: Rejoice always; pray without ceasing; in everything give thanks; for this is God's will for you in Christ Jesus (1 Thessalonians 5:16–18).

PRECIOUS *One,*

Should you stop praying? Stop crying to the Lord because He doesn't seem to be hearing? Because it appears He isn't going to answer?

Should you stop praying because God hasn't made right that which is wrong? Because it seems that He isn't going to stop the destruction we see about us in the world?

No, I don't think you or I should stop praying and crying for righteousness, for justice.

Why?

Because we know God hates sin and loves righteousness.

Because we have the parables in Luke 11 and 18 in which our Lord assures us that we "ought always to pray and not faint."

Because if anything is going to be done about it, ultimately God has to do it.

Because it keeps us

in communication with our Father.

"The smoke of the incense with the prayers of the saints" will someday soon go "up before God out of the angel's hand" filled with "the fire of the altar" (Revelation 8:3–5) and "the kingdoms of this world will become the kingdom of our Lord and of His Christ, and He will reign forever and ever" (Revelation. 11:15).

Hallelujah! Keep praying. Give God no rest until He establishes and makes Jerusalem a praise in the earth (Isaiah 62:7). And you can know with an absolute certainty He will because Israel, His covenant nation, is precious in His sight.

Listen to His promises for someday His elect will all come home to the land of Israel, as promised in

covenant to the descendents of Abraham, Isaac, and Jacob for an everlasting possession.

But now, thus says the LORD, your Creator, O Jacob, and He who formed you, O Israel, "Do not fear, for I have redeemed you; I have called you by name; you are Mine!

"When you pass through the waters, I will be with you; and through the rivers, they will not overflow you. When you walk through the fire, you will not be scorched, nor will the flame burn you.

"For I am the LORD your God, the Holy One of Israel, your Savior; I have given Egypt as your ransom, Cush and Seba in your place.

"Since you are precious in My sight, since you are honored and I love you, I will give other men in your place and other peoples in exchange for your life.

"Do not fear, for I am with you; I will bring your offspring from the east, and gather you from the west.

"I will say to the north, 'Give them up!' And to the south, 'Do not hold them back.' Bring My sons from afar, and My daughters from the ends of the earth,

"Everyone who is called by My name, and whom I have created for My glory, whom I have formed, even whom I have made" (Isaiah 43:1–7).

Precious ONE,

The hope of God has sustained His people for about six thousand years through circumstances very much like yours and mine— through governments gone mad, through inexplicable pain from our fellow man, through seemingly impossibilities, through situations and circumstances that would otherwise have been unbearable, driving us insane.

It is a hope that those who have gone on before us would shout from the portals of heaven were it necessary. But it isn't necessary, for God has recorded many of their stories in His Word and then woven through their accounts His pearls of promises, which are "yea and amen."

Do you know how pearls are formed? Pearls, which rank among the most precious of jewels, are formed when a grain of sand or some other irritating source gets inside the shell

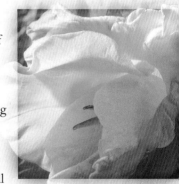

of an oyster. The oyster covers the irritated part with a beautiful milky substance called mother-of-pearl. The pearl is formed by many layers of tiny crystal minerals. These thin layers partly transmit and partly reflect

light,
their
blended
reflections giving the pearl
its beautiful, delicate luster.
This is not an overnight
process! It takes years, but it
is worth the wait, for the
oyster produces a pearl of
great price.

The pains, trials, tribula-
tions encased layer by layer
with the truth and promises
of God have formed magnificent examples among the
believers, pearls who caught
and reflected the resplendent
glory of the Lamb. This is
your destiny. This is your

HOPE! This
is why, Beloved,
having been justified by faith
we can exult in the hope of
the glory of God—and hope
does not disappoint.

And not only this, but
we also exult in our tribula-
tions, knowing that tribulation brings about perseverance; and perseverance,
proven character; and
proven character, hope; and
hope does not disappoint,
because the love of God has
been poured out within our
hearts through the Holy
Spirit who was given to us
(Romans 5:3–5).

PRECIOUS *One,*

If you will make the will of God your focus day by day, if you will seek to please Him alone, then you will find yourself satisfied with life. Misery will slip away like a whipped puppy with its tail between its legs.

Life will take on purpose. God will meet you right where you are—not demanding or expecting you to live by the standards of the world, but simply in His power.

The will of God for your life is nothing more than to submit yourself to Him each day and say, "Father, Your will for today is mine. Your pleasure for today is mine. Your work for today is mine. I trust You to be God. Now lead me and I will follow."

Take one day at a time.

Commit your way to the LORD, trust also in Him, and He will do it (Psalm. 37:5).

Precious ONE,

Are you hanging on by your fingernails? Too worn, too weary, too weak to cry out to God anymore? Are you ready to give up, to stop praying, to stop believing, to walk away?

If I didn't know what I know about God, I might tell you to call it quits and get on with your life. But because God is who He is, because our times are in His hands, and because He's the God of all flesh and absolutely nothing is too hard for Him, I have to tell you not to give up. Don't become passive. Instead "humble yourself under the mighty hand of God that He might exalt you at the proper time, casting all your anxiety upon Him, because He cares for you." (1 Peter 5:6–7). Be still. "Wait, on the Lord."

How do you wait on the Lord? It begins by learning to sit at His feet and know Him. Learn of Him, learn from Him, from His Word, and you'll always have something to hang on to.

"My soul, wait in silence for God only, for my hope is from Him.

He only is my rock and my salvation, My stronghold; I shall not be shaken.

On God my salvation and my glory rest the rock of my strength, my refuge is in God.

Trust in Him at all times, O people; pour out your heart before Him; God is a refuge for us" (Psalm 62:5–8).

Second, tell God you want only what He wants—whatever that means. Then, whatever He says to you. Do it . Do it with confidence and without hesitation.

"So I shall have an answer for him who reproaches me, for I trust in Your word.

And do not take the word of truth utterly out of my mouth, for I wait for Your ordinances.

So I will keep Your law continually, forever and ever.

And I will walk at liberty, for I seek Your precepts" (Psalm 119:42–45).

PRECIOUS *One,*

If you have failed, made a mess of something, run to God. You can do it because He loves you and always desires your highest good. You need not be afraid. Confess your failure—name it for what it is. Call it nothing less. Don't sugarcoat it or gloss over it. Be honest; be blunt. Say it aloud, "I acknowledged my sin to You, and my iniquity I did not hide. . . . And You forgave the guilt of my sin" (Psalm 32:5).

Tell God you want to succeed, not fail, and that you know only He can do that. Tell Him you are willing to do whatever is necessary if He will simply show you what to do by laying it upon your heart, putting it in your mind.

If you have the assurance that what you hear in your mind is in accordance with the whole teaching of the Bible, then do whatever God leads you to do. When you are convinced of what God

wants you to do, then cling to Him, to His promises . . . and watch what He does. Observe to do according to all He tells you. Don't turn to the right or to the left. Then you will have success, for it is God's intent that you succeed rather than fail.

And what will happen? You will become a man or woman renown for praise and for glory. Listen, it is not only God's promise to Israel; it was also written for your instruction and encouragement in these final days:

"For as the waistband clings to the waist of a man, so I made the whole household of Israel and the whole household of Judah cling to Me," declares the LORD, "that they might be for Me a people, for renown, for praise, and for glory; but they did not listen" (Jeremiah 13:11).

Listen, Beloved. Listen and cling.

Precious *One,*

Have you prayed and prayed about something and God hasn't answered?

Maybe you've been agonizing over a son or daughter, your husband or wife, or even a grandchild. Maybe you've been asking God to deliver you from a stressful situation or to provide some need, and nothing has happened.

One of the major keys to answered prayer is persistence. In Luke 11:9 Jesus said, "Ask and it will be given to you; seek, and you will find; knock, and it will be opened to you."

The tenses of the verbs tell us to keep on asking, seeking, knocking. In Luke 18:1–8 Jesus told His

disciples a parable to show that at all times they ought to pray and not lose heart. Prayer is to be persistent!

Isn't this where we often fail? It's easier to quit than to per-sist. We don't like to wait. When our prayers are not answered right away, then we take things into our own hands and try to do what, in reality, only God can do. And when we get impatient and do it our way, we mess up in one way or another. Yet God tells us to hold on in faith, to not let go until we receive what we're asking for.

If there is a delay, you can be sure it's because God has a pur-pose. His ways are not our ways. His timetable is not the same as ours. So, Precious One, persist unless He tells you to desist!

PRECIOUS

I don't know what you may have heard in Sunday school about the courage of David, the simple-hearted shepherd boy who squared off against the Philistine Giant by the name of Goliath, but often the stories just don't do this moment justice. Here was an untrained young man fresh from the sheepfolds, who found  himself standing virtually unarmed in the shadow of a nine-foot, battle-hardened warrior who was armed to the teeth.

Even King Saul, the man who ought to have stepped forward as the champion of his people, tried to dissuade David with human logic. "You are not able to go against this Philistine to fight with him; for you are but a youth while he has been a warrior from his youth" (1 Samuel 17:33).

It was like a fair-haired choir-boy climbing into the ring with the heavy-weight champion of the world. Ridiculous! Suicide!

Even Goliath got a good laugh out of it.

But David knew the battle was not his, it was God's. God had delivered David from a lion and bear—so what was an uncircumcised Philistine who taunted the armies of the living God!

David knew there was a weapon more powerful than sword or spear or javelin in the hands of a nine-foot raving warrior. Listen to David's response to Goliath's threat, " I come to you in the name of the LORD of hosts, the God of the armies of Israel, whom you have taunted."

David knew that it was not a contest between a shepherd boy and a giant. Goliath was contending with God. David was merely God's stand-in—called on stage to testify to all generations

that "the king is not saved by a mighty army; a warrior is not delivered by great strength, a horse is a false hope for victory; nor does it deliver anyone by its great strength. Behold, the eye of the LORD is on those who fear Him, on those who hope for His lovingkindness . . . . He is our help and our shield" (Psalm 33:16–18, 20).

Is this a truth you need to remember, Precious One? The battle is His—not yours.

PRECIOUS *One,*

Are you discontented? Unhappy? Feeling horribly inadequate?

Maybe, just maybe, it's because your thinking has been colored by the world! Maybe it's because you're off truth's center and are unable to see things from God's perspective.

I believe if you could see things His way—look at your situation objectively rather than subjectively—then your unhappiness would fade and discontentment would turn to joy. You would know that it is all part of God's bigger purpose.

Yesterday as I walked and prayed, I realized how influenced we are by the movies and television programs we've seen, by the books and magazines we've read, by the family members, teachers and peers to whom we've listened, and by the songs we've sung until their words lodged deep in our hearts.

If you don't want your thinking to be colored by the world, then you must obey Romans 12:2, "Do not be conformed to this world, but be transformed by the renewing of your mind, that you may prove what the will of God is, that which is good and acceptable and perfect."

To do that you must get into the Word of God and meditate upon it day in and day out. It is the bread of life, a light unto your path, the plumb line by which you measure what the world says. You need never feel inadequate, Beloved, because your adequacy is in Christ! It is a place where you can rest in peace and contentment.

Precious ONE,

Are there times when a thousand why's reverberate in your mind? "Why didn't I?" "Why did I?"

Or maybe even more difficult why's such as, "God, why did You allow it?" or "God why didn't You stop it when I cried out to You?"

And then what's and how's follow the why's, don't they?

A proud heart would raise itself against God's sovereign ways. Haughty eyes would deny the sufficiency of God and His promises. We would sit in judgment on His character saying, in essence, "If I were God I would never had …" or "I wouldn't allow that."

In contrast, a humble heart would accept that God does not always let us know His ways. It would agree with Romans 11:33, "How unsearchable are His judgments and unfathomable His ways," and accept the fact that His judgments are unsearchable, His ways unfathomable. It would not seek to resolve great matters or difficult things that God has chosen not to make known to us.

Oh, Beloved, quiet your soul in the Word of God. Put away the why's, what's, and how's. Rest in your heavenly Father's arms. Rest in Him from this time forward, for He birthed you into His family. Your El Shaddai, your all-sufficient One, has provided everything you will ever need. And He loves you with an everlasting love.

PRECIOUS *One,*

Do you realize that if you keep looking back at your past, at your failures, you will never win the race set before you! Although it is wisdom to evaluate where

and how you failed for the purpose of learning and growing, the past is never to be your focus. If it is, Beloved, it will cripple your future.

So let's talk about failure for a minute—why and when we fail, for we all do.

We fail when we try to do something we are not capable of doing. Romans 12:3 tells us we are to have "sound judgment" in respect to ourselves, and not to think more highly of ourselves than we ought.

So take an honest and objective look at yourself and recognize your limitations. Just don't undersell yourself. Like every true child of God, you are gifted

by God so you can achieve His purpose in His kingdom. "As each one has received a special gift, employ it in serving on another, as good stewards of the manifold grace of God" (1 Peter 4:10). "You are His workmanship created in Christ Jesus unto the good works that He has ordained for you" (Ephesians 2:10).

We also fail when we try to do it "our way."

When we don't follow and live by God's precepts. We need to put ourselves on the altar as Romans 12:1–2 bids us to do, and tell God He can direct us anyway He desires.

The secret to recovering from failure is to run to God, confess your failures, throw yourself on His mercy, and cling to His promises, which are "yea and amen." Amen means "so be it"!

PRECIOUS One,

Does listening to the news do you in? Do you find your stomach in knots? Your blood pressure rising? Are you dismayed and frustrated by the blindness, the stupidity, the insanity, the twisted logic, the prejudice, the tolerance of evil, the hatred of righteousness? Do you feel overwhelmed, discouraged—impotent to do anything about it?

How well I understand. This is when I pause, take a deep breath and recall what I know about our God and His ways. Peace is restored, my frustration ebbs when I open my New Inductive Study Bible and look at the truths I've recorded about God—His character, His ways, His power, His sovereignty in its ample margins under a purple triangle colored yellow, my symbol for God.

During the all the confusion and frustration of the United States Presidential elections in the year 2000, I kept returning to Psalm 33 where I was reminded that God would have His way. Good or evil, God sets up the "kings" according to His blessing or judgment on the nations.

Let me share a few of

the verses that brought me peace as I waited for the outcome. As you read them, notice how God has the psalmist remind us that God is the creator—and that He did it simply by the power of His Word! Awesome! Then He gives us the assurance that no matter what man thinks or plans, it can't happen if its' not God's will and won't serve His purpose either to judge or to bless.

"By the word of the LORD the heavens were made, and by the breath of His mouth all their host.

"He gathers the waters of the sea together as a heap; He lays up the deeps in storehouses.

"Let all the earth fear the LORD; let all the inhabitants of the world stand in awe of Him.

"For He spoke, and it was done; He commanded, and it stood fast.

"The LORD nullifies the counsel of the nations; He frustrates the plans of the peoples.

"The counsel of the LORD stands forever, the plans of His heart from generation to generation.

"Blessed is the nation whose God is the LORD, the people whom He has chosen for His own inheritance" (Psalm 33:6–12).

Be still, my heart, our God is on His throne.

PRECIOUS

So often, when we need love we forget that others need the same—especially those who don't realize that Christianity is a relationship rather than just a religious option, or who think it is only for those who need a crutch to make it through life.

The people of this world need love—unconditional, unwavering love. Yet they don't know where or how to find it.

And this is where you and I come in.

There are two ways they  can get the message: either from exposure to God's written Word or from interacting with God's living epistles "known and read by all men." According to 2 Corinthians 3:2 those living epistles are you and I—genuine children of God. The real thing—not the counterfeit!

And which are they more likely to "read"? The Bible, God's written Word, or us? Us, of course! At least initially!

Do you remember what Jesus told His disciples in the Upper Room, just before His pending arrest in the Garden of Gethesmane? Listen to the words of the Son of God: By this all men will know that you are My disciples, if you have love for one another (John 13:35).

Love is what distinguishes us from the world. Lived out in us it is irrefutable. There is no argument against it, no explanation for it—but God. Not the *phileo* type of love that loves because it finds the other person loveable, because that person or personality attracts and pleases, but the *agape* type of love that looks beyond the likeable, the attractive qualities to the person's deepest need—the need for unconditional love that simply desires another human being's highest good.

It's the love demonstrated by the One who was about to be crucified because God so loved the world. It's the love that in His moment of greatest

torture would have the eternal well being of His perpetrators at heart. A love that would cry out on their

behalf, "Father, forgive them for they know not what they do."

I believe, Precious One, in your struggle, in your need for love that you will find fulfillment in simply loving others as Jesus commanded us to do when He said, "A new commandment I give you, that you love one another even as I have loved you" (John 13:34).

Walk in love. Focus on others' needs to be loved with His unique love and see what happens!

PRECIOUS *One,*

Are there times when you wonder just how much God really cares about you? Maybe because of what is happening right now, you don't feel very precious to God.

I understand. Sometimes our circumstances seem to overrule our thinking. So let's reason together for a moment. I believe it will help.

If you weren't precious to God, Christ would not have suffered and died for you, "the just for the unjust" (1 Peter 3:18)!

When you are in a trial, your adversary, the devil, wants you to think you are suffering because God is angry with you, doesn't love you, or doesn't even care enough to hear your prayers and rescue you.

Whatever you are feeling, thinking, or experiencing, Beloved, you must remember that you are precious to God. That will never change. You have been chosen by God. According to 1 Peter 2: 9 you are a chosen race, a royal priesthood, a people for God's own possession.

Stand firm in God's grace—no matter the trial, no matter the suffering. Glory will follow. The only way to have victory is by believing and obeying God no matter what you think, no matter how you feel. God's grace is there. Stand firm! Remember He said, "My grace is sufficient for you, for power is perfected in weakness"(2 Corinthians 12:9).

Precious ONE,

What do you do when you fail after you've been saved?

The first thing you must *not* do is say there is no hope, no way out. To say that, Beloved, would be to deny the power of the One who has rescued you from the greatest failure of all. God is always there for you. To not believe this is to insult Him . . . to say He does not mean what He says and does not watch over His Word to perform it.

What do you do when you fail? First, remember there is hope because God is God.

Second, recognize that God did not restrain you from failure either because you chose to fail since you did not choose to obey Him, or because He wanted to teach you something.

Third, if it is moral failure, repent, throw yourself on God's mercy and grace, and then go and sin no more.

Fourth, like the Apostle Paul, said, "press on toward the goal for the prize of the upward call of God in Christ Jesus" (Philippians 4:14).

And press on—forgetting those things that are behind.

It's done and when you confess as 1 John 1:9 says, it is under the blood.

Precious ONE,

Are there times when you wish you could be more for the Lord? When you realize that you could have done more than you've done?

What keeps any of us from really being used of God? Is it our lack of educa-tion? Our lack of training? Who or what we were or are? The damage that was done to us? Our past? Our circumstances?

It's none of the above, my friend. If it were, the circumstances of our lives, and the actions of others would limit God's power and dilute His promises.

No, these are not the things that keep us from being mightily used of Him. Not being used of God, not being the conqueror over all goes back to one thing: not taking the time to know Him and then in strength and courage walking in the obedience of faith. Nothing more! Nothing less!

Why? Because in any case, in any situation, in any circumstance, Jesus is the only answer, the only solution. It all boils down to whether or not we have been with Him enough to know Him and what He says and then to live and act accordingly.

Listen carefully: "For this is the love of God, that we keep His commandments; and His commandments are not burdensome. For whatever is born of God overcomes the world; and this is the victory that has overcome the world—our faith. And who is the one who overcomes the world, but he who believes that Jesus is the Son of God?" (1 John 5:3–4).

PRECIOUS

Do you look at your inadequacies, your ineptness, your personality, or even your past and think that because of certain "things" about you there is no way you can excel?

You, your personality, your background, are nothing to a sovereign, omnipotent, omniscient God! God demonstrated that in the disciples, in the prophets, in the kings, in all the various men and women He has used since Adam and Eve.

The disciples were not perfect. They were not loved and appreciated by the world, nor even by everyone in the church. Their lives were not without difficulties, challenges, trials, accusations, misunderstandings, and setbacks. Yet those who opposed them often marveled.

Why? Because what they saw could not be explained or rationalized—they did not "fit the bill." The disciples had a confidence that gave them godly boldness and enabled them to live above and beyond what they were in the natural. The only explanation was the correct one—they had been with Jesus.

Just remember, beloved of God, "God has chosen, the things that are not, so that He may nullify the things that are, so that no man may boast before God. But by His doing you are in Christ Jesus, who became to us wisdom from God, and righteousness and sanctification, and redemption" (1 Corinthians 1:28–30).

Precious ONE,

What a calling the Lord has given to us as the children of God! We must seize the day, seize the opportunity! There's a needy world out there, and people need hope. They need answers. The answers are found in the Word of God, man's textbook for life. Neglect the textbook, and you will fail the exam.

What are we to do? What is our responsibility? It is to know the Word, to obey the Word, to live according to the Word—and then to proclaim it in season and out of season. Did you get the last part of that sentence? This is where so many fall short.

I see you and me in the same role as John the Baptist. John came saying, "Repent for the kingdom of heaven is at hand" (Matthew 3:2). We also need to call people to repent—to have a change of  mind. We need to present to them the Christ— the God who will love them, save them, forgive them, transform them. We need to love them enough to confront them with their sin; at the same time giving them hope of forgiveness and eternal life.

We need to gently help them see that any belief or action that is not in accordance with the Word of God is sin. That's why we are to proclaim the Word!

And if we are going to proclaim it, then we must know it . . . and live it! Even if the world hates us. Love is willing to risk being hated, rejected for the sake of another's highest good.

So as you go about your God-given duty, remember what Jesus said, "If the world hates you, you know that it has hated Me before it hated you. If you were of the world, the world would love its own; but because you are not of the world, but I chose you out of the world, therefore the world hates you" (John 15:18–19).

Precious ONE,

Do you realize that Christ's resurrection is your guarantee that death is no longer the victor, that sin has been conquered, that your personal defeat has been made null and void? Through the resurrection, the devil has been rendered powerless because your sin was paid for in full. It is sin that gives Satan power. However once your sin is dealt with by believing in Jesus Christ, Satan no longer has the power of death. Thus, those who believe that Jesus is the Christ, the Son of God, who confess Him as Lord and who believe in their heart that God has raised Him from the dead, will live forever and ever.

Why is understanding this so vital? How will grasp-ing and living by this truth enable you to face each day, to live through every trial, to overcome every incident of life?

When you remember that Jesus has been raised

from the dead, you remember that whatever you are facing—it is not the end. Not the final chapter. Not the last word. Not the last analysis. This is momentary. Eternity is on the horizon.

Night is almost past. "The sun of righteousness will rise with healing in its wings; and you will go forth and skip about like calves from the stall.

"You will tread down the wicked, for they shall be ashes under the soles of your feet on the day which I am preparing," says the LORD of hosts.
(Malachi 4:2–3).

A new day is coming. Our "momentary, light affliction is producing for us an eternal weight of glory far beyond all comparison, while we look not at the things which are seen, but at the things which are not seen; for the things which are seen are temporal, but the things which are not seen are eternal" (2 Corinthians 4:17–18).

God, stamp eternity upon our eyes.

PRECIOUS

Do you realize that because of identification with Christ, no born-again child of God is a second-class citizen in His kingdom! The same power that raised Jesus Christ from the dead has raised you and given you the same Holy Spirit that came upon Jesus!

Put your past behind you, my friend. Jesus is raised from the dead! Raised because of your justification. You have been totally, absolutely, completely justified—declared righteous —because of the total sufficiency of Jesus' atoning death. The blood of the sinless Lamb of God satisfied the holiness of God. Sin was paid for in full! You have a clean slate. You are on equal footing with every other child of God! Now go and proclaim His resurrection. Proclaim it by living in the full assurance of complete forgiveness, allowing the resurrected Christ full reign in your life, giving your all to Him, and sharing the Good News with others who desperately need it.

Walk in newness of life as a first-class citizen in God's kingdom! Remember "If anyone is in Christ, he is a new creature; the old things passed away; behold, new things have come" (2 Corinthians 5:17).

Precious ONE,

Whatever you do, wherever you are, whatever you are going through, whatever emotions or feelings you are dealing with, don't fail to spend time with God. It will be a battle, everything that can happen will happen in order to keep you from spending time with Him. It is the one thing you dare not neglect! Your well-being and ability to cope in a Christ-like way depend on it. It's the foundation— the only foundation that holds, the only foundation you can build on, the only foundation that won't give way in the earthquakes of life. And the earthquakes are not going to lessen!

I don't know your pains (physical or emotional), your problems, your doubts, your fears, your inadequacies, your plights, or the obstacles before you, Beloved, but I do know that there is a solution, there is an answer. And while time with Him won't necessarily deliver you out of your specific situation, it will carry you through your situation as more than a conqueror.

The solu-

tion is simple, available to all who will take or make the time to be with Jesus. Just like Mary, when she sat at the feet of

Jesus, listening to Him. Jesus told Martha, when she complained about Mary, that Mary had chosen "the one thing that is needful" which shall not be taken away from her. (Luke 10:42 KJV)

It's a choice, Precious One. A choice you alone can make. It's a matter of priorities—yours!

I wonder what is going on in your heart or in your life and if it is difficult to deal with . . . or maybe a little scary. First Corinthians 13:12 says: "Now we see in a mirror dimly, but then face to face; now I know in part, but then I will know fully just as I also have been fully known."

The word *dimly* literally means "in a riddle." What we see, what we experience now may seem like a riddle, something hard, difficult, scary, hurtful, or incomprehensible. And for the life of us we may not understand why God would allow it, or we may not be able to imagine what possible good could ever come from it. Little can we realize what God is doing, what He has in store, or how He is going to use the riddle in His eternal purpose. But we don't have to see—all we have to do is trust.

C. S. Lewis wrote, "The next moment is as much beyond our grasp, and as much in God's care, as that a hundred years away. Care for the next minute is just as foolish as care for a day in the next thousand years. In neither can we do anything, in both God is doing everything."

Someday, we will realize that "as for God, His way is perfect." Oh how we will rue the hours we spent fretting and fussing over things we had no control over, things that could not be changed by our "concerns."

Helen Keller said, "If the blind put their hand in God's, they find their way more surely than those who see but have not faith or purpose."

"The steps of a man are established by the LORD; and He delights in his way.

When he falls, he will not be hurled headlong, because the LORD is the One who holds his hand" (Psalm 37:23–24).

Precious ONE,

Are you familiar with Proverbs 18:10, "The name of the LORD is a strong tower; the righteous runs into it and is safe"? This is a day to find shelter in God's name, Jehovah-sabaoth.

This name of God is ours to use in the time of conflict and warfare. And believe me, Precious One, our warfare is going to get more blatant, more intense, more severe as the day of our Lord's return draws near and the enemy realizes his time is short.

The word *sabaoth* means a "mass." In this case, it refers to a mass of heavenly beings, a mass of angels, or an army of heavenly hosts. It is our Jehovah-sabaoth who rules over all the angelic hosts, over all the armies of Heaven. He is Lord over all powers, all principalities, and all rulers in high places.

In fact, in Ephesians, the New Testament epistle on warfare, God tells us that He has seated Jesus Christ "at His right hand in the heavenly places far above all rule and authority and power and dominion and every name that is named" (Ephesians 1:20–21). They are in subjection under His feet. He then goes on to tell us Jesus is the head of the church which is His body. So where does that put the enemy in relationship to our position? You've got it ! Under us because we are in Him! Wow! Jehovah-sabaoth!

This is the Name to whom we run when, from our perspective, there is no other help. And we don't have to run far because we are "seated with Him in the heavenly places" (Ephesians 2:6).

PRECIOUS *Grace*

Have you been disgraced unjustly? It's hard to deal with isn't it? The scene constantly replays over and over in your head and each time you can almost taste the bitterness of the whole affair.

Have you stopped to remember that someday the situation will be righted. Not only will the disgrace you bore be understood,

but if you walk in faith and do not allow bitterness to overtake you, God will bless and reward you for your steadfast walk of faith.

Think of those who bore unjust disgrace—like Mary, the mother of Jesus who was accused of bearing a bastard. Think of the years she kept herself pure, as she chose to live her life in a way pleasing to God no matter what her peers did, no matter what her flesh may have desired. Little did she realize at that time that she would be the one chosen by God to bear in her body the very Son of God, the long promised and awaited Savior of the world.

Think of the scorn felt by Mary's cousin Elizabeth because she, a daughter of Israel, the wife of Zacharias, a Levite who served the temple, was childless. Little did she realize that eventually the Lord would "look with favor on me, to take away my disgrace among men" (Luke 1:25)—that she would bear the forerunner of the Messiah as promised in Malachi. That her son, John the Baptist, would be called by Jesus the greatest among men.

Do you remember how Jesus rode into Jerusalem on a donkey, weeping over the city because the Jews, for the most part, did not realize "the time of their visitation." Little did they realize that on that very day Jesus was fulfilling the prophecies of Zechariah and Daniel that proved He was the long-awaited Messiah.

I wonder, Beloved, if we realize how short our time is before Jesus returns. And that when He comes, He'll bring His "reward with Him to give to everyone according to what they have done" (Revelation 22:12). Then all will know that you have walked faithfully before Him. Persevere, Precious One. Don't be overcome by evil, but overcome evil with good.

Precious ONE,

When reality crashes in—a reality you never planned for, expected, or could have dreamed of—what do you do? Well, if you're like many, one of your reactions will be to ask why. Why me? Why my family? Why my child?

In praying for those who are facing these heart-wrenching realities, God spoke to my heart three powerful words that contain as much meaning as any three words ever spoken to me: "I remain God."

I think these words had an even greater impact on me because from time to time I have noticed the many ways people sign their letters. A friend of mine always signs her letters, "I am warmly yours." So when those words, "I remain God," invaded my heart, it was as if God had said to me that His signature is on all that happens in our lives. These words remind me that nothing is there without His permission. It is all filtered through His fingers of love.

God still is—and always will be—God! So hide in Him. "God is our refuge and strength, a very present help in time of trouble" (Psalm 46:1).

PRECIOUS

How does one recover from failure? Stumbling? Falling short of God's standard?

The answers will be varied according to where and how you failed, but the source will always remain the same: GOD AND HIS PRECEPTS FOR LIFE.

That is why you must read the Word of God on a consistent basis. I know I've said it more than once, Beloved, but as Paul wrote, "To write the same things again is no trouble to me, as it is a safeguard for you" (Philippians 3:1). You have to determine that you are going to take advantage of what God has made available to you—truth, wisdom, insight,

knowledge, healing.

Do not give in to despair, Beloved. God is your redeemer. He buys back, buys out, rescues, sets free, and protects. He is the God of another chance to all who genuinely have a change of mind and throw themselves into His outstretched arms and bury their heads in His all-sufficient breast. He sends His word and heals them and delivers them from all their destructions. (Psalm 107:20)

Just remember, failure can either be a stumbling block that flattens you to the ground or it can be a stepping stone to a life of success built upon the unmovable Cornerstone. It is all a matter of faith. The remedy for failure is faith—faith's obedience, faith's trust in the One who stands behind every word of His holy book, the Bible.

Precious ONE

We can be overcomers. We can be more than conquerors, because in the midst of the conflict of ministry, in His unjust suffering, our Lord Jesus Christ never turned away from His calling (Isaiah 61:1–3).

Now then, how can you be an overcomer? You need to make it your practice to familiarize yourself with the whole counsel of God.

As Joshua set out to conquer a land occupied by the enemies of God, corrupt to the core, God gave him the key to success, the path to victory.

Listen carefully, Beloved.

"Only be strong and very courageous; be careful to do according to all the law which Moses My servant commanded you; do not turn from it to the right or to the left, so that

you may have success wherever you go. This book of the law shall not depart from your mouth, but you shall meditate on it day and night, so that you may be careful to do according to all that is written in it; for then you will make your way prosperous, and then you will have success. Have I not commanded you? Be strong and courageous! Do not tremble or be dismayed, for the LORD your God is with you wherever you go" (Joshua 1:7–9).

Things may get worse around you, but life can be better, sweeter, more fulfilling, more exciting, more wonderfully challenging and expansive IF you will simply choose this day whom you will serve, and serve Him unflinchingly!

Precious ONE,

Do you ever get frustrated with people? Maybe they're unloving, rude, unkind, inconsiderate, distant, or just unnecessarily contrary. Frustrating, isn't it?

How are you responding?

There's one thing you must do, Beloved: CONSIDER JESUS. God has not left you alone. He hasn't abandoned you. He's still there. He's still the same. Neither His character nor His promises have changed. God does not alter with the circumstances.

When life becomes frustrating, when things go wrong, it's not because God has changed, forgotten you, or lost control of the situation. It's not that He doesn't love you anymore. He still rules, He still cares, He still loves. It's the very nature of His being. He provides what you need before you need it. God's name is Jehovah Jireh—the God who provides. He has made provision for you through His Son, to move you through whatever you are experiencing as more than a conqueror, not returning evil for evil, but doing good, blessing those who curse you. "Therefore be perfect, as your heavenly Father is perfect" (Matthew 5:43–48).

PRECIOUS *Enemy*

Are you experiencing a situation you never expected to go through?

How are you dealing with the pain, the trauma, the loss, the fear, the uncertainty?

Let me share some insights that might help.

First, every situation of our lives that is frustrating, unpleasant, or tragic in one form or another is a test from God—a test that will do two things: reveal whether or not you are going to believe and obey God or whether you will choose to walk in unbelief's disobedience. If it is the latter, then out of love, I have to tell you this is nothing less than sin.

Second, it is a test that will demonstrate to those who are watching or involved whether or not having a relationship with Jesus Christ, being a real Christian, makes a difference. It will show whether or not Christians can live on a higher plane—one that transcends circumstances.

So in the midst of your situation, stop and consider the One who loved you so much that He laid down His life for you. Why would you not consider Him and His glory in this test? Not only is Jesus there for you, Beloved, not only does He live to make intercession for you, but—if you want to be faithful, you can, Beloved. You really can.

Why? Because Jesus is not only your example but your enabler. He felt and experienced the same things you do—and He was faithful. Therefore, because He is in you and you are in Him, you can be more than a conqueror. Remember His words to His followers and walk through this in a way that honors the One whose name you bear.

"In the world you have tribulation, but take courage; I have overcome the world" (John 16:33).

PRECIOUS *Mercy*

Have you ever felt betrayed, misunderstood? Are you wondering if you can survive the situation or if it will be your undoing?

You shake your head in wonder. Your heart aches. You go through the motions of your days as if nothing

has happened, as if all is well.

But it did happen. And all isn't well!

What are you to do in the face of betrayal? Misunderstanding?

Whatever you have experienced, no matter how sur-

prising, how disillusioning, or how great the pain, God can and will sustain you if you will but cast your burden on Him. You have His promise—He will not allow you to be shaken. He won't let you totter. He won't let you fall if you will but hold on to His promise in faith's obedience. Go to the Psalms and read until you find the same situation you are dealing with— then watch how the psalmist dealt with it, how he found the resources, the strength to not despair in the land of the living. Remember, God loves you and He is for you. Nothing can separate you from His love.

"Cast your burden upon the LORD, and He will sustain you; He will never allow the righteous to be shaken" (Psalm 55:22).

Precious ONE

What a day we're living in! What an hour is ours! There's a stirring in my soul.

Although marriages, relationships, hopes, and dreams are being shattered and our "Humpty Dumpty" lives have had such a great fall that nothing seems to be able to put us together again, there is God!

He is the Redeemer, and He can put back the most shattered of lives. Even that which we marred by our ignorance, carelessness, or rebellion can be remade into an exquisite vessel if we'll just put ourselves into the Potter's hand.

Difficulties, challenges of our faith, trials, impossible situations are merely opportunities for the child of God to show the reality of the faith he or she professes. Stop and look at your trials with the eyes of faith? Don't be overwhelmed. Be challenged!

Listen to God's words to a nation under siege because of sin and take hope: "For I know the plans that I have for you," declares the LORD, "plans for welfare and not for calamity to give you a future and a hope" (Jeremiah 29:11).

PRECIOUS

The more you know your Lord, the more everything else in this life will grow dim and unimportant in comparison to the surpassing value of knowing Jesus Christ and the power of His resurrection (Philippians 3:10). Lay hold of that for which Christ laid hold of you.

God has a purpose for your life, a work for you to do. Nothing in your life will be allowed to hinder that purpose; rather, God our great Redeemer will use it for His purpose.

"We have obtained an inheritance, having been predestined according to His purpose who works all things after the counsel of His will" (Ephesians 1:11).

Your responsibility is simply to make yourself available—to be spiritually prepared and ready to go. He will let you know, if you will but listen. Be faithful in the small things—humble yourself under His mighty hand and in due time He will exalt you when He knows you can handle it without walking in pride.

Precious ONE,

When you think about serving God, do you look at who you are, where you are, what you have, or what you don't have, and say, "No way—forget it. Someone else, but not me!"

Your lack of confidence can be centered around your flesh—around what you have achieved or didn't achieve, around what you were or weren't, or in the light of what you have done or what has been done to you!

Quit placing confidence in your flesh and start putting your confidence in God. Do as Paul says in

Philippians 3:"Count all things as loss for the excellency of knowing Christ." Let knowing Christ Jesus your Lord be what you value more than anything else in this world, even your service for the Lord.

"Forget what lies behind." The past is over, done; there is no changing it. You can learn from the past but you can never reconstruct it, Beloved. So stop focusing on the past for it will cripple your future.

"Reaching forward to what to what lies ahead, I press on. . . ." Never cease to reach forward to what lies ahead. Don't live on past failures, achievements, or laurels.

Keep your eyes, Precious One, on "the goal of the upward call of God in Christ Jesus."

Precious ONE,

Are there ever times when you wonder if you are prepared for what tomorrow or even later today will bring? Do you think, "If only I knew what was coming . . ."?

I understand. Rarely does God ever let us know what He is going to do in our personal immediate future.

And really, He's under no obligation to let us know. We don't have to know—because God does! All we have to do is walk.

However, you and I are responsible, by His Spirit,
  To move at His command,
  To speak at His urging,

To pray at His prompting,
To receive whatever He filters through His fingers of love,
  To lean not on our own understanding, but in all our ways to acknowledge Him that He might direct our paths.

Does He not say, "I will instruct you and teach you in the way which you should go"? (Psalm 32:8).

PRECIOUS

We have talked about the various types of love before, but did you know that agape is a love that loves first—it's the aggressor. Listen to 1 John 4:10: "This is love, not that we loved God, but that He loved us and sent His Son to be the propitiation for our sins."

It's a love that called us beloved when we were not beloved (Romans 9:25).

It's a love that does not end, for what He says to Israel, He says to you. "I have loved you with an everlasting love . . ." (Jeremiah 31:3).

It's a love that endures. It "bears all things, believes all things, hopes all things, endures

all things." It never fails (1 Corinthians 13:7–8).

This is a love that you and I not only have received from the Father and the Son, but it is a love that we possess if we are truly children of God. You may not feel this love, you may not be allowing it to flow through you, but if you are a child of God, it is there because every child of God has the Spirit of God dwelling within. When you became a child of God, He poured out within your heart the love of God (Romans 5:5).

So, Precious One, do what is precious in His sight; love others with His love.

Precious ONE,

Are you touched, as I am, by Paul's expectation and hope that "Christ shall even now, as always, be exalted in my body whether by life or by death"? (Philippians 1:20)

How I long consistently to consecrate to Him everything that I am and everything that I do, no matter how significant or insignificant. I long to be aware always that I am not my own, I am bought with a price and have but one calling— to be filled with and led by His Spirit.

Have you noticed that there's such an inner sense of peace and confidence when you consciously begin and sustain every day and every situation this way? It breeds a quietness and confidence that become your strength in the varied situations of life.

Remember that whatever today or tomorrow holds, GOD IS. His name is "I AM," and He is there for you. He is everything and anything you will ever need. Now be there for Him. Let everything in His temple, your body, say "Glory to the Lord."

If this will be your passion, then Christ will be exalted in your body.

PRECIOUS

Do you know how critical it is that you and I know who God is and what He says and then make it our goal to live accord- ingly in every circumstance of our lives?

This rules out passivity. Instead, it means charting our course under His direction.

It means making sure that we are consistently, continuously in His Word so that we know that GOD IS. It means staying in consis- tent and continuous com- munion with Him in prayer so that we will know that He knows that our hearts and our ambitions, which we have verbalized, are pleasing to Him.

It means not leaning on our own understanding, but committing our way unto Him, trusting Him, and waiting for Him to bring His will to pass. It demonstrates to God that ours is not a one-way love affair—but a genuine love that longs to be pleasing to Him.

When we come to the end of our life we want to be able to say with Paul, "I have fought the good fight, I have finished the course, I have kept the faith" (2 Timothy 4:7).

Precious ONE,

Let me ask you, Precious One, when do you run to God the most? When do you pray the most? Isn't it when you're hurting the most? When you're disappointed, stressed, pressured, then you fall back in dependence upon the Lord instead of upon yourself.

God works in affliction! Don't despise it. Embrace it. The times when we're afflicted are the times when we're open to see His Work, to learn His Word. We have no other place to go, no other to turn to who can deliver us.

If you go to Psalm 119 you will see the heart of someone who truly understands this as he goes through severe trials. In verse 67, the Psalmist writes, "Before I was afflicted I went astray, but now I keep Your word." In verse 75 he goes on to say, "I know, O LORD, that Your judgments are righteous, and that in faithfulness You have afflicted me" (Psalm 119:75).

In God's wise care, it is good for us that we are afflicted. Oh I know, Beloved, sometimes we think we won't survive, but eventually we see that "it was good for me that I was afflicted, that I might learn His statutes" (Psalm 119:71).

PRECIOUS *Grace*

In the light of all that is going on in our nation, in our world, in your own life, do you find yourself having to deal with despair? Or trying to help others who are dealing with despair?

At times do you or your loved ones find your hearts failing you for fear—fear of the future? Wondering how you can or even why you should keep going on? Thinking, *What good would it do? What does the future hold anyway? More of the same?*

What is God's Word to you in these days? It is a word of HOPE, my friend. Sure HOPE, unfailing HOPE! Not the world's kind of hope, but God's kind. God's hope has no maybe. When we hope in God, when we cling to His promises, to what He says in His Word, we have a sure word of promise: a word that cannot be shaken by the circumstances of life. A word that cannot be nullified by man— no matter how hard he tries. A word that is as certain as the unchanging character of our God.

Just know that in respect to the future of the nations and mankind God assures us in Amos 3:7 that "surely the LORD God does nothing unless He reveals His secret counsel to His servants the prophets."

If you want to know, Beloved, what the future holds then study the Old Testament prophets and the book of Revelation. Because you are a child of God, loved by the Father, indwelt by the Spirit, you have the mind of Christ. You can understand the Word of God; He has not left you in the dark—nor without hope.

"For in hope we have been saved, but hope that is seen is not hope; for who hopes for what he already sees? But if we hope for what we do not see, with perseverance we wait eagerly for it" (Romans 8:24–25).

Precious O N E ,

Have you failed?

You didn't measure up.

You didn't achieve your goal.

You didn't hit the standard.

You didn't accomplish what you thought you should.

In a sense, this is where life begins—in a state of failure. Because to sin is to miss the mark, the standard set by God. Consequently, we are all slated for failure unless we turn to God. Romans 3:23 confirms this!

But do you realize, Beloved, that Christianity is God's means of bringing us out of failure? But it is a process—and that is what so many of us forget in our relationships and dealings with others—and in our understanding of ourselves and where we are in the process of sanctification.

By sanctification, I mean living our lives in such

a way as to know, believe, and embrace what God says so that we order our actions and thoughts according to His precepts. In this way we experience success rather than defeat.

Just remember, my friend, the world's definition of success is far different from God's. So you must not measure yourself or your success by the world's standard. You are in the world but not of the world. "He who is spiritual (that's you) appraises all things, yet he himself is appraised by no one. For who has known the mind of the LORD, that He should instruct Him? But we have the mind of Christ" (1 Corinthians 2:15–16).

Precious ONE,

Do you realize that you are to hope in God, not in what you see, what you feel, or what you experience? God reigns in sovereignty over all events. In His time He will vindicate His own, and He will justly judge the unrighteous. You need not play God; you must only rest in who He is. Remember, He will never cease being God; not for a second.

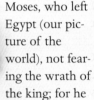

What seems unending, unrelenting now, has an end. A glorious, victorious end! An end that is merely a beginning—a beginning of a new life without tears, without death, without mourning, crying, pain, as Revelation 21:4 assures us— for He makes all things new!

So do not despair, precious child of God. He is the God of all hope. Be like Moses, who left Egypt (our picture of the world), not fearing the wrath of the king; for he endured as seeing Him who is invisible (Hebrews 11:27). You shall soon see the King of kings face to face in all His glory when He comes to rule and reign.

Remember, "faith is the assurance of things hoped for, the conviction of things not seen" (Hebrews 11:1). Keep your hand in your Father's and hope in Him, for "hope does not disappoint."

PRECIOUS

Could you do with a little hope? A little joy? Hope for a brighter tomorrow? Have years of waiting for these things dragged on and on? Long years seemingly never-ending years?

Don't faint, Precious One. Soon in the midst of the darkest of days, maybe even sooner than you think, your day of Jubilee is coming for the fullness of your redemption is yet to be experienced.

Your Kinsman-Redeemer, the Lord Jesus Christ, will soon step on the throne of God and take the seven sealed scroll from the right hand of the One who sits upon the throne as described to us so vividly in Revelation 5:1–7.

And what is this scroll? Why did John weep until the Lion of the Tribe of Judah, the Root of David came forth. Why was no one in heaven, or on the earth, or under the earth, able to open the book, or to look into it?

I believe it's because that scroll is the title deed to the earth. We lost our dominion when Adam sinned and the serpent of old, Satan became the prince of this world. No one could ever win it back but a perfect man. The Lamb was the perfect man who conquered sin and death, and dealt a mortal wound to the head of the serpent.

Now with the breaking of the seals of the scroll, every unjust action, word, or deed against your Lord and against you and all those who belong to Him will be brought into account. All those who have scorned your Christ and your commitment to Him will acknowledge that God has loved you and will continue to love you for all of eternity.

So stand strong in faith, Precious One. Don't faint or lose hope in the day of adversity. You have a righteous and just God who will bring all this about in His perfect timing. The night may be dark, but joy comes in the morning for those who are beloved of God.

Going Loco

Dr Tom Smith

Going Loco

Further adventures of a Scottish Country Doctor

First published in 2009 by
Short Books
3A Exmouth House
Pine Street
EC1R 0JH

10 9 8 7 6 5 4 3 2 1

A CIP catalogue record for this book
is available from the British Library.

ISBN 978-1-906021-68-9
Printed in Great Britain by Clays

Characters referred to in *Going Loco* are composite characters,
and essentially the author's inventions,
although everything that takes place
is based on real incidents.

To my family

JIMMY AND JENNY

J immy's big blue eyes looked up at me from the couch, worried, near to tears. His big sister, Jenny, at fourteen all of
three years older than him, handed me a small grubby piece of
card. It was an opened-out cigarette packet. On the outside was
that jolly sailor with his head inside the lifebelt – the one with
Senior Service printed on it, proving to its addicts that if it was
good enough for our stalwart sailor lads, it was good enough
for us.

That wasn't what interested me. On the plain side, that had
been the inside of the packet, there was writing. Not easily
decipherable, as it was a doctor's, and everyone knows what
their writing is like, but eventually I made it out. It was brief
and to the point: Dear Doc, Appendicitis? Yrs R Patrick.

'Is this all?' I asked the girl.

'Yis' she replied, Brummie accent well to the fore. 'Will he
need an operation?' glancing fearfully at Jimmy.

'Let me look at him for a minute, and I'll know better. How
long has he had the tummy pain?' I was at my kindest and least
frightening, but I knew the two kids were terrified. As I moved
forward to talk to Jimmy, she pushed herself between us,

defending him from my attack.

'You're not going to touch him, are you?' she asked.

'Well, I have to,' I said, 'to find out what's wrong with him.'

'Dr Patrick doesn't do that. He's a prescribing doctor, not an examining one,' she replied.

'You mean he didn't put his hand on Jimmy's tummy?'

'Course not,' she said indignantly. 'He don't have time for stuff like that. Once he knew that Jimmy had stomach pains he sent him here. It's up to you, he said, to find out what's wrong.'

Wow, I thought, but I smiled at her.

'Well, maybe he's right,' I said. 'I suppose I'm the examining doctor, then, not the prescribing one.'

She grinned back at me. 'That's all right then,' she said, 'but don't hurt 'im.'

I took off my white coat, so that I was in my shirtsleeves, and sat beside Jimmy, our faces level. He had the blue scarf of Birmingham City around his thin neck, to keep him warm. I tugged a little at it, for fun, and smiled again at him.

'I'm a Villa man myself,' I told him. 'You don't mind one of the enemy examining you?'

He smiled. So the doctor was human. Divested of my uniform, I must have been a lot less scary.

'So how long have you had the pain?' I asked again.

'A few days,' he replied. 'I think it's because I haven't been. It's cold in the dunny and I don't like going out to it.'

Light was dawning. It was February; we were in one of the coldest winters Birmingham had ever known. The frost had penetrated so far through the ground that the water mains had frozen and water was being delivered by truck. Jimmy's house was one of thousands with no inside toilets – and the journey out to a cold 'dunny' had been too much for the lad. He didn't have a scrap of fat to keep him warm and his clothes were threadbare.

'Can I feel your tummy?' I asked him.

He nodded. I unbuttoned his jacket, he rolled up his jersey, and I opened his shirt. Underneath he had a vest, and under that was a sheet of thick brown paper tucked around his chest and waist like a tube. I had seen that before – brown paper had a great reputation for keeping children free of chills. Finally, I got to his skin.

I gently laid my right hand on his flat stomach.

'Where is the pain?' I asked him. 'If you can, point to where it is with just one finger.'

Jimmy's shaky right index finger positioned itself over the lower left side, just above the groin.

'I think you are right, Jimmy,' I said. 'You haven't been for a while, have you?'

It was an easy diagnosis. He had about a week's worth of constipation in his gut, and being small and thin, he was bound to find that pretty painful. I straightened up and smiled at both children.

'We'll just help you a little,' I said, 'and you can go home. Don't worry.'

I arranged for a gentle enema for Jimmy, and a cup of hot tea and buns from the canteen for both of them while sister, in the background, tried to find out why their parents weren't with them. Dad was at work, and Mum had seven other children to look after. Jenny, the oldest, had taken the role of carer for the visit to hospital. They had come in by bus, straight from the doctor's surgery.

I looked at the cigarette packet again. I took my biro from my white coat pocket, scored out 'appendicitis', and replaced it with 'constip'. I wrote 'yrs T Smith' underneath, and gave it to the waiting hospital car driver. These two weren't going home by bus if I could help it. They would be driven in style, after eating and drinking their fill. The driver would deliver the note to Dr Patrick's surgery a few doors along from their home.

Later, relaxing in the mess over coffee with other duty housemen, I brought up the subject of Dr Patrick. His single-handed practice was famous, but not for the right reasons. For years now he had been sending in messages like this, without the courtesy of phoning beforehand. He didn't seem to care when a consultant blasted him out for wasting the hospital's time. And no one could remember when the 'old guy' had made a correct diagnosis.

I wasn't sure about that. Obviously, it was a big mistake to mix up constipation with appendicitis – and he hadn't even felt the child's abdomen. But Jimmy had needed our attention, so I was glad that Dr Patrick had sent him in. Give him his due, he had served his time – some said more than 40 years – in the poorest district of the city. He deserved brownie points for that.

Manu Tailor, a long-time friend as a student and now a fellow houseman, had been reading the noticeboard.

'Hey, Tom,' he called across the room, 'you get Saturday off next week don't you?'

'Yes,' I replied, 'but I have plans for it.'

'Like sleeping all day?' laughed Manu. With one day off every three weeks, we usually spent it catching up on lost sleep. 'What about doing a locum instead?'

'Not on your life,' I replied.

'Even if it's for Dr Patrick? You could learn a lot for all of us.'

I walked over to the noticeboard. There was a typed request for a locum to cover his practice for a day, from 9 am to 9 pm. It would involve a morning and evening surgery and calls between times. The typing wasn't great – there was plenty of evidence of erasures and smudges where errors had been corrected. These were the years before Tippex. The paper was cheap and so thin that there were spots where the force of the keys had made holes in it. It was signed by Mrs Patrick, in a hand nearly as shaky as the good doctor's had been on the cigarette packet.

My only experience in GP had been during training, but I had to start sometime, and in those days, once you had finished your first hospital year after qualifying, you could legitimately do any GP job you pleased. Two years into the profession, I felt I should surely be able to tackle a day in practice. I decided I needed to know this guy, so I stepped across to the outside line telephone and dialled the number on the letter.

The following Saturday, I arrived by bus (I didn't yet have a car) at the surgery doorstep. It was ten to nine. The front door of the three-storey red brick terrace house was still locked. A forlorn line of beaten-looking people was standing on the pavement, waiting patiently. I bid the queue a cheery 'good morning' and was greeted by a few half-hearted replies. I rang the bell. An elderly lady answered: she was thin, careworn, with grey hair tied neatly in a bun, and a deeply lined face. They weren't laughter lines. She had a cigarette hanging from her lower lip. I wondered how she managed to keep it there: maybe it was stuck there by the smear of lipstick.

'And you will be the locum?' she said. The cigarette still hung there as she spoke. 'Please come in.' She glanced at the patients waiting out in the cold, ushered me inside, then shut the door behind me, leaving them there to deepen their impending hypothermia. I mattered, it appeared, but they didn't.

She must have seen my concern.

'It's a practice rule,' she said, 'that the door doesn't open until nine sharp. If we don't keep them under a firm hand, we couldn't get through the day. I'll let them in shortly, after I've explained things to you. The doctor is away for the day, so he has left me to show you the ropes. I'm Mrs Patrick.'

I looked around. There was a large hall that hadn't been redecorated since the house had been built 60 years before. The wallpaper was peeling in several areas, where there were patches of black mould. Around the wall were wooden chairs of different design, not a cushion on any of them. The carpet was threadbare, in some places with holes in it, so that anyone unsure of his or her footing might easily trip. This served as the waiting room, I was told. The first door on the left was the consulting room. Mrs Patrick showed me in.

In the centre was a large desk, in dark wood, probably mahogany, behind which was Dr Patrick's chair. In front of it was the patients' chair, an armless upright dining chair. It looked like the sort of chair that gave you backache if you sat in it for more than a few minutes. Maybe that was its purpose. There was nothing to encourage you to stay in that room a minute longer than you needed.

In one corner was an examination couch, very dusty, with a sheet as a cover. Beside it was a sink and towels, and all round the walls of the room were cupboards, presumably to hold his equipment. Each one had a sheet of foolscap tacked to it, on which the contents were listed in large print. To one side was a door with the label 'Dispensary', and on the other side was another one labelled 'Toilet'. Each of the drawers on the doctor's desk was also labelled – 'sample bottles', 'syringes', 'hospital letters', 'biochemistry', 'haematology' and so on.

I began to thank Mrs Patrick for having gone to all the trouble of labelling everything: it would be a great help to me.

She cut my thanks short.

'I didn't do it for you,' she said. 'I did it for him. He is a bit forgetful these days – the labels help him to find things.'

Stunned, I didn't know what to say. It was time to start the surgery, and the doctor's wife left the room to call the first patient. Curious, I opened the drawer marked 'hospital letters'. It contained five packs of twenty Senior Service. No writing paper. I walked to the doorway to shake hands with the patient and introduce myself.

The surgery went well. The patients were pleasant and happy to see me, and hoped that their 'real doctor' wasn't ill. They were genuinely fond of him. As I sorted out their problems, I had a strong sense that this was a happy practice, with good relationships between the doctor and patients. Yet with each prescription I signed, the patients frowned. When it happened the first time, I asked why.

'Oh, it's Mrs Patrick that usually writes the prescriptions,' he said. 'The doctor just chats with us: it's his wife that really treats us.' I didn't know what to say. There were a few notes written by Mrs Patrick on the desk giving directions to the houses of patients I had to visit. I hadn't thought much about them at first, but now I had heard about the practice's peculiar arrangement, I scrutinised them again. The writing looked familiar. It was the same as on the cigarette packet. It was the wife, not the doctor, who had sent Jimmy to me. Jenny must have been in on the secret, and had known when to tell a discreet lie.

I finished the surgery, and asked Mrs Patrick for the list of visits. I wondered where the doctor usually parked the practice car: there was no parking space in front of the house, and being mid-terrace, I didn't see a way round the side to the back, where presumably the car was kept.

'Oh, there's no car,' she told me. 'The practice is very compact. The doctor does his rounds on foot. No one is more than a quarter of a mile away. You'll find it easy. I've mapped out a route for your visits.'

Naturally, I thought. She couldn't risk him getting behind a wheel. I hadn't planned for a hike around the frozen wastes of Nechells with my bag and prescription pad, but needs must. I made the visits, completed the evening surgery and called on Mrs Patrick at the end of the day. She gave me a cheque 'for my trouble', and saw me to the door.

'You will be discreet, Doctor, won't you?' were her last words to me. She didn't need to say more. She knew the tightrope she and her husband were on, and how easily I could cut it down from under them. I got on the bus, turning over and over in my mind the ethical dilemma I was in. Was it really possible that a doctor's wife, unqualified in any way, could have taken over her sadly demented husband's practice and run it successfully? Apparently for years? I didn't tell my fellow junior doctors, but I spoke to my consultant. I couldn't let things stand as they were.

Three weeks later, Jimmy and Jenny appeared again at the hospital casualty department, this time with their mother. It was

Dad's turn, on his day off, to look after the other children. They weren't sick. They were angry, and their anger was directed straight at me.

'It was you, wasn't it, that got the surgery closed down?' said their mum. 'You did a locum, didn't you, for the day? It was after that we heard that we had to get another doctor. Dr Patrick is away in a home, and Mrs Patrick is beside herself. Why did you do it?'

I tried to find words that would both excuse myself and comfort them, but there weren't any. They had lost their precious doctor, and I was to blame. They went off, deeply unhappy, and I was left to muse on my first day as a locum. I didn't know it then, but there were many more years of 'locuming' to come.

Moving On — Writing and Research

It's strange how careers develop. Mine didn't go to plan. At the children's hospital I thought I would become a paediatrician. Then getting married took precedence and a quick shift into general practice seemed the best way to achieve a decent family life. Hospital jobs then meant 'living in', in single quarters, and shifting locations every six months or so. It's amazing how uncomfortable a single hospital bed can be when the mattress has been moulded into a permanent trench by the countless housemen before you, and when two of you are trying to sleep in it; when every move and squeal of the bedsprings is heard through the cardboard walls of the residency, and all the other housemen are trying to do the same. Or are, perhaps, trying to use the bed for its other purpose while making the minimum of noise.

That isn't a recipe for a happy marriage. So, soon after we married, Mairi and I gave up the hospital life, and after a year in the Birmingham suburbs, we headed for a practice in our native Scotland. I've covered the first six years of that in *A Seaside Practice*, so if you would like a glimpse of a hapless English-trained doctor in a West of Scotland single-handed country practice, then please read that. What follows here is my – still hapless – journey through the minefield of locum medicine, mixed with my travels first in medical research, and then as a writer.

I'd better explain. Leaving my practice in Collintrae was a wrench, but we needed a break from the permanent on-duty hours. Today we would call it 24/7 on call, and no one would dream of doing it. We did it for five years, and decided that was enough. So medical research beckoned, in the shape of a job in Southampton. It was good while it lasted, giving me plenty of experience in organising clinical trials of new drugs and an insight into the business mind that few doctors ever achieve in their normal lives. It also led me to break the law, but more about that later.

What I prized most about my life in research, however, was the opportunity it gave me to write. That wasn't planned, either. It all started with my being asked to make up the numbers at a business lunch. We were a new company in Britain, and the aim of the lunch was to introduce us to the staff of medical journals in which we hoped to advertise our drugs. As a purely medical man, I wasn't involved in commercial matters, but I was there because I could answer technical or clinical questions about our drugs. I didn't get any to answer.

One journal had sent its medical man, too. Hertzel Creditor, who wrote for *Pulse*, a weekly newspaper for GPs, sought me out and sat beside me. He was intrigued that a young man with his own practice in the West of Scotland had given it up to enter industry. My story would be of interest to his readers, he said. Could I supply him with a few anecdotes?

A couple of glasses of wine later, with both our tongues loosened, Hertzel gave me an offer I couldn't refuse.

'Give me 700 words, and if they are any good, you can fill half a page each week for us', he promised.

I wrote them that evening, Mairi typed them for me, and I sent them off to *Pulse*.

Three weeks later, I had heard nothing, and assumed that I had failed. Having had six years of hardly any family life in practice, for the first time we had weekends free to enjoy it. So Saturday mornings were devoted to doing things with the children, Catriona, now aged seven, and Alasdair, aged five. Priority number one was to clean out the guinea pig hutch. We didn't run to dogs or cats, assuming that guinea pigs were easy to keep, didn't need taking out for walks, didn't mess up the lawn, and wouldn't catch the goldfish in the pond. The only chore was the weekly hutch-refreshing ritual: that done, we had the rest of the weekend to ourselves.

Guinea pigs appear to excrete several times their body weight of droppings every day, so we didn't take the ritual lightly. We took off the top layer of mess, then the layer of straw, underneath which was sawdust, and finally the newspaper pages that kept the base of the hutch reasonably clean and hopefully free of rot. I had chosen *Pulse* for my base the previous week, and was gingerly lifting the congealed gooey mess from the floor when I noticed words on the page that seemed familiar.

It was my article. Somehow I had missed it when I had flicked through the journal on its arrival. But it didn't have my name on it. Instead, someone called Dr Desmond Wetherley had written it. Who was this guy? How had he managed to steal my work? I couldn't wait until Monday morning to phone Hertzel. I was blazing.

Mondays weren't my favourite days at the office. They

started at 8.30 with a meeting of all heads of department, under the chairmanship of the managing director. He needed a report from each of us in turn, on how well we had achieved our objectives set the week before, on our ongoing projects and the goals we were setting for the next week. It was a very Dutch way of doing business. I sat through these meetings, listening to marketing, sales, technical, logistics and pharmaceutical experts, before chipping in with my contribution on research. Most of it was irrelevant to me. That morning, the sales and marketing people were at odds over an advertising campaign that had gone wrong, and their efforts to curry favour with the boss extended the meeting to well beyond midday. I was desperate to cut and run, to get to the phone and have my say about this Dr Wetherley.

So I was steaming when I eventually reached the telephone.

'What's this about?' I raged at Hertzel. 'How could this Dr Wetherley steal my work?'

I could hear Hertzel laugh.

'Didn't we tell you?' he asked. 'You are Desmond Wetherley. We have a list of names that don't appear in the *Medical Directory*, so that we know they aren't registered doctors. We choose one for each of our doctor writers, because we can't use your real names. Got a piece for this week? We'd like to have it. Tomorrow, if possible.'

It turned out that *Pulse* paid its contributors a month in retard, which is why I hadn't yet received notice that my first piece had been accepted. The following day, I received the official confirmation from the editor that I was to write a weekly column. Desmond Wetherley was on his way.

With the letter was my first cheque – a whole five pounds.

That night, I told Mairi that I wanted to write for a living. She didn't comment, but she did ask for the cheque: she said she had a use for it.

Tuesday passed as usual. When I came home from work on Wednesday evening, there was a new picture on the wall. It had a small label on the bottom right-hand corner, with '£5' on it. It was a print of Hogarth's 'The Distrest Poet' – the one about the budding writer. I'm sure you have seen it. The scene is a dilapidated attic. The poor writer is sitting at the window – the only source of light in the room. He is scratching his head with one hand, his feather pen in the other. There are pieces of scrunched-up paper all around him. The *Grub Street Journal* is on the floor. A miserable-looking cat is feeding a kitten, lying on his jacket on the floor. The waste-paper basket is full. The baby is in a cot in one corner under the sloping roof, howling. His downtrodden wife is sewing his rags, the dog has just grabbed the last piece of meat in the larder, and the landlady is standing in the doorway with her tally stick, demanding the rent that he can't possibly pay. The rhyme underneath is:

> Studious he sate, with all his books around
> Sinking from thought to thought a vast profound
> Plung'd for his sense, but found no bottom there,
> Then writ, and flounder'd on, in mere despair.

It is still on my office wall, a tribute to Mairi's keen sense of business. I may have earned my first professional crust as a writer, but she didn't want to end up in a garret.

I killed Dr Desmond Wetherley a few months later. All medical writers owe a debt to Dr David Delvin. Before he made his stand, no doctors could write under their own names.

The General Medical Council considered it to be 'advertising', a sin for which the only penalty was to be struck off. Hence the *Pulse* list. David had the courage to challenge the GMC, and deliberately wrote under his own name. Hauled up before the Disciplinary Committee, he made the case for all of us. We were on tenterhooks until the ruling. Most of us expected the worst – but David won. We now have more than 400 British doctors writing regularly and broadcasting under our own names, thanks to David.

It took five more years for Mairi and I to establish enough of a writing business to go it alone, and to turn our backs on industry, but the seeds of that decision were sown in that guinea pig hutch. In the meantime, I had to learn the craft of being a medical researcher.

THE INTERVIEW

The transition of country-doctor tadpole to full-adult research-doctor frog hadn't taken long. You could say I was chucked into the deep end of the muddy pool and left to mature by myself. The mud meant, of course, that I couldn't at first see the predators cruising about in the pool alongside me. So happy frog that I was, I took to the new life with zeal.

I had an easy entry to the industry. My British 'interview' for the job was conducted under the branches of an ancient yew tree into which were embedded about a dozen slates and a bullet from a gun. You will need to read *A Seaside Practice* to understand why. It was a simple interview: I was told I had the job as soon as I had been carried off a roof, where I had had an unusual consultation with an elderly ex-GP. It had been his gun, and bullet, that had been the turning point in the decision to hire me.

Two weeks later, I was on my first plane to Amsterdam – the first of hundreds I was to make over the next seven years – on my way to meet the bosses of Huizens Pharma in the Netherlands. That journey wasn't a good start. The Glasgow-Amsterdam route was serviced by a KLM Fokker Friendship

22

27: a noisy, shaky, small plane with about 30 passengers. I noticed when boarding that the regular travellers, hardened Scots to a man, were surprisingly overdressed for the journey. It was April, after all, and the winter chill had gone even from Glasgow. We would surely expect even warmer weather in Amsterdam. Yet my fellow passengers were dressed in heavy winter coats, some with furry hats, and most of them were wearing sturdy, even fur-lined boots.

We took off on time for our two-hour journey. When we got to our cruising height, I understood only too well why most of my companions looked like Laplanders. The Fokker had a design fault. The heating system kept the cabin air temperature just around the lowest a normal human could tolerate, but whatever material was used to insulate the floor from the sub-freezing hold temperature underneath didn't work. It was like sitting with my feet, in my best, but lightweight, shoes, in a deep freeze. I hoped that the seven cups of hot coffee I drank over the next two hours would prevent frostbite.

So the Huizens chauffeur meeting me at Schiphol watched curiously as this man from the Glasgow plane stumbled and stamped his way on still-frozen and anaesthetised feet towards him. We smiled at each other, said hello; he took my briefcase from me, and opened the back door of a gleaming, huge, black American car. He introduced himself as Willem, put my brief-case on the front passenger seat and invited me to make myself comfortable in the back. Willem spoke excellent English, and was svelte and sophisticated. I was suitably impressed. Huizens had pulled out the stops, treating me as a VIP. I complimented the driver on the beautiful condition of the car.

'It's a Studebaker,' he said. 'We got delivery of it this morning. You are the first to ride in it. Beautiful, isn't it?'

I agreed with him.

'Are you in pain, Doctor?' he added. 'I notice you are limping and finding it difficult to walk. Is there anything I can do for you?'

I explained that my feet were still frozen from my time in the plane, and that if I could get a little heat directed to the floor of the back seat, I would be delighted.

'*Verrekte lullige ijskoude Fokkers,*' Willem said, grinning from ear to ear. 'But this car has everything: we will soon put that right.'

I relaxed back into my seat, feeling the hot blast around my legs, and slid my shoes off. Bliss. I mused that I'd heard my first words of Dutch, though they weren't necessarily those that a language school would teach, at least in the first few lessons. I began to think about the meetings ahead, and let my mind drift.

It didn't drift for long. About 200 yards along the airport road, there was a massive bang, the car lurched hard to the left, and to my immediate right there was a small white van with a large angry man gesticulating at me. The extended middle finger in an otherwise closed fist didn't suggest that he was welcoming me to Holland. That wasn't surprising, because his van's front left wing was crumpled into the Studebaker's rear right one.

Willem was incandescent. He wound down his window and leaned out, facing the man, who was already halfway out of his cab.

'*Klootzac!*' Willem shouted. This wasn't pleasing to the ears of our assailant, who was, amazingly for his near seven-foot stature, very quickly at his side.

Willem, all of five feet six, made a snap judgment and sped

away, leaving our van driver friend far behind, looking at his wrecked vehicle in despair.

We didn't talk much after that on the 30-kilometre journey to the Huizens factory near Hilversum. It turned out that Willem wasn't as fluent in English when raging mad as he was when welcoming visitors to his country. The new Studebaker would need substantial bodywork repairs, and he had lapsed into a contemplative silence. He continued to mutter words in Dutch under his breath, but not loud enough for me to understand their meaning. That was a pity, I thought, as in my caffeine-soaked condition, I reasoned, I could probably learn the language quite fast from him. After all, I had learned colloquial Scots quickly from my Collintrae patients. Couldn't I learn Dutch in the same way?

About 40 minutes later, still high on my shots of Douwe Egbert's strongest coffee so liberally supplied by KLM, I was ushered into the boardroom of Huizens' pharmaceutical research building. It was impressive, but not quite what I had imagined.

I had thought I was coming to a state-of-the-art modern research facility, a concrete and glass hi-tech space-age wonder, with men in white coats and clipboards scurrying between glass-doored laboratories, through which I might be able to glimpse medical research going on at a frenetic pace. There would be benches with retorts and distillation systems bubbling, steaming and squirting their contents into glass bottles labelled with the names and numbers of the new drugs, the knowledge of which I would soon be privy to. I could feel my heart beat fast against my chest with rising excitement.

It wasn't like that at all. Huizens Pharma research was conducted in a Victorian building that had once housed the biggest chocolate factory in Europe. It was a dead ringer for one of those derelict cotton mills in the Lancashire industrial heartlands. Red brick walls, tiled floors and long corridors dotted regularly with solid closed wooden doors greeted me, as Willem guided me along to the boardroom, where I was to meet my Dutch employers for the first time.

The boardroom door was bigger than the others. Willem knocked, a voice from within bid me enter, and I strolled in, still aware of the pumping inside my chest. Six men were sitting around an oval table, and I was invited to join them at the only vacant chair. I sat facing the window, looking due south, straight into the midday sun. The glare stopped me from seeing clearly the faces of my inquisitors: only their outlines, silhouetted against the sun, were discernable.

The fat one in the middle welcomed me to the team. He, Professor Arendt, apparently, was my boss's boss's boss, the man at the top of all the drug research for Huizens Pharma worldwide. He introduced me to the others, one by one. They included the international directors of clinical medicine, pharmacy, animal research, chemistry, statistics and public relations. They sounded very important, but as they all seemed to have long Dutch names, and I wasn't hearing very well – I was getting noises in my ears and feeling a bit dizzy – I told myself that I would brush up on their names later. All I had to do at this meeting, I thought, was to answer any questions as brightly as I could.

They asked me about my medical career so far, and seemed pleased with the answers. I sat forward in my chair, feeling I was on top form, answering their questions fast and slickly, and hopefully with some humour. I was ideal for them, they eventually said, because I had some knowledge of the problems doctors faced in general practice, and they had no one as yet on their payroll with that experience. I seemed to be doing well.

Then came the crunch. Professor Arendt asked, 'And have you started to learn Dutch? If you are intent on a career with us, that's essential.'

I grinned. I had the perfect answer.

'I haven't had the opportunity so far,' I said, 'as this is my first visit to the Netherlands, and I've been too busy in practice since I was offered the job. But I have started today. I've learned a few phrases and words from your chauffeur'.

'That's great' he said, 'I was hoping you two would get on well together. What were these phrases?'

'They sounded something like "*verrekte lullige ijskoude Fokkers*" and "*klootzac*",' I said.

There was total silence in the room: the atmosphere chilled almost back to Fokker Friendship level, as the others waited for the professor's reaction. Then he burst out laughing and the rest followed.

'Dr Brand', said Professor Arendt, 'I'm not sure you have started Dr Smith on the right foot, but we will forgive you just this once. Please take him away, show him around, and teach him some Dutch that might be more usable in professional company.'

Willem was sitting behind me: I hadn't noticed him coming into the room after me and seating himself on a chair near the wall. I turned to see him: luckily, he was laughing. I hadn't put him in the board's black books, but I could have. He explained to the board in flawless English about my freezing feet and the litre or so of Douwe Egbert's best that I had consumed.

Our chemistry specialist took out a piece of paper, jotted a few figures on it, then came up with my likely blood caffeine level, assuming that I had drunk the strongest Douwe Egbert brew. It was way beyond the normal limits, he announced, and explained, he said, why 'Dr Smith is, how you say in English, high as a kite'. They all laughed again. 'We know how cold you can get in those "*ijskoude Fokkers*", but old widow Egbert makes a coffee that you haven't yet experienced in Britain. Be careful with it – and welcome to our group.'

So I was in. '*Ijskoude Fokkers*' simply means 'freezing Fokkers'. I won't directly translate *verrekte* and *lullige*, as they rudely refer to people's lack of married parentage and of sexual self-control. As for *klootzac*: *kloot* means ball, and *zac* means bag. Enough said.

Willem Brand turned out to be not the chauffeur, but one of my research colleagues-to-be. The regular chauffeur being off sick, he had volunteered to drive to the airport in the new company car to meet me. It wasn't surprising that he hadn't talked much after the crash: the other drivers and doctors had predicted it.

You see, Willem is Belgian. The Dutch and the Belgians have a healthy disrespect for each other. They tell the same story about the other's driving sense. The Dutch say that when Belgians come to a crossroad they speed up, on the perfect but dubious logic that the shorter the time they are actually on the crossing, the less likely they are to hit another vehicle. The Belgians say exactly the same about the Dutch. It turned out that the crash was Willem's fault. In Dutch road law, the priority at road junctions has to be given to the vehicles entering from the right. Our giant white van man knew that: Dr Willem, the Belgian, didn't.

We got on well together after that. For seven years we often travelled together, and he never let me forget that once I thought he was my chauffeur.

I spent the rest of that day with Willem. He showed me around the labs: behind the wooden doors I had passed earlier were the research teams I had imagined. He explained what each team was doing and how the two of us were to relate to them. He waxed lyrical about receptors and blockers; antibodies and antigens; bacteria and antibiotics; viruses, vaccines and antivirals; muscle spasms and antispasmodics; dilators and constrictors of blood vessels and airways; abnormal heart rhythms and anti-arrhythmics; biochemistry, pharmacology and microbiology. I would have to be up to speed in all of them.

The enormity of what I had done – to leave a rural general practice for this – was dawning on me. I was way out of my depth. It didn't help that my brain was fast running out of caffeine, and I was now drowsy, and maybe even a bit depressed. Dropping caffeine levels do that, I reminded myself, and forced myself to think more positively.

Willem sensed that he was making me uneasy, and grinned at me.

'Come on,' he said. 'I'll treat you to a decent meal before you get on to the plane.'

We left for Amsterdam, this time in Willem's own tiny rubber-band-driven DAF. We ate Indonesian-style in a restaurant called, in Dutch, the Five Fleas. During the meal, Willem popped out for a minute, to return with a large box. In it were thick socks and a pair of fleece-lined boots.

'Try them on,' he said. 'I can take them back if they don't fit.'

Willem was a good judge of feet. They were perfect: I kept them on and put my other socks and shoes in the box. He wouldn't let me pay for them.

'Compliments of Huizens' research department,' he said. 'We all wear them on Fokker Friendships.'

On the 9.45 flight home to Glasgow, at least my feet were warm. Mulling over my day, I accepted a Douwe Egbert from the hostess and added a whisky to it. I reasoned that the combination would dispel my doubts about being able to do the work.

I had a taxi waiting for me to take me home to Collintrae (we hadn't yet moved south). Billy, the driver, looked curiously at my feet.

'New boots, Doc?' he asked.

'It's a long story, Billy,' I replied.

THE TRANSITION

Leaving Collintrae was hard. Mairi, the children and I said goodbye to close friends and hundreds of patients, leaving tearfully with their good wishes ringing in our ears. We vowed that some day we would be back, and to reinforce the vow we had bought a cottage in the district, between Kilminnel and Braehill, with the money that Mairi had inherited from her mother.

But we were looking forward, too, to a life in which we could be more of a family, enjoying free time together in the evenings and weekends, something that the practice could never have given us. London was only three-quarters of an hour away, and we wanted to make the most of the big city and the new life.

In the weeks before the move, I had spent a day buying a house in Oakley, a commuter village just outside Basingstoke, a ten-minute drive to the office. A ticky-tacky box like hundreds of others on the new-build estate, it was a far cry from the doctor's mansion in Collintrae, but it would have to do. I hoped Mairi and the children would accept the change. My salary was going to be well under my income as a GP, but I was prepared to take the drop while I was learning my new trade.

We drove down over a weekend, moved in on the Monday and took the next three days to settle in and to get to know our neighbours. I had been asked to report to the office on the Thursday morning, at nine.

That first day I met the 'reps'. It coincided with the annual sales conference, so that the 70 or so salesmen and women from all over Britain and Ireland were in the conference room. Vivian Lewis, my former tutor at medical school, and now Huizens UK medical director, paraded me in front of them. Seventy pairs of eyes scrutinised me: I knew that their owners were asking themselves if I was up to the task. The Scots and the Brummies applauded a little louder than the rest, when they heard my background. Bill Black, the rep that visited Collintrae, was there, in the middle of them. He had obviously given his mates the low-down on me and it seemed to be favourable. He winked and smiled: I was grateful to him, feeling a little less on my own. I resolved to seek him out at the bar afterwards.

Vivian then led me to the managing director's office, where I met James Montrose of Linlithgow. I learned later that everyone gave Mr Montrose of Linlithgow his full title. He was around 50 years old, well over six feet tall, with no hint of a stoop, still fair-haired rather than grey, with piercing blue eyes made larger by his rimless glasses with thick lenses. He was on the gaunt side of slender: if I had seen him in the surgery I would have guessed at serious illness in his past. His wrinkles, however, were laughter lines rather than careworn, and his face broke into a welcoming smile as he rose to meet me.

'*Dag, dokter Smith, je bent wilkom,*' he said, offering me his hand. He must have seen my slight frown at the language, so he switched to English – with a strong Dutch accent.

'We have heard so much about you from Dr Lewis. He says you aren't much good with heights. Nor with Dutch coffee, according to Professor Arendt. We will have to keep you off roofs, out of Fokkers and restrict you to tea.'

He had obviously been well briefed.

The room was furnished with comfortable chairs, but no ostentation. I got the feeling that this was a place for business, not egos, and that he was a man who was straightforward and friendly. Status didn't matter to him, a fact that I found curious, considering that he was the British boss of a very large company.

Vivian left us alone, and James M of L offered me a seat at the table next to his desk. He sat beside me, still smiling.

'I can see you are curious about my name. Seven generations ago, one of my Scots ancestors found himself on the losing side of one of their wars against the English, and fled across to Holland. The name has survived, but the Scottish connection has long gone. With lands confiscated and my family on the 'most wanted' list, we settled first there, then in Indonesia. I'm the first to come back to Britain. So I'm Dutch with a smattering of Scots genes – but they are pretty diluted by now. I'm sure we are going to get on well.'

I was sure we would, too, and listened intently as he began to explain what he expected of me as the second doctor on his team. At last I began to warm to the job. It was more varied than I had expected. For the team in Hilversum there was the research. They produced the new drugs, and tested them to the level at which they could be used in humans. I was to find doctors in Britain who could do the first trials of them in humans, and to plan, organise, and eventually help analyse, their results. For the team in Basingstoke, I was to teach the reps about the drugs, so that they could present them fairly to the doctors on their 'patches'. I was also to 'vet' the advertising copy for the drugs, to make sure the company wasn't straying outside the law. I only found out later how important that job was – it was I who would go to jail if we couldn't back up our claims.

Later that evening, at the bar of the hotel where the reps and I had been booked for the night, Bill Black filled me in on James M of L. Everyone respected him: he had been a guest of the Imperial Japanese Army during the war, and had spent three years on the notorious Burma railway. Several of the reps, Bill among them, had suffered with him, and he had sought them out after the war, when he knew he was establishing a sales force in the UK. I wasn't surprised that they were fiercely loyal. His gaunt look was the aftermath of beri-beri, malaria and a digestive system that had never recovered completely from his years of starvation.

Around ten o'clock, James joined us in the bar. Whatever the Japanese had done to his stomach, it hadn't spoiled his taste for good whisky. He sat down among our little group of Scots and West Midlanders, and paid for a round of Glenmorangies. We sipped them slowly, appreciating his generosity.

'How did you like your visit to Hilversum?' he asked me.

'To be honest,' I replied, 'I thought I'd made a mess of it. Your board was very tolerant. And I love my furry boots. I'm curious, though, about the buildings. Willem Brand told me that it had been an old chocolate factory. It wasn't purpose-built for drugs research.'

'That's how the whole pharmaceutical firm started,' said James. 'You know our parent company is Huizens of Huizenhoven – the biggest electrical and white goods company in the world?'

'Yes'.

The tall Dutchman took a paper hankie from his pocket, wiped a tiny drop of whisky from his upper lip, and leaned forward a little towards me. 'Why do you think a huge company like Huizens diversified into pharmaceuticals? Do you think it was planned? Did the great and the good in the board at Huizenhoven decide one day to add pharmaceuticals to their portfolio?'

Huizenhoven, I knew, was the city in the south of the Netherlands where Huizens Electrical was based. Virtually all of its 100,000 breadwinners were Huizens employees: its Dutch premier league football team was Huizens SV – the company's 'sports club'. One of the top three Dutch teams – the others were Ajax of Amsterdam and Feyenoord of Rotterdam – HSV had won the Dutch league dozens of times, and the European Cup once. Everyone knew about HSV, and most women around the world had Huizens products in their kitchens.

Huizens Pharma wasn't so well known. I hadn't even heard of it myself until I had had to prescribe some of its drugs.

'I don't know,' I replied. 'I suppose I hadn't thought about it.'

'It was entirely by chance,' James said. 'The chocolate company had gone bust after the war. Huizens wanted another factory to make light bulbs. We bought the buildings, expecting to get permission for change of use, but were refused. The rules were that the factory had still to make chocolate – it was too soon after the starvation of the last years of the war for the authorities to lose a food-producing factory. And there were still tons of chocolate raw material in the stores, waiting to be processed.'

James tasted another sip of Glenmorangie, ran the tip of his tongue around his lip to make sure none was wasted. It dawned on me that the muscles around his mouth weren't quite normal – probably a residue from the years on the railway. He hid his weakness very well.

'I did notice a whiff of chocolate when I was there,' I said. 'I wondered about it.'

'At times it's not just a whiff,' he replied. 'We still process chocolate there, but not for confectionery. That's how we make our hormones. Our chemists found loads of plant steroids in the chocolate residue, so we make our hormones from the stuff that the chocolate manufacturer used to throw away. The rest goes for fertiliser.'

'You mean all that chocolate goes to waste?' I said.

'Not to waste, exactly. We do need the fertiliser. But we need the steroids more. They make much more profit for us. If we didn't make them we would have gone the way the chocolate manufacturers did. And it means we still buy cocoa beans from Surinam, so we keep the Dutch West Indies happy. It's just that we make better use of them.'

I wasn't sure that making hormones out of cocoa was a better use than making chocolates, but I could see his point. I knew of the Huizens hormone product. Called Huizogen, it was a progestogen, a female hormone whose only licensed use so far had been to ease painful periods. I hadn't prescribed it much in Collintrae: my sturdy Scots Presbyterian women patients had borne their period problems with biblical fortitude and rarely discussed them with me.

'You said hormones,' I said, 'but isn't there only one – Huizogen? Do you have more in research?'

Vivian Lewis, who had joined us a few minutes before, answered for James.

'We did have,' he said, 'but we've run into a little problem. Working on them seems to have sterilised the women researchers and feminised the men. It didn't help that the women couldn't conceive and that the men started growing breasts. And when they all lost their sex urge, everyone got alarmed.'

'I'm not surprised,' I said. 'What was happening?'

'It was when we started to build up their production. Going from small lab production to bigger production lines to make pills for trials meant the people working with the raw material were much more exposed to it. Even a few milligrams of the new female hormones were so potent that they stopped women ovulating. Despite all our precautions in the old factory building, we couldn't prevent our employees, male and female, from inhaling the dust. Over months, the amount they inhaled was enough to cause havoc with their sex lives. So we stopped all development until we could build a production line that hoovered up everything, and we could kit out everyone with space-suit protection. That will take a year or two.'

I thought for a moment about the implications of Vivian's story.

'So the new drug is an oral contraceptive?' I asked Vivian.

'Looks as if it's the best yet,' he replied, 'but that raises a big problem for us. We can't market a contraceptive. It's written into our company rules.'

'Why's that?' I said, astonished.

James answered for Vivian.

'Old Franz Huizens — son of the founder of the company — objects on ethical grounds. He is a member of Moral Rearmament and doesn't believe in birth control. As he is still the major shareholder, we must bow to his will.'

'So why carry on with the hormone research?' I asked him.

'We could license it out to another company,' said James. 'Apparently, that wouldn't offend Franz's business code. As long as we don't promote it ourselves, it seems we can do the research and then sell the expertise to another firm. It's our business to make profit where we can.'

The conversation was turning serious: it was the first time I had come face to face with the new priorities my job would impose upon me. It dawned on me that my prime aim was no longer the drive to help the sick: instead, it was to help Huizens make a profit. Of course, if I could help the sick by doing so, that was acceptable. But was it?

'At least,' I said, 'we aren't making de Witt's pills.'

'What are they?' asked James.

'They were marketed for bladder and kidney infections. Little, round white pills – around 30 in a box. The instructions were to take three a day until your urine turned blue: that was a sign that you were cured. Sometimes it took three days, sometimes just one. They were popular for more than a hundred years.'

'And did they work?' James asked.

'Every time,' I replied. 'People swore by them: they made millions for de Witt and his descendants – until the regulations for medicines were tightened. You see, every sixth pill contained the harmless blue dye, methylene blue. It passes straight through into your urine. You couldn't tell from looking at a box of pills which of them carried the colour. Taking three a day, you were almost bound to swallow one of them in the first three days, and the cure became obvious. Most urinary infections clear up in three days anyway, so the appearance of bright-blue urine related well to the improvement in symptoms. Everyone was easily convinced that the pills worked.'

Vivian grinned at me.

'You have a lot to learn, young Tom,' he said. He was all of ten years my senior, and still saw me as one of his students. 'Maybe we aren't so far from de Witt as you think. A few weeks at your job and you may wish you had something as simple as his pills to work on.'

That puzzled me, but I let it go.

Seeing my frown, the man sitting to Vivian's left introduced himself to me. Middle-aged, balding, well rounded, I would have placed him as a schoolmaster if he hadn't been part of the company.

'Hi, Doc,' he said, offering me his hand to shake. 'Oliver Davies. Training manager. We are going to see a lot of each other. I teach the reps how to sell and you teach them what they are selling. More important – what they aren't selling. Did you ever hear about the Beecham's Pills advertising around the turn of the century?'

I couldn't say I had.

'Everywhere they were promoted as 'Worth a guinea a box'. On billboards, in newspapers, on the boxes themselves, over the early radio and in silent film cinemas. It was the best-known pharmaceutical slogan in the world. Yet they only cost a shilling a box.'

'Why was that so wrong?' I asked.

'It just so happened that the standard charge for a back-street abortion at the time – of course, abortion was a serious crime then – was a guinea. Beecham's pills contained a small amount of quinine. Someone worked out that if you swallowed a whole boxful, you got enough quinine inside you to make you miscarry – and not enough to poison you. The margin between the two doses is fairly narrow. So the public got the message that if you swallowed a whole box of the pills at once, you would abort – without the need to fork out a whole guinea. Women actually thought that the guinea-a-box slogan was an undercover message about abortion. The strange thing is that Beecham's themselves had no idea that their slogan would be taken that way. As soon as it was pointed out to them, they stopped it.'

'Are you saying that it's going to be my job to stop Huizens making a similar mistake?'

'It depends on how you assess a mistake. When the pills were 'worth a guinea a box', Beechams sold millions of boxes. When the advertising was dropped, sales slumped. What was the mistake – commercially? The slogan or dropping it? Let's take a show of hands around this table. Who says the first?'

Two hands went up – mine and James's. Vivian had moved away from the table to speak to a man sitting on a stool at the bar, who had just arrived, and whom I hadn't seen before, so he didn't take part.

'And who says the second?' Oliver continued.

Nine hands were raised, including Oliver's.

'So you see, Doc, that at times you may have a fight on your hands. Welcome to the fray.'

I looked at my half-glass of Glenmorangie and decided that it was time to take another sip. James M of L saw me raise it to my lips and raised his too, holding it towards me for the briefest of moments in a silent toast. We swallowed together. I was fairly sure no one else around the table noticed.

Vivian brought his friend to the table.

'Can I introduce you all to a good friend of Huizens – Professor Peter Mawson, of St Bart's?'

I'd heard of Professor Mawson. His unit was famous for the

study of new drugs, their benefits and particularly their side effects. His reputation was above reproach, and so was the work of his team. The two men sat down together, opposite me. The professor politely refused an offer of a drink, looked at me and smiled.

Vivian turned to him and gestured towards me.

'Here's your newest recruit,' he said. 'Tom Smith.'

Peter leaned across the table and shook my hand.

'Very pleased to meet you,' he said. 'We are looking forward to seeing you at Bart's on Monday.'

I hadn't a clue what he was talking about, but Vivian was quick to enlighten me.

'I haven't had time to tell you yet, Tom, but Peter and I have arranged for you to work in the lab at Bart's for the next six weeks. It'll give you an idea of the nuts and bolts of research, and you will be working on one of our drugs, too. We are throwing you in at the deep end.'

'I'm sure he can swim,' the professor added.

I wasn't sure that I could, but I was going to give it a good try.

Baptism of Fire

Mairi, the children and I spent the weekend getting used to life in a commuter's estate. The views were the houses opposite and the sea was 30 miles away. They were the minuses. The pluses were that I could spend the whole weekend with the three of them and not once worry about the phone. Those early days were bliss, as I found my family again. We had the whole of the south of England to explore and we were looking forward to doing it, the four of us.

Naturally, I was looking forward, too, to Monday. I had a new company car, a train ticket for the next six weeks, and a totally new working life for which I felt great enthusiasm, but also a little foreboding.

That first morning I left the house at seven to catch the 7.29 from Basingstoke to Waterloo. The Vauxhall had that new-car smell of aerosol-produced fresh leather (I would have to be higher in the Huizens hierarchy to merit real leather seats) but I didn't mind the plastic. I drove happily to the station, parked among hundreds of other commuters' cars and waited on the platform for the express from Southampton. With no bowler and no pinstripe, in my grey suit I stood out from the crowd of almost exclusively male City-bound commuters.

When the train arrived, I found myself at the door for the dining car, and climbed in. A waiter with a white cloth over his arm welcomed me with a smile.

'Are you for breakfast, sir?' he asked.

'Why not?' I thought, and sat down on the last empty seat at a table for four. The three men didn't bother to look up, intent as they were on their bacon and eggs and their *Times* or *Telegraph*.

'Good morning,' I said, brightly, to them.

There was a chorus of 'Hrrrumph' in reply. It seemed that chat with a newcomer wasn't on their agenda. I ordered a full breakfast, then opened my *Guardian* and read until it arrived. I had been warned that commuters weren't communicators, so I settled for my own thoughts and company.

Five minutes later, I was looking down on my three rashers and two fried eggs, with a slice of fried bread, some baked beans and a cup of steaming black coffee. I started to cut my bacon when the man opposite me leaned forward.

'Lift up your coffee cup,' he said. 'Like us.'

I looked at him. He was smiling and nodding across, first at me and then at the others. They too were smiling at me, and had their cups, mostly half empty, in their hands, a few inches above the cloth.

I put down my knife and lifted my cup.

At that precise moment, the train rocked and jolted violently. I had a hard job keeping the cup steady, to stop the coffee from spilling. If I had left the full cup in its saucer, on the table, it would surely have spilled all over the cloth, and maybe even over me.

'Thanks,' I said.

The three men put their cups down. I had a sip at my coffee, and put mine down, too.

'It's the points here,' he said. 'The train always judders over them. You have seven minutes before the next lot – I'll warn you.'

I thanked him profusely, and the four of us started to talk. It turned out that they had 90 years of commuter experience among them, from Southampton and Brockenhurst in the New Forest. They knew every wrinkle in the train travel business and were happy to welcome me to their little band. They occupied the same seat every day, and my seat was empty only because its previous occupant had retired on the previous Friday. It seemed I was a fit replacement for their friend.

The silence broken, we soon exchanged names and professions. My informant about the points was Arthur the architect. By the window opposite was Billy the banker – 'never call him Willie' said Arthur mysteriously. The others laughed – it took me years to work out why. Sitting beside me was Charles the chartered accountant. Amazingly, the fourth member, the one who had just retired, had been Donald the dentist. They were truly disappointed to hear that I was Tom the doctor. Dom, they said, would have fitted better.

Hearing that I was bound for Bart's, they decided to take me in hand. Billy and Charles worked in the City, which meant that the three of us were to catch the 'Drain' from Waterloo. They had been doing so daily for more than 30 years and thought nothing of it.

The Drain is well named. It's a shuttle underground service between Waterloo and Bank. Walking on to the platform, I was struck by the queues of men waiting two abreast at around fifteen-yard intervals. They snaked around the platform in disciplined order. When the train came, the carriage doors stopped exactly at the head of each queue. The men filed onto the carriages like paratroopers who had been ordered to leap out of a plane, in perfect marching time. Billy and I boarded together, with Charles just behind. I was astounded to find that there were no seats: the carriages were for standing occupants only. We stood there, crammed together like sardines, clutching loops of leather hanging from metal rails in the roof, or holding onto metal uprights, swaying as we sped the few miles to the City. It occurred to me as we did so that if anyone had a heart attack on the journey, he would have remained propped up until he fell over as we got out.

Happily, no one died, and we all made for the exit. I had to take another tube one stop to St Paul's, and walk from there to the hospital. My two new friends wished me luck and said they would keep a seat free for me on the next day's morning train. It was a good start, I thought, as I turned towards the Central Line platform.

It was a fresh, sunny morning, and my walk led me around St Paul's Cathedral and across to the square between the front of St Bart's and Smithfield Market. I needed to get to Little Britain, a street running along the side of the ancient hospital buildings, and had to pass the front entrance of the hospital. My attention was drawn to a massive plaque on the wall beside it. At the top was the saltire, the white-on-blue diagonal cross of Scotland. Under it, in Gaelic and English, was a dedication to William Wallace and to the fact that he had been hanged, drawn and quartered at that spot. As a Scot I didn't take it as a good omen.

I arrived at the pharmacological research department exactly on time, at 9 am. It was already a hive of activity. Young men and women in crisp white coats were taking blood samples, measuring blood pressures, taking notes on clipboards, watching other men and women jogging on dangerous-looking makeshift running machines or hitting 'yes' or 'no' keys in answer to questions that were flashing on and off TV screens placed in front of them. In one corner, there were the remains of an ancient Austin 7 car, the wheels, sides and roof of which had been removed. In the driving seat was a young man, wired up to machines recording his electrocardiogram, his blood pressure and his heart rate on paper rolls that were neatly forming piles on the floor near him. One roll was recording how fast he was reacting to hazards in the road on the screen in front of him. Cars, houses, trees, stray pedestrians and animals, sudden road warning signs, blind bends were all flashing towards and past him. He didn't seem to be doing so well. In the minute or so I was watching him, he crashed twice.

I glanced at the paper recordings. His heart rate was fast and erratic, his blood pressure ranging from high to low as he met and missed or hit each obstacle. He was breathing 24 times a minute – about twice as fast as normal. Yet he was showing no signs of stress. In fact, he had a huge grin on his face even when he had apparently become a 'fatal' and had to start again at the beginning.

Peter Mawson tapped me on the shoulder. I hadn't noticed him approach, so engrossed was I in the scene. I turned to face him.

'That's one of yours,' he said to me, smiling. 'He is taking H7316, one of your drugs, and from the look of him a fairly high dose of it. You'll be running these trials for us.'

The subject stopped his driving, stepped out of the car and stood up. Then fell flat on his face. He was still grinning as he shakily got to his feet.

'I think you have a bit of a problem with it,' Peter added, 'at least at that dose.'

He invited me into his inner sanctum. I sat down in an easy chair, and he began to tell me my role in his department. I'll cut out the details, as this isn't a textbook on how to conduct research. It's enough to say that most of the time you are measuring, taking notes, making calculations and drawing conclusions. The rest of the time you are writing them up for publication. It wasn't, I thought that day, my first choice of jobs, but it would be an education. It would be my task to supervise the studies done in Little Britain with the drugs Huizens had in research – before they reached patients. The main purpose was first to see that they were safe, and second that they were effective.

The drug taken by the driver was certainly effective. It was an antidepressant: and if his wide grin was anything to go by, he was deliriously happy. But it didn't seem to be safe, at least for anyone getting behind a wheel. I would learn a lot in the next six weeks about safety, including my own.

The subject that day was one of two dozen volunteers for the H7316 study. Some were taking the drug, some weren't. Those who were on the drug were taking different doses. I had to monitor all their physical constants, before and at set times throughout the day after they took their daily tablets. I wasn't to know which dosage group they were in until after all the results were printed. We had to stick to these rules, to avoid any bias.

The study ran smoothly for my first two weeks. I heard that other human trials had gone so well in Holland and Germany that a licence had been given for its first trials in patients, in

Leeds. They were all severely depressed inpatients in a university psychiatric department, and I didn't see any harm in that. They wouldn't be driving.

So, at the beginning of my third week, I set off from home to St Bart's thinking I'd have a normal day. It didn't turn out that way. Half a mile from home, smoke started to fill the windscreen. It was coming from under the bonnet. There was a garage to the right, about twenty yards ahead of me, with, luckily, a space in the oncoming traffic that I could use to swing suddenly into its forecourt. Before I could stop the engine, a mechanic had rushed out with a fire extinguisher and a big blanket. He had the fire out in seconds, but the engine was wrecked. He offered to drive me to the station, and promised to have things fixed by the end of the day. I managed to catch the train with a minute or two to spare.

I sat with my travelling companions, out of breath and covered with soot from the smoke. I must have smelled acrid, but they were too polite to mention it. True to type, although they must have been curious, they didn't ask me a thing. My arriving dishevelled and filthy didn't faze them, or, for that matter, our steward, at all. As usual, a huge breakfast was put down in front of me, and I began to eat. Ten minutes into the journey from Basingstoke, with all four of us tucking in, the train suddenly stopped. The steward stood at the end of the dining car and shouted at us all to get off. The galley was on fire, and it was spreading. I didn't wait for a second announcement. Being in the aisle seat, near the door, I was the first on the trackside.

The others followed. They had their briefcases in one hand and their breakfasts, on trays, in the other. Arthur the architect had thoughtfully put my breakfast on top of his.

48

'Couldn't see you goin' hungry, old lad,' he said. 'Can't waste good food.'

We sat down on the embankment together, eating and watching the railwaymen putting out the fire, and wondering how late we would be. Half an hour later, we were back on the train, on our way. It meant arriving late in Bart's, but Peter didn't mind about that: he was too concerned about another piece of news he had received.

'We have two dead dogs,' he said. 'You had better tell your bosses...'

Which was why, later that day, I was taking a flight to Amsterdam.

OF DOGS AND DIAMONDS

The man in the aisle seat was nervous. Maybe he was just a natural fidget, but he couldn't sit still. Every few moments he shifted in his seat, as if his back hurt, or his legs were seizing up. He kept picking up the airline magazine from the pocket in the back of the seat in front of him, and leafing through it. Then he would put it back, finding nothing of interest in it. Time and again he did it, as if he was missing something of vital importance, yet never finding it.

He was sweating, too. I could see beads of sweat glistening on the back of his hands. He was in the aisle seat, I was at the window, so when the stewardess asked if we would like tea or coffee, I took the opportunity, as my head turned towards her, to glance at his face. The same beads were on his temple and forehead. He could just have been nervous about flying, but I put the thought aside as unlikely. He had too much of the well-travelled businessman about him. A little too heavy, with not a hair out of place; what remained of it was expensively styled. His pinstripe suit, starched white shirt shaped to accommodate his expanded waist, gold-flecked silk tie and cufflinks just the right length below the jacket sleeves proclaimed his affluence.

Surely he wouldn't fear air travel. Something more important must have been bothering him.

The cufflinks were the big give-away. If they had been ordinary, say, the usual gold, to go with his tie, I might have paid less attention to him. But they weren't. Each had two brilliant white diamonds set in gold. Big ones. The flash from one had caught the corner of my eye as he moved his hand back and forward to the magazine. It was after that I saw the rest of his jewellery. Two diamond rings on each hand, on his fourth and little fingers, even bigger than the ice on his cuffs. A bracelet on his right wrist was encrusted in diamonds of different colours, blue, yellow, rose and clear in repeated regular order around it. On the back of his left wrist was a plain-faced watch, wafer thin, a stark contrast to the diamonds studding the gold strap that held it there. The diamonds didn't stop there. Through the middle of his tie was a stud, a single diamond, even bigger than the others.

Even then I hadn't seen the last of his diamonds. Our flight was the KLM 4.30 from Heathrow to Amsterdam. It took only three-quarters of an hour, and as a British national, there was no paperwork for me on entering Holland. It was different for my companion. As the stewardess passed down the aisle handing out landing forms for non-Europeans, he took one. He pulled out from his inside pocket a diamond-studded pen and started to fill in the little squares. It didn't work for long. After a few fruitless efforts, he turned to face me. Leaning slightly over the two parcels strapped into the seat between us, he spoke for the first time.

'My pen seems to have run out of ink. By any chance do you have one I could borrow for a moment?' I wasn't sure about his accent. It could have been American, but there was a hint of the eastern European about it. Had he learned his English in a Russian-American school?

He flashed a smile as he spoke. Flash being the appropriate word, for in the middle of his left upper front tooth – the central incisor for the technically minded – was yet another of his diamonds. Like the others, it caught the light, this time making me uneasy, perhaps because of the pain he must have gone through to have it so neatly inserted into the tooth.

I handed him my tenpenny Biro, and was happy to see that it worked well. He offered to give it back to me, but I told him to keep it. I had another in my breast pocket and dozens more back at the office. He thanked me and fell silent again. He obviously didn't want to talk.

We landed a few minutes later. We rose from our seats when the engines shut down. He took his briefcase from the shelf above us; I picked up my two boxes from the seat between us and started to lug them, with some difficulty, along the aisle towards the front exit.

The boxes had been awkward – not just for me to carry, but because I had to resist several attempts from airline staff to relieve me of them. The check-in staff had wanted to put them in the hold, saying they were too big for cabin baggage. I showed them my two tickets, one for me, the other for the boxes, and they relented. My boxes had paid for their seat, and I was not going to let them out of my sight or hands. Getting onto the plane, I had a similar problem with the steward. He had wanted me to put them in the hold: I again showed the two tickets. That puzzled him, but he had let me stagger along the aisle to the two seats, and helped me to strap them in.

Getting off the plane was simpler. I walked into the sleeve, up the covered gangway, into the airport, carrying one package in each hand. I had no other hand luggage. All I had was my passport, my return ticket for later that day and a sheet of paper folded in my breast pocket. The diamond man and I walked together, through passport control, past baggage reclaim, towards customs. It seemed we were both travelling light. We were the first passengers from the plane to reach the little group of customs men at the glass doors that led into the airport arrivals hall.

They were waiting for us, eager to meet us. Three large men in grey uniforms, one with a gun on his belt, looked up from behind their bench and beckoned us towards them. I knew I wasn't sweating as much as my companion. The betablocker I had taken before leaving for Heathrow made sure my face was dry and my heartbeat slow. There was no beating pulse at my neck or sweat on my brow to raise the slightest suspicion.

Two more men appeared from behind a metal screen and walked briskly towards the diamond man. He looked at them, then shrugged. He held out his hands, and one of them hand-cuffed him. They walked together towards a side door, and he was gone. No one had said a word.

Which left me facing the man with the gun.

'Are you with that man?' he asked.

'No. We sat beside each other on the plane, that's all,' I said, keeping calm.

He seemed to accept the answer at face value.

He stared at my two boxes. 'What is in the two packages?' he asked.

'Medical samples,' I said, pulling the letter from my inside breast pocket. 'I have the list of content here.' On it were lists of chemicals, serum samples, test equipment and documents, all of them with permits to allow them into Holland. There were about 30 items, described in medical or chemical terms almost certainly outside the man's experience or knowledge.

He took his time reading it. 'You from Huizens?' he asked.

'The British end, yes,' I replied.

He took out a small, pointed steel knife.

'You don't mind if I open it?' he said. It wasn't a question, but a demand.

Before I could answer, he stuck the point of the knife into one upper corner of the first box.

'Please don't do that,' I said, beginning to be alarmed.

What looked like a jet of steam was now issuing from the hole, like a kettle on the boil.

The customs man withdrew the knife and peered closely at the steam.

'Why is this steaming?' he asked.

I replied, as calmly as I could, 'That's not steam; it's liquid nitrogen. It's used to keep the serum samples cold. You have punctured the inner seal. That's why it's leaking. We need to get it to the lab as soon as possible before it's all lost. If you open it here the samples may be spoiled. More to the point, you could freeze your face, or even an eye. The liquid nitrogen will spill all over the place, and it's many degrees colder than the inside of a deep freeze.'

He stepped back a metre or two, and reread my document. He stroked the stubble on his chin.

'Well, I suppose if it's from Huizens, it's OK. Go on through.'

I lifted the packages and began to walk up to and through the automatic sliding frosted-glass doors, and, without looking back, into the open concourse of Schiphol Airport to meet my Huizens contact.

I never met the diamond man again. I don't know why he was taken away. I presume it was to do with fraud, maybe on a big scale. But he couldn't have imagined the scale on which I was working. I had got my two deep-frozen beagle dogs – highly illegal material – through the Dutch customs. Over 200 million pounds were resting on my successful delivery of those dogs to our animal pathology experts. His diamonds were chickenfeed compared to my contraband. It was my first venture into crime, and I sincerely hoped it would be my last. I was a million miles from Collintrae and my life as a country doctor.

A Dog's Life

Bringing a new drug into the medical market involves coordinating several strands of research. The initial chemistry, which gives a clue to its possible properties, benefits and side effects, is followed by laboratory studies of what it does to cells and cultures of tissues. If it passes them without mishap, the next step is in animals. Whatever you think of animal research, the rules can't be broken. In the 1970s, the Committee on Safety of Medicines (then called the CSM: it is now the European Medicines Commission, but the rules are the same) laid down the species of animals to which the drug had to be given, in what range of doses and for how long. These studies had to be completed, or nearly so, and any doubts about safety dispelled, before the first studies in humans. Whatever you think of this – and I know that many readers will naturally be offended by it – the dog studies had to be done. It was part of my job, along with many others, to ensure that it was done as humanely as possible.

Beagle dogs are ideal. They are affectionate, seem to lap up every chemical known to man, and will tolerate all that the researchers can throw at them. For every potential new drug, dog lifetime studies, eight years for beagles, had to be performed before the drugs could pass on to the next stage, first in human volunteers, then in patients. So for six years before I joined the Huizens research team, 24 beagle dogs had been happily munching H7316 without anything untoward happening to them.

The dogs had been so well that the CSM had allowed us to start on the human studies – which was why our obliviously happy drivers at Bart's were crashing their cars every morning. It was also why, 200 miles to the north of us, in the Leeds University Department of Psychiatry, a small group of very seriously depressed men and women were coming alive again after years of Stygian gloom. The excitement about this drug in the company was palpable. It was an entirely different molecule from the current crop of antidepressants, and we were confident that it would have far fewer side effects than they did.

The worst side effect is, of course, sudden death. People tend to tolerate an occasional dry mouth, or the odd bout of indigestion, and even a bit of a shake, but sudden death is a tad more difficult for a company to present as a risk for their new drug. If a dog had died, couldn't a human do so, too? We had to find out the cause, and to be certain that it wouldn't also be relevant to patients. One dog's death might have been a coincidence, unrelated to the drug, but two, found dead in the morning of the same day, was a real concern.

My instructions were clear. We had to examine the corpses as soon as possible in the company's own labs in the Netherlands. I was the most responsible employee: I had to be the courier. The company would supply me with the false paperwork, and I would have to bluff my way through all the red tape. Getting a licence to ship the dogs out of the country would take too long: we needed answers yesterday. We had started to give the drugs to humans: we couldn't afford for any of them to go the way of the dogs.

So while I was wending my way to Amsterdam, Vivian, my old tutor and now my boss, was on the train to Leeds, with the distinctly more unpleasant job of persuading the eminent professor there that he had to stop his patient trial forthwith. Stopping a trial suddenly when it is producing spectacular results is always difficult. When it involves pitching people who feel wonderful for the first time in years back into their life of unending deepest misery, it verges on the impossible. It isn't easy to balance the probable tiny risk posed by the drug against the considerable risk of suicide when it is stopped. So Professor Amey, our contact in Leeds, would put massive pressure on Vivian to let him carry on with the trial at least until we knew what had happened. After all, the dogs had survived six years on the drug: the patients had only had it for a month.

That wasn't my immediate concern. There was another curious fact about those dogs. Beagle fur is a mix of black, brown and white patches. Our 24 had started off the usual colour. As they had grown older, however, the black areas had faded to a light brown, so that they were now two-coloured rather than three-coloured. Even the brown patches were lightening: if they survived to their usual eight years, they were in danger of becoming all-over blonds. Very pretty, but not very beagle-like.

Once I was through the airport security, I was delighted to find Willem waiting for me. He was in a hurry. He explained that the dogs needed to be in the lab within the hour. A team was waiting for them, and its members would be working through the night on them. We would have some answers within a few days, and even that wasn't soon enough for our triallists. More than a hundred people were taking H7316 in hospitals around Europe. We had to know fast how much danger they were in.

I handed my parcel over, and, job done, shook hands and said '*tot siens*' to Willem, intending to turn back towards the departure area to catch my plane back to Heathrow. He kept hold of my hand, scrutinising it, then turned his eyes to the rest of me.

'Have you been having a barbecue?' he asked, laughing. 'Your shirt and your tie – they are covered in soot.'

I looked down at myself. I was still a mess from the morning's fires. Yet no one I had met that day, until Willem, had bothered to comment on it. Not the Bart's staff, the people at the animal lab from where I had collected the dogs, the airport check-in and aircraft crew, the diamond man or even the customs officers. Maybe they thought that I was just some nutty professor, who always travelled looking like this.

I told Willem about my day. He laughed and patted me affectionately on the shoulder.

'We suspected you might be a walking disaster,' he said. 'Take care on the way home. I could get you a new shirt where I bought the boots for you, but it's too far out of our way. Maybe next time.'

With that he left with the dogs to find his car. I caught my plane, wondering what the next day would bring.

It brought a lot. First a phone call to Peter at Bart's to stop the car studies, and to apologise for my non-appearance at the lab. I had a meeting to address at the office that took precedence. He understood and wished me well. Then a few frantic phone calls with Willem, to catch up on progress, and a call to Vivian, who was having a torrid time in Leeds.

Huizens gave the British part of the firm plenty of autonomy, the Dutch trusted James M of L's judgment implicitly but this was too serious for national organisations to go their own way. I faced the managers around the table that morning knowing I was delivering very bad news. H7316 was to be our flagship drug: our first move into antidepressants, it had given us only good news from the start of its use in humans. All the studies so far had confirmed that it didn't carry the side effects of the standard treatments, and that it worked really well. Its main advantage was that it also worked fast – it raised mood within a few days of starting it, in considerable contrast to all other known antidepressants. The sales team were looking forward to a bonanza that would pitch the company into the top six in the country. I had to tell them that the bonanza had disappeared. James gave me the floor.

I was short and stark. 'We have lost H7316. All trials are stopping. We can't risk what happened to the dogs happening to patients,' I said.

'But we've spent a quarter of a billion on it already. Do you mean that has all gone for nothing?' That was Oliver Davies, our training manager. 'Can we do nothing to retrieve the drug? What actually killed the dogs?'

'They developed ulcers in their small intestines. In each dog, one ulcer broke through the gut wall, and they got peritonitis. It killed them within hours – probably the whole process started and ended overnight, while the dogs were sleeping. There were no symptoms beforehand.'

'Why do you think it could happen in patients?'

This time it was James.

'It's the way the dogs "handle" the drug,' I replied. 'For the drug to work, their liver has to "conjugate" it. That is, it has to add another chemical to it. There's a choice of three of them. Humans, for example, add sulphate or glucuronide to it. It's only active when combined with one of them. The dogs do that too, but they can also acetylate it. And that was the trouble with the two that died. The acetylated drug caused the ulcers: the two dead dogs were the only acetylators among the 24.'

'So the others don't have ulcers?' asked Oliver.

'That's right,' I said. 'They have been checked and they are healthy.'

'And people don't acetylate it?' again from James.

'Our best guess is that only one person in a thousand will acetylate the drug,' I told him.

'Then what's wrong with marketing the drug, but testing people for acetylation before they take it?' asked James.

'Loads.' This came from Andrew Watson. He had been listening intently, without speaking. I remembered him from the meeting at the hotel, and he hadn't spoken a word then, either. He was the technical director, in charge of laboratory practice and small-scale manufacture of drugs for trial purposes. He had been lured from academia, and it showed.

'Tell me, then,' said James.

'Practically, it would mean putting every new patient through a biochemistry work-up before starting the drugs. And who would want to take it knowing that some people might die from it? Our competitors would have a field day. Can you imagine the CSM agreeing to license a drug on that basis? You would have to let GPs prescribe the drug freely to depressed patients regardless of the way they metabolise it, or you don't market it at all.'

Oliver leaned forward in his seat, chin on hands.

'If we do that, what's the risk? How long would it take for your one in a thousand patients to develop an ulcer, and how long for it to perforate? It took the beagles six years. Does that mean 40 years for humans – on the basis that dogs age seven times faster than we do? If that's the case, where's the harm?'

I couldn't believe what I was hearing.

'How many patients do you think will be given this drug in the first few years after marketing?' I asked him.

'Around three million,' he said.

'At one in a thousand at risk, that's 3000 potential sudden deaths on this drug – we don't know when. But you can be assured that when the first one dies, because of the drug or not, the lawyers will be looking through our files. People will die coincidentally from perforated ulcers, irrespective of whether or not the drug caused them. When the lawyers read about the dogs, they will have a field day. You would be looking at billions in damages.'

That seemed to end the discussion.

Until Andrew spoke again.

'As a matter of interest, what colour were the two dogs that died?'

'Odd you should ask that,' I said. 'They were the only two of the 24 that had kept their black markings. All the rest were going blonde, some were almost white. Why do you ask?'

'So the acetylated drug didn't affect the dogs' skin colour?' he continued.

'That's right.'

'Then could you use the change in skin colour as a marker of safety – that if you turn paler on the drug you would be free of risk?'

'I suppose that's true – but just think of the political impli-cations of marketing a drug that lightens skin colour. It's not on the Huizens agenda.'

'Not yet,' said James. 'We may have to wait a few years for that.'

H7316 never did make the market. It took a further five years for the Huizens research team to change the molecule into one that wouldn't cause ulcers. It turned out to be a matter of switching a chlorine atom for a fluorine atom. The new drug was on the prescription pads in the mid-1980s. It was good enough, but didn't work quite as spectacularly or as fast as H7316. Maybe twenty million people are being prescribed it around the world today. So far none have died from taking it.

But there is an illegal drug in circulation with a very similar formula to that of H7316. I don't know how the secret got out. It isn't used for depression, but it does lighten skin. I'm told it blocks the action of the melanocytes – the cells in the skin that produce melanin. It has never been given a licence, as far as I know, in any developed country. But is it being used in coun-tries where skin lightening is sadly very much in demand? I have my suspicions.

The Spy?

The loss of H7316 didn't prevent me from finishing my six-week stint at Bart's. I was given another drug to work on: this time it was a betablocker. Huizens thought it might have special advantages over its competitors. I had to show it didn't make people wheeze – one of the major problems with this class of blood-pressure-lowering drugs. After working out a new protocol for it, I settled back into my former routine of measuring, recording and writing up. It gave me plenty of time to ruminate on where my life was taking me – assuredly well away from practising medicine. Did I really want that?

Around eleven o'clock one morning, three weeks into the new trial, Peter called me into his office. He had a visiting doctor from Bulgaria for me to meet. A consultant physician from the University of Sofia, she needed some experience of conducting clinical trials. Could I show her the ropes, and perhaps let her do some of the testing?

Anna Petranova was 30-something, with long black hair, hooded eyelids, a full, oval face with just a hint of a double chin. She would have passed as good-looking, if not beautiful, if she would only have smiled. She didn't, even when Peter introduced me to her. I tried to make light conversation with her, but she replied only with a shrug, or a 'yes' or 'no'. It was clear that either she didn't understand me, or that she simply had no time for small talk. I decided that it must be the latter, and took her into the lab to show her what we were doing.

As the bulk of the work in studying a betablocker is largely a matter of taking blood pressures every hour or so throughout the day, I was glad to have her with me. The machines we used, however, were different from the ones used in surgeries. They were 'fixed' so that the readings they showed were not the real ones. A code had to be broken at the end of each study to find the true blood pressure. That way there was no possibility of bias. Having two doctors measuring the pressures was a bonus: it made the results even more watertight. So I was happy to have the silent Anna with me, if only for the corroboration.

Except that there was no corroboration. Anna's measurements didn't at all correlate with mine. My measurements and hers were so far apart that I was beginning to believe that I had lost my touch. Accurate blood pressure measurements depend on catching the exact instant when the heartbeats in the artery in the arm suddenly fade away. With experience, the listener can be accurate within one or at most two millimetres of mercury – but you need to be in complete control of the air in the cuff to achieve it. Anna's readings were often ten millimetres or more wide of mine – both above and below them.

This worried me a lot. I tried to ask her how she was measuring the pressures: what she was hearing as she let the cuff down, but she either did not understand me, or thought that I, as a lowly ex-GP, had no right to question her abilities. Nor did she seem to want to discuss the trials with me. She was in a world of her own: when she wasn't taking pressures, she didn't talk to any of the other researchers or to the volunteers. That was unusual, because we all got on well together, and humour was a great reliever of tensions. I began to wonder if her silence sprung from ignorance, that she might not know, in fact, how to take a blood pressure correctly. As the technique had been initially developed by the Russian physician, the great Dr Korotkov himself, a hero of the Soviets, she should surely have been very familiar with it.

The next morning on the train, I mentioned Dr Anna to my three friends. Billy the banker put aside his *Financial Times* to listen intently. He had contacts with Sofia, he said. He might just make a telephone call and find out a little more about Dr Anna.

I was horrified. I didn't want to stir up trouble, I told him. She was, after all, a guest of St Bart's, and I was only a 'temp'.

Mid-afternoon on the next day, three men in grey suits appeared in our room. Peter was with them. He was full of apologies, but he said that Anna was to go with them. She had to do as they asked.

She stood up from the seat where she had been entering numbers into columns and slowly stared at each man in turn. To the amazement of everyone else in the room, she tried to run past them through the open door. They closed ranks, took hold of her and escorted her out of the room. She didn't return.

On the home-bound train that evening, the headlines were about a man who had been stabbed in the leg with the point of an umbrella in broad daylight in a busy London street. Later, it transpired that the poison was ricin, a favourite of the Bulgarian Secret Service. The killer was never caught.

The next morning, Billy asked about Anna.

'How is Dr Petranova?' he asked me.

'I wouldn't know,' I told him. 'She went away with three men yesterday afternoon, and the prof doesn't think she will be back. Why do you ask?'

'It's curious,' Billy replied. 'The only Dr Anna Petranova in Sofia is still in her clinic there. Or was yesterday, when a friend of mine telephoned her. And she is 55 years old. That's a little older than your Anna appears to be. Yes?'

The 'yes' wasn't a question. It was confirmation.

'Yes,' I said. It was now clear as crystal that Billy was more than a banker, but I let that thought pass through my head, then float away. Now my blood pressure figures would be scrapped, and I'd have to restart the trial. I asked the steward for a refill of the strong black coffee and began to think again.

'Don't let her worry you,' said Billy. 'I have a proposition for you. There's a doctor friend in Lymhampton who needs a break for a few days. Would you like to stand in for him? You did say, didn't you, that your contract lets you practise medicine several days a month?'

'I'd be glad to,' I told him. I was really needing to put things into perspective, and a few days of going loco would help me to do just that. Which was how, two weeks later, I found myself in practice in a coastal town on the Solent, in a charming house overlooking the Isle of Wight.

Practice — South-Coast Style

The river Lymm empties itself into the west end of the Solent, facing the Needles. At its mouth is Lymhampton. The town's romantics fancy that it has a long history of mystery and intrigue, that they are descended from smugglers of fine French wines and silks, and even of pirates who made good enough to escape the gallows. Several families claim descendancy from the man they describe as the 'real' Scarlet Pimpernel, dismissing the fact that he was a creation of a French noblewoman who had never heard of the place.

The rest of the population have no time to speculate on their ancestors. Boat-building and repairing don't make you rich unless you own the business, so there was little enough time for romance in their lives. These days, the town's main industry is servicing the flourishing yacht trade. Its focus is on the harbour and marina, and the townspeople are a mix of the wealthy boat owners and those whose living depends on them. The doctors reflect that mix: the two practices that serve the community are as divided as their patients. One serves, and shares the spoils of, the relatively rich: the other looks after the artisans and others. The two don't meet much, on any level.

Naturally, my contact being Billy the Banker, the practice I had been asked to locum for was the wealthy one. Dr Haswell lived in a beautiful Tudor mansion, with an acre of ground around it. The lawns were dotted with magnificent trees planted more than a century before by one of those Victorian explorers whose overwhelming urge was to outdo his peers in their collections of exotica from the Far East. The good doctor employed a gardener and a maid, and had built a swimming pool by a patio next to the breakfast room. He was well into his sixties, and believed that his morning cold dip was the basis of his rude good health.

My task was an easy one. All I had to do was to look after the practice for a long – Friday to Monday – weekend while he was away to visit relatives. Mairi, the children and I were to stay in the house and take full advantage of the facilities. It was June, the weather was set fair, the children eyed the swimming pool with great glee, and we looked forward to living the life of luxury.

There were two snags. One was that it was mainly a private practice. I had not only to treat patients: I had to make sure that they paid, or at least hand them a bill, for each consultation. I had never had a private patient and had no idea what the going rates were. I decided to leave detailed notes for each surgery visit and call and leave it to Dr Haswell to sort out later.

The other snag? The doctor had a flock of geese that had to be corralled into their house at night and let out in the morning. They also had to be fed and watered. Catriona, in her eleven-year-old's enthusiasm for all animal life, volunteered for the post of chief goose attendant. Alasdair, much wiser than his nine years, left her to it. The birds, like those in the Roman capitol 2000 years before, were Dr Haswell's burglar alarm.

Friday morning started well. Being 'private', Dr Haswell had a beautifully furnished waiting room. His wife usually prepared coffee for the patients: there was a notice asking them to pay 'a little' towards each cup, in a large soup bowl on the table in the middle of the room. Naturally, she had started off the 'collection' with a few strategically placed 50-pence coins, then left Mairi to continue the practice. The odd twenty pence was thrown in, too, just in case that seemed a bit over the top. But no coppers. There was also, being private, no fixed appointment list. It was 'come when it is convenient to you': the doctor would always be at your service. Of course, the fee for seeing people outside surgery hours at the house was double the standard two pounds. Calls, depending on the distance the doctor had to drive, were ten pounds or more.

This was new to me. In Collintrae no one had paid a thing. It wasn't going to be easy to set a fee per consultation. I decided to note down each consultation on a list, and leave it to Dr Haswell, when he returned, to organise the money. I started the surgery, a little fearful, not of the consultant process – that was what I was trained for, after all – but of how I would relate to the patients.

My first patient was delightful. She was 90 years old, slim as a pencil and bursting with good health and bonhomie. She was also titled. On the inside of her notes there was a warning in red ink on how she was to be addressed. 'Your ladyship' or 'My Lady' was apparently appropriate, although in fact, 'Your Grace' (said the notes) would have been more correct. She did not want to stand on ceremony, she had said, so the lower titles were acceptable to her. Apparently, she didn't want to descend quite as far as 'Mrs'.

All she was in for was an official note to say that her

eyesight was good enough for her to drive. I asked her to read the chart behind my head. She read it perfectly without glasses, with each eye in turn. I squinted at it myself, with my specs off. I couldn't read beyond the third line.

'I'm happy to sign the note,' I said, and filled in the form accordingly, signing it neatly at the bottom.

'You look a fit young man,' she said, eyeing me up and down. 'What are you doing this lunchtime? Would you like a game of squash?'

I'd never played the game in my life.

'I'm sorry; I'm on call until Monday. I can't manage, though thanks for the offer.'

'That's a shame,' she said. 'I could do with a game myself. It's a bit of a bore having to practise on my own.'

I wondered if I should have signed the form, after all. She must be living in the past, I thought, with all her talk of squash games. There was nothing about dementia in the notes, so I let it pass. I led her to the door and ushered her out, still wondering if I had done the right thing.

Patients two to twelve were all over 80. They seemed to have nothing wrong with them, and were remarkably well. They needed their blood pressures measured, their heartbeats recorded, their hearing checked, their joints examined, their chests heard, their reflexes tapped, the soles of their feet scratched. They were seeing Dr Haswell every three months or so, 'just to keep them healthy', they said. Not one of them had anything that I could say was a sign of illness. The odd creak with age, but that was all.

I finished the surgery, thinking that I had never had an easier morning, and went through into the kitchen to have coffee. Mairi, Alasdair and the maid were there to join me.

The maid, Annie, was smiling.

'I see you had her ladyship in this morning,' she said. 'Did she invite you for a game of squash?'

'As a matter of fact, she did,' I replied.

'You should play her some day,' Annie said. 'She has a full-size squash court, and she practises every day. She used to be the British champion, you know – in the 1920s. Dr Haswell has given up trying to beat her. She asks all the locums, but none of them take her up on it. She will be quite disappointed.'

Naturally, I was taken aback: I had thought of her as a 'bit doted'. She was obviously anything but.

In the silence that followed, as we all ruminated on the vision of a 90-year-old still playing competition squash, I wondered where Catriona was. It wasn't like her to miss the morning coffee break. Alasdair was sitting in a corner, nose in a book. I wandered to the window, to see if she was in the garden. In the middle of the manicured lawn stood a massive cedar tree. She was about ten feet up in the branches, looking down at the army of geese that had gathered below her, encircling the trunk. The boss goose – I suppose he was the gander – was taking front stage, hissing up at her and flapping his/her wings threateningly.

Annie and I went out with a large broom and tried to shoo the avian attackers into their pen. We weren't natural goose herders. The big one – the leader that had tried to kill our daughter – made a beeline for the swimming pool. The others followed in line astern, honking as they went. The pool was surrounded by a wattle fence, about four feet high, which presumably served the dual purpose of windbreak and barrier to toddlers. The gate in the fence was open, and our enemies swept imperiously through it, to settle on the water. Annie and

I secured the gate and left them to their swim, hoping that their wings were clipped enough for them not to fly over the fence. They hadn't shown much inclination to use their wings as anything other than deadly weapons. We assumed that they were as harmless there as they would be in the enclosure.

Catriona had been in the tree, apparently, for about an hour, the double glazing of the windows preventing us from hearing her cries for help. She likes geese now, but preferably at Christmas and well done in plenty of gravy.

There were two house visits for me. One was an 'urgent': two small children with 'stomach problems', and the other was one that Dr Haswell had listed for me to see as a routine follow-up. He had left a note to say she was someone he saw regularly, 'just to make sure she was OK'. He didn't expect any problem with her. I finished my coffee, noted the two addresses and went on my way.

The first call was to a terrace house in the town. The square of small front garden was laid with gravel. There was not a weed to be seen, and the outside of the house was spotless. The door had a brass knocker in the centre: there was no bell. Usually, when people are expecting the doctor to call, they leave the front door off the latch, so that we can walk in without having to wait. It wasn't so in this case. I couldn't turn the door handle: it was locked from the inside.

I lifted and dropped the knocker twice. I had to wait maybe half a minute before I heard someone unbolt the door: one above, the other beneath. Then a key turned, and the door opened, only a few inches. A woman of about 30 peered through the gap at me. I was carrying a bag and had a stethoscope poking out from my jacket pocket, so it must have been plain who I was. She had a cloth in her hand, which she extended around the door edge to polish the sweat from my offending hand off the knocker.

'You're not Dr Haswell,' she said, unnecessarily.

'No,' I replied. 'I'm Doctor Smith. I'm here to see the children.'

'I'd rather see Dr Haswell,' she said, still not opening the door any further. It was my turn to look her up and down. What's sauce for the goose is sauce for the gander, I thought, then wondered why I had thought it. Those geese were preying on me.

She had short black hair and a narrow, fierce face that hadn't often smiled. The corners of her mouth were turned down as if she had been permanently angry from birth. And she was obviously angry now.

'Well, you will have to wait until Monday,' I said, and began to turn around to go. I knew the action was offensive, and that I shouldn't have done it, but there was something about her that was ringing alarm bells.

'I'm standing in for him over the weekend,' I added, ' so if you need to see the doctor, it will have to be me.'

'Oh, all right then,' she said. 'Take your shoes off and come in.' She opened the door more widely, and I got a glimpse of polished parquet flooring in the narrow hallway beyond.

'Pardon?' I said, astonished. Had she actually told me to take my shoes off? Without even a 'please'? 'Take my shoes off?'

'Yes,' she said. 'No one comes in here from the street in their outdoor shoes. They will carry germs from the pavement into the house, and I'm meticulous about that. I won't take risks.'

Howard Hughes came to mind. I didn't respond verbally: I don't think she saw me shrug my shoulders. She was already halfway along the hall, making for the bottom of the uncarpeted wooden stairs at the end of it.

I took off my shoes and left them on the doorstep. I was glad it wasn't raining, and hoped no one would nick them while I was visiting. I took my first stocking-soled steps across the floor. It was like an ice rink. She was wearing moccasins, the soles of which obviously had more grip than my socks. As she reached the bottom of the stairs, the phone rang. She went into a side room to answer it, saying as she did so that the children were upstairs in their bedroom, and could I go on ahead.

If anything the stairs were slippier than the floor. I struggled up them holding onto the banister to make sure I didn't slip. At the top there was a small landing that led to a short corridor. The children's room was straight ahead of me: I could see a cot in it with crumpled bedclothes on it and the sides down. There was no child in it.

The children were in the first room on the left. It wasn't a bedroom: it was the toilet. There they were, Silas, aged five and Samantha, aged three, with their backs to me, bending over something. I walked in, to find that it was the bidet. One was pressing the button, the other bending over the little fountain, lapping up the water from it and from the pool of water lying in the bottom. They obviously had a raging thirst, because they didn't notice the stranger among them.

I waited for Mum to arrive, so that we could discuss the scene. When she did, all hell broke loose.

'I've told you two that you mustn't drink from there,' she screamed. She rapped poor little Silas around the backs of his legs with the palm of her hand, then picked him up roughly and almost tossed him into the bedroom. He didn't cry: just kept silent. He looked stricken but determined. I gathered he was used to this sort of treatment. Samantha toddled after them, silently, unhappily, to climb into the cot.

I kept quiet, too, assessing what I had seen, and not wanting to act too hastily. I wanted to be sure that I was saying the right thing when I did decide to speak.

'They have had diarrhoea and sickness for three days,' she said. 'They won't eat a thing, and they will only drink water. I've left water by them, but they won't drink it out of a cup.'

I looked at the two children, and they looked at me in turn. There was just a hint of a smile on Samantha's face. Silas was holding back tears, but being brave in front of the new doctor. They looked terrible, with sunken cheeks and big black bags under their eyes. They were pale, rather than flushed, and there were tiny beads of sweat on their foreheads. I told them I would like to feel their tummies, and they both nodded to me. They were astonishingly good kids, I thought, despite their mother's temper. She hadn't broken them, so far.

Their stomachs were distended with gas, and they winced while I gently explored them with the flat surface of my fingers. I could pick up a fold of skin and watch as it stayed there, like a tiny mountain ridge, for seconds before collapsing back. They were badly dehydrated and toxic. I smiled at them, and they smiled back at me.

'Could you open your mouths for me?' I asked them. Two little mouths opened wide.

'Now stick your tongues out at me,' I added. They each mustered a grin and stuck their tongues out. They enjoyed that, I thought. Doing something rude in front of their mum. I was sure that they were kept under strict rules of conduct, and sticking tongues out would be forbidden. I had warmed to the two of them, but I didn't like what I saw. Their tongues were red and raw and had patches of white material on them that my gentle touch with a wooden spatula didn't shift.

I stood up and faced Mum.

'I'm going to have to send them to hospital,' I told her. 'They are toxic, badly dehydrated and may have a combined bowel infection that needs to be identified and treated urgently. They will need drips and antibiotics.'

'Oh no, they won't,' she replied. 'They are not having antibiotics or drips. I'll look after them at home. You can go now. I will wait until Dr Haswell comes back. He will know how to treat them.'

'Then you won't mind if I call the social services,' I said. 'It's my professional opinion that these children are in real danger if they are kept at home. If you won't consent to them being admitted, then I will see that someone else makes the order.'

'How dare you,' she replied. 'I am a much better mother than most, and I won't have my children taken away from here without my consent.' She was furious, almost spitting at me in her anger.

I stayed calm.

'It is your choice,' I said, slowly and calmly. 'You either let me send them in, or the social services will be visiting you, possibly with the police. Remember, I have seen the children drink from your bidet. They definitely have thrush, and probably an E.coli infection, too. Both are serious infections in children of their age. The bidet is a pretty solid bet for their source. That would have to go in the report. Oh, and by the way, when the health officials do arrive, be nice to them. You would be wise to let them keep their shoes on.'

She thought for a few seconds, then gave in. The ambulance took less than ten minutes to arrive, and I saw the kids off in it, their mother with them, still glowering at me. There was no word of thanks for my trouble, but none, after all, was expected.

I had taken a lot longer on that visit than planned, but there was still time to make my second call before lunch. I put my shoes on, then sat in the car for a minute or two, taking deep breaths and letting my anger seep away. The next call would be less stressful. What could go wrong with a routine visit to an old lady?

Plenty, it turned out. She lived in what estate agents would call a cottage of character in the New Forest, next to another that was bigger and better maintained. Her home had seen better days. The thatch needed tidying and there were holes in it near the edge of the roof that I hoped were the results of squirrels or birds, rather than rats. The garden was neat, with a small lawn and a flower border leading up to the front door. It was one of those dark panelled wooden doors with beer-bottle-bottomed glass insets in it, through which you could vaguely see the light streaming from the room inside. I rang the bell and opened the door, saying 'it's the doctor' as I walked in.

Mrs Musgrave was standing in the hall, looking at me, puzzled.

'Are you from Dr Haswell?' she asked.

'Yes,' I said. 'The doctor asked me to call in on you, just to check you were all right. I'm Doctor Smith.'

'Then you aren't supposed to be here,' she replied. 'My son will be very annoyed. Although I'm glad to see you. Please come in.'

I didn't know what her son had to do with my visit, but let the remark be. She showed me to an easy chair in the living room and sat opposite me on the couch. I was about to ask her how she was feeling when a man who I guessed was in his late forties burst into the room.

'Who are you?' the man asked me.

'It's the doctor, dear. He is standing in for Dr Haswell,' Mrs Musgrave said.

'Then you can get out, now,' the man barked. 'I've told Haswell I don't want him here – and that applies to his stand-ins, too.'

'I'm sorry,' I said, 'what have I done wrong?'

Mollified by my apparent contrition, the man calmed down.

'I'm sorry, too, Doctor,' he said, 'but you obviously don't know what is going on here. Haswell has been visiting my mother for years, and she has never been ill. She keeps on paying his bills, and they are mounting up, for absolutely no medical treatment at all. She doesn't need this extra expense, especially now that her life savings are draining away, mainly into Haswell's pocket. I've written to him saying that he is no longer my mother's doctor, but he won't listen. So you are welcome as a visitor to this house, but not as a doctor.'

Things began to fall into place.

'Does that apply to you, too, Mrs Musgrave?' I asked her.

'Well, I am a bit worried about his bills,' she said. 'The last one was for more than a hundred pounds, and it's difficult to pay on my pension and my few savings.'

She was being polite, but her body language was plain enough. She was truly uncomfortable with my visit. It was only another financial burden on her dwindling purse. I didn't want any of it.

I turned to her son.

'I'll pass on your strong feelings to Dr Haswell when I meet him on Monday,' I said. 'I do understand them, and I'll make sure this visit isn't charged for. Off the record, you might try speaking to a lawyer if he persists in visiting.'

'That's just where I've been,' he explained. 'I moved in next door a few months ago, and was astonished by the number of visits the doctor made – and the cost of them. I've asked my lawyer for a legal letter to stop them.'

I didn't stay long: I took just enough time for the Musgraves to show me around their small garden to stroke their cat, give them my good wishes, and leave. I wondered how many of my surgery patients that morning were in the same financial boat. This weekend wasn't the pleasant relief in country practice I had expected it to be.

I arrived back at the Haswell mansion just before one o'clock, ready for lunch. The family was waiting for me. The sun was hot, and Mairi had spread a picnic on the patio table. The kids were already wolfing down baked potatoes and sausages.

I looked at the pool, longingly. I had the afternoon off until four o'clock, when the evening surgery would begin.

'Anyone fancy a swim later?' I asked.

Alasdair laughed.

'Not likely, Dad,' he said. 'Have a look at it.'

The geese were gone. Mairi, Alasdair, Catriona and Annie had combined forces in a goose drive while I was away. They were back in their pen, though by the continuing honking it seemed they weren't pleased to be there. The water in the pool had been crystal clear that morning. The geese had left their imprint in it.

It's odd how much around two dozen geese can excrete in an hour or so. We were now looking at a muddy grey pool, with a mixture of floaters on the top and sediment just visible through the murk, on the bottom. It was very clear what the 'floaters' and the 'sinkers' were made of. If that wasn't bad enough, there were feathers everywhere, in and around the pool.

At that moment, Mairi came out with a piece of paper she had found in the kitchen. We hadn't noticed it before, as it had been swept up in a bundle of newspapers. It stated that on no account were the geese to go anywhere near the poolside. The fence wasn't a windbreak or to keep toddlers from harm. It was an anti-goose fortification, never to be left open to their marauding. Goose poo, apparently, was the one thing that the pool's delicate filtration system couldn't cope with. Somehow we had to clean it out and have it ready for use by Monday.

There was a telephone number for a pool maintenance service in the hall. I left it for Mairi to ring and use her soft Scottish voice to charm the men to come quickly to deal with it. We were staggered by the estimate – as much as I was being paid for the weekend – but we had no choice.

The GPs in the district held regular meetings to discuss new treatments and medical politics at one of the pubs. That evening was one of their dates. When they heard that there was a locum in Dr Haswell's practice, they invited me along. I was glad to go, as I wanted to meet them and make new medical friends. They would also be sounding boards for research projects and ideas, so I was looking forward to it.

It was a pleasant evening, with great food and a good speaker. Relaxing afterwards with a few of the Lymhampton doctors, I found they were curious about my links with Dr Haswell. I said that I hadn't met him, and that a mutual friend had arranged the weekend job. I had known nothing about his practice beforehand. I then mentioned my problems with Silas, Samantha and their mum, not leaving out the episode of the bidet. They all started to laugh. I couldn't see why it was so funny. Dr Kilmartin, one of the older doctors, put me wise. They all knew the family. Mum had arrived in the town in the previous year to set up a health food shop. She had written articles in the local paper extolling the virtues of alternative medicine in all its varied incarnations, and warning readers that orthodox doctors were charlatans and peddlers of dangerous medicines that would always do more harm than good. The citizens of Lymhampton should come to her, instead, if they wanted to keep healthy.

The articles had been frankly libellous, but the consensus of medical opinion was to leave well alone. People like her would never be shut up, and the doctors reasoned that few readers would be persuaded, anyway, by what they considered her ravings. Somehow the story of the bidet would get around and she might even be so humiliated that she would move away. I had to endure lots of backslapping by my delighted colleagues.

On a more serious note, they were concerned about what they saw as Dr Haswell's 'soaking' of the finances of old and vulnerable patients. They had had their suspicions, but couldn't see what they could do about it.

The rest of the weekend went well, except for my test on the squash court. I decided to accept her ladyship's offer of a game of squash. I had a vague knowledge of the rules, and she was gracious enough to give me a short tutorial on them before we started playing. I didn't score a point. She dominated the centre of the court and somehow managed to reach the ball without seeming to move. She could place the ball, every time, so that it was always just out of my reach. I lasted about half an hour, during which time I must have lost half a stone chasing a little round ball but never catching it. She was as cool and fresh at the end as she had been at the start.

Humiliated? Not at all. I had learned a lot from her, and we became good friends.

By Monday, I was glad to leave. Private medicine, I had always suspected, wasn't for me. That weekend proved it. I handed his practice back to Dr Haswell in reasonable order. I told him about Mrs Musgrave and her son, and about Silas and Samantha and their mother. He made no comment, except to thank me and pay me a cheque. I drove to the pool-cleaner's office, signed it on the back and handed it to him. Then we went home. I didn't do another stint for Dr Haswell. He didn't ask me to.

About a week later, I heard he had been admitted to Southampton General Hospital with severe gastroenteritis. The weird thing was that the bacteria that caused it had never before been found in human infection. When I mentioned it to my vet counterpart in Huizens, he recognised it immediately.

'It's endemic in geese,' he said. 'Kills quite a lot of domestic flocks in Europe.'

Maybe I shouldn't have paid that pool cleaner quite so much.

OF FARTOMETERS AND PLAGIARISM....

My stint at Barts finished a week early, and I returned to my work for Huizens. I was sorry to part with my commuter mates, but they all remained friends, and they even visited us when we returned to Scotland, seven years later. Strangely, Billy the banker never mentioned either Dr Petranova or Dr Haswell again.

It was part of my job with Huizens to find ways of measuring the immeasurable. Some diseases are difficult to quantify. That is, it's hard to find ways of measuring the symptoms so that you can calculate with mathematics and statistics the degree to which your drug may help. Take two illnesses for examples – irritable bowel and premenstrual tension.

We had drugs in research for both diseases, but for the life of us we couldn't find ways of measuring their severity or of assessing how much difference the drugs might make. I suppose that most people have experienced irritable bowel. It causes bloating, stomach pains, diarrhoea, constipation, wind and flatus, but not necessarily all at the same time nor all the time.

We assumed that there was some way of measuring all these symptoms. Perhaps patients on trials could keep diaries and put numbers to their symptoms. Then we could compare the numbers when they were 'on' and 'off' their drugs or the placebo comparisons. That didn't work so well. Irritable bowel is so erratic that the numbers fluctuated too much from day to day, making meaningful comparisons hopeless. We had to find a solid measuring system, like the blood pressure machine for our high blood pressure studies, or a glucose test for diabetes, that would define how well the treatment was going.

We needed a good gastroenterology researcher who was steeped in the disorder to devise such a machine. We came up with the name of John Comyn, at Reading University. He had his 'fartometer' up and running, and was desperate to use it in drug trials, if only to prove its worth. It was simple enough. It consisted of a microphone attached to a strap that wound around the middle of the abdomen like a belt. It led to a recording tape. The patient wore the belt for 24 hours and the tape recorded the sounds from the abdomen. We needed 40 volunteers with IBS to take part. They would wear it for three separate days – one on no treatment, one on placebo and one on our drug. At the end of the trial, we would be able to correlate the sounds with the symptoms – each patient wrote a diary – and with the drug. Simple. I spent a week devising the trial protocol, then put it to the test.

Oh, and there was one other minor thing. During the test days, the patient swallowed an electronic 'pill' that recorded pressures inside the gut as it travelled from mouth to anus. That would be useful, we reckoned, in linking pressures with sounds and symptoms. The only problem was that the pill was expensive, and had to be retrieved, washed and used again for the next subject. I don't know if John told his subjects that, but it was supposed to be part of the 'volunteer information pack' given to them before the trial. I still doubt to this day that he did.

Suffice it to say that when we collected our tapes, and started to listen to them, we became the world's experts in recognition of bowel sounds. They come in various grades, from soft, musical gurgles to loud rasps and long-lasting rumbles. We had the world's biggest collection of farting sounds: John even thought of telling the *Guinness Book of Records* about them.

Did the study come to a useful conclusion? Well, no. Some people rumbled like trains going through a very long tunnel; others were as silent as the grave. Yet others could have done as well on the stage as the Victorian Le Pétomane (I think that was his name) who, it was said, could mimic the battle of Waterloo with the noises from his nether end. Yet we were never able to correlate the noises with symptoms – the quiet ones had just as much discomfort as the noisy ones, the drug days didn't pan out differently from the days on no drugs or the placebo, and the pressure-measuring pill simply didn't work. In fact, we even lost two of them. We hoped that they had been expelled but there was no evidence for the expulsion. That's 30 years ago now. As the electronics were similar to those of a pacemaker, I hope the devices don't show themselves for the first time in a crematorium. The deceased may go off with a bang.

What did we do with the tapes? Let's say that some people found them amusing enough to take copies. How they were used I can't tell. But I've heard very similar noises on the occasional TV comedy programme late at night, and I wonder how they got there. Maybe John and I could have insisted on copyright, and shared the proceeds with the volunteers, who sadly, despite all their trouble, made no contribution at all to our understanding of irritable bowel syndrome.

If anything, dealing with pre-menstrual tension (PMT) was more difficult than with IBS. It's strange how when we don't understand a disease, we reduce it to its initials. Maybe we talk about IBS, PMT and that other favourite, ME, because doing so seems to diminish them, and makes them less of a challenge.

My entire knowledge of PMT as a medical student was that it was written on the buses in Stoke-on-Trent and stood for Potteries Motor Transport. Mea culpa. Told to find subjects for a trial of a new treatment for it, I helped draw up a plea for volunteers to be placed in a popular woman's magazine. We got 12,000 replies, the biggest response to any advertisement in the magazine's history. One woman even flew down from Shetland to see us, to make sure she was one of the subjects.

It didn't take long for me to realise, when talking to many of these unfortunate women, that PMT really existed. If I had known my medical history better, I would never have been in doubt about it. Just before the First World War, the French legal system established that a wife was not guilty of a capital offence because her premenstrual state had made her temporarily insane at the time she stabbed her husband to death. The fact that she stabbed him more than 50 times tended to support, rather than count against, her lawyer's successful claim. She walked free, with the sympathy of every woman, but very few men, in France.

PMT goes a long way back in history. Pliny, a doctor as well as a writer and philosopher in the first century AD, wrote that in the days before her monthly bleed, the best place for a woman was at the bottom of the garden. The goddess Juno didn't approve, apparently, because when he travelled to Pompeii, she arranged – she was the goddess of volcanoes – for the town to be covered by around 50 feet of hot pumice. Maybe she was premenstrual at the time.

However, none of this history was relevant to my task. How could we enumerate the symptoms of PMT, so that they could be analysed for clinical trials? We reckoned that they fell into two types – the physical and the emotional. There was the bloating. Many women had two wardrobes: a thinner lot of clothes for the first part of the month, and a fatter lot, maybe two sizes bigger, for the second half. They put on half a stone or more in the last week or so, only to lose it within two days of the period starting. The women listed headaches, irritability, tenseness, mood swings and changes in sexual feelings towards their partners as the main emotional problems for them. Some felt less like sex, others the opposite. That was curious because they felt at their sexiest at a time when their irritability drove their partners away. Frustration was the name of the game for them and their partners – and for that matter, their children, who saw their mums as alternating between angels and demons every two weeks.

Eventually, we worked out ways to measure all these symptoms, turned them into a 'PMS score' (PM tension had become PM syndrome in the meantime) and started the trials. Amazingly the trials did show that the drug, a progestogen, worked. It helped women physically and emotionally and we were granted a licence for it.

The next stage was to get the good news to doctors. That meant organising a series of meetings throughout the country about PMS and its treatments, one of which, of course, would be our drug, Huizogen. As the doctor involved in the planning of the trials, it fell to me to be the first speaker.

Stories about avoiding the guillotine if you kill your husband at the right time of your month (plus the idea of going to

France if you want to kill your husband), and of goddesses with premenstrual problems and a bit of a temper seemed the right way to start off the meetings. There were plenty of boring talks laden with statistics and guidelines to come after me: at least the meetings would start off with humour.

The first talk was in Bristol. It seemed to go well, as it did in several hospitals and health centres in London and Glasgow. The next was in Birmingham. There the format was different. The organisers there wanted their local psychiatrist to give the first talk. He was particularly interested in the relationships between women's hormones and their mood. Could I chair the meeting instead, and maybe sum up at the end? I didn't mind. Pliny, Juno and the guillotine could wait: it would be just as good to send people off with a laugh as to start with it.

I opened the meeting and invited the first speaker to the podium. He seemed taken aback when he saw me, then swallowed nervously, and asked for the first slide. I was fascinated to see it was one of mine – a picture of Pompeii. I became less fascinated when he started to talk. Pliny, Juno, the French and all my anecdotes, word for word, poured out of him. Slide after slide, in exactly the same order as my own, were flashed on the screen. I caught the eye of Wendy Cooper, a friend and one of my fellow speakers – she had written a bestseller on female problems – sitting in the front row. She had been at all the previous meetings.

Wendy's mouth was wide open, aghast at what she was hearing. Then she grinned at me and made a paper-ripping gesture with her hands. Obviously, I would have to tear up my intended talk. I stood up at the end, summarised the whole show as well as I could and brought it to a close. I then made a beeline for the psychiatrist. I was too slow. He was out of the building before I could get to him.

It turned out later that he had been at the Bristol meeting. He had taped my talk, noted down my slides, and copied them for his own use. Asked to talk in Birmingham, he hadn't known that I would be there too, and had simply repeated my talk as if it were his own. I would have been flattered if I hadn't been so outraged.

Wendy thought it was a hoot. She thought I had ad-libbed well at the end. She asked me to work with her on a book she was writing – *Human Potential, the Limits and Beyond*. She needed medical input: while she did the 'journalist bit', I would do the 'scientific bit'. We wrote it together over the next three months. It was the start of my involvement with books and of a twenty-year-long friendship with her.

Another man, whom I didn't know, approached me as I was leaving the hall. He was one of the conference organisers. Would I be interested in reporting conferences for his company? I didn't know whether or not my contract with Huizens allowed me to, but I told him I would look into it. James M of L, the next day, decided it would be a good thing for the company, and for me, to do so and gave me a free hand. It was a brilliant decision, and led ultimately to my next career.

As for the psychiatrist, as far as I know he is still giving my talk, although I fear that it is a bit out of date now. I hope he has found someone else's data to add to it.

...AND A SWISS RAILWAY ENGINE

Tom Wells was the president of the Royal Society of Medicine's Ear, Nose and Throat section. You would expect a man of such distinction to live in a big city, running an academic unit of the highest regard in a well-known medical university.

Not Tom. He was the sole ENT surgeon in Omagh, County Tyrone, and people came from all over the world for his advice. He had been invited many times to fill professorial chairs all around the world, but had declined. He wanted to live in his beloved Northern Ireland, and if people wanted to take advantage of his expertise, they would have to come to him. They did come, in droves.

Tom's big claim to fame among us researchers was that he had a Swiss railway engine under the floor of his consulting rooms. He was better known to patients and to other doctors as the world's greatest expert on dizziness.

I'd better explain about that engine. It was fixed to the floor of the room below his office by steel in concrete. Switch it on, and it was silent: he would tell his friends that it was the smoothest engine known to man: far smoother, he said, than the engine in the best Rolls Royce. It wasn't going anywhere, of course. Its axle was sticking up through the floor and fixed to a chair in the centre of the room. People sat in the chair, and the engine spun them round, slowly at first, then faster, until they became dizzy, or not, as the case might be.

By applying sensors around the subjects' eyes and making records of how they reacted to the spin and at the same time monitoring their nervous and circulation systems, Tom could precisely diagnose the type and cause of virtually any case of dizziness. He had lectured all over the world on the subject, and being the only one with such a precise 'rotatory chair', he was in huge demand from companies developing drugs for dizziness. If you could get Tom to give you some of his 'chair time', you were at least one step ahead of your competitors.

Not that Tom was competitive. He was generous to a fault. He was only interested in drugs that might help his patients, and not in the money or glory. So we were lucky that we had one that seemed, from the animal studies, to be specific for a condition called Menière's disease.

Menière's is devastating. Its main symptom is a constant noise in the ears. It may be a whistle, a roar, or a hum, but it is always intrusive. The noise keeps people awake at night and distracted through the day. Imagine living next to the Birmingham to Manchester motorway without double glazing, and never being able to get away from the traffic noise at any time of day or night, and you get the picture. But that's not all. Along with the noise comes dizziness and deafness. Doctors look on it as the DDD disease – dizziness, deafness and din. When I began to interview patients with it, I added a fourth D – despair.

The main cause of the DDD is high pressure inside the inner ear, the organ that combines hearing with balance. This isn't a medical textbook, so I won't go into more detail. It's enough to know that our drug was known to reduce the fluid pressure in the inner ears in animals, and we wanted to know if it did so in humans with Menière's. Tom was the obvious person to approach.

I met him on one of his monthly visits to the Royal Society of Medicine in London. In his early sixties, just a little chubby, with red cheeks and laughing eyes, I warmed to him immediately. I was surprised that he had an English accent: he explained that he had moved to Omagh 30 years before from Oxford, and wild horses wouldn't drag him back. He was Irish now. The conversion hadn't been painful, he said.

This was 1975, and Northern Ireland was at the height of its troubles, with bombings, shootings and sectarian warfare in the news daily. I wondered how an Englishman managed, especially in a place like Omagh, where the rural community was as deeply divided as it was in Belfast. I wasn't so rude, of course, as to ask him: I felt that it was his place to talk about it if he wished. I didn't want to pry.

I was thrilled when he agreed to study our drug. One of the Huizens rules about setting up trials, however, was that the company doctor had to visit the units doing them and to assess whether they would be performed correctly. I had to meet him in Omagh.

It wasn't a journey to be undertaken lightly. Anyone from the rest of the British Isles visiting Northern Ireland then was warned beforehand about the risk. You might be a target simply because you came from the mainland, or you might be caught in the crossfire or bombs that were an everyday occurrence for the resident population. I had two small children, and a wife who definitely wouldn't want me to go.

So I decided not to tell her the truth. Because the trial discussions would take all day, I had to be away overnight. I made the big mistake of telling her I would be in Dublin, and that I would phone her from Ireland that evening. I reasoned that I would be so well looked after that she need never know I had put myself at risk. Tom had told me that the car meeting me at Belfast airport was recognised as a 'safe' taxi by both sides of the sectarian divide, and that it would deliver me direct to the hospital.

Everything went like clockwork. I had a great afternoon in Tom's department meeting his staff and having a trip on the famous chair. We discussed details of the trial and drew up an agreement on timing, finances, numbers of subjects, analysis, writing it up and a probable publication. It was nearly seven o'clock before we could call it a day and go out for dinner together.

He had arranged for me to stay at the best local hotel – the Loughgannon Castle Hotel – and we had a wonderful meal there. At the next table were three men in clerical clothes who knew Tom. They were pleased to see him and were delightful to me. When they heard what we were planning, one of them volunteered to be one of the subjects. He had been dizzy and deaf himself since a little incident with a loud bang a year or two before.

The others laughed at this, leaving me mystified, but I let it go. It was obviously an Irish joke, the details of which shouldn't be shared with someone from across the water. I assumed it was something to do with the troubles. They did, however, share their whisky. It went down very well, and I went to bed feeling, shall we say, mellow and at peace with the world. It was only then that I realised how late it was – well after midnight, when

Mairi, who had to take the children to school in the morning, would be fast asleep. I thought it better not to waken her, especially as I might not sound absolutely sober, and decided to phone in the morning.

The phone ringing by my bedside wakened me. It wasn't Mairi: it was the receptionist. She told me that my car was there to take me to the airport. I looked at my watch. It was nearly 8.30. I had slept in: the school run would already be in full swing. I couldn't call home. I washed, shaved and threw on my clothes as fast as I could, and ran downstairs. I said a cheery 'good morning' to my three new friends of the night before, whose stomachs were obviously made of sterner stuff than mine. They were tucking into a huge fry-up with all the trimmings in the conservatory that served as a breakfast room. I wasn't sure that they had seen me, but I didn't have time to check. The car was already nearly twenty minutes late in starting its journey: we would have difficulty catching the Heathrow plane.

The journey was not as easy as that of the day before. For the first fifteen minutes we were in the rush hour traffic: we had to travel through the centre of Omagh before reaching the main road to Belfast. On the way out of town, the scene changed for the worse. Suddenly, there were police sirens all around us, and armoured cars full of soldiers bristling with guns were speeding past us. We hit the first road block on the outskirts of town. There were four more on the way to the airport.

The driver didn't know why we were being held up so much and so often. He assumed that there must have been an 'incident' that morning, and that the army was looking for someone. He didn't dare to ask: being curious about the reason for a road block was a sure way to get arrested, he said. Just keep mum, he told me. I did what I was told. The delay meant that I had missed my plane: the next one was in another four hours. My plan to return to the office in Southampton before going home was dashed: even if I drove straight home I would be late.

At Belfast and Heathrow airports I tried time and again to speak to Mairi, but the phone was constantly engaged. It wasn't like her to talk for hours, so I assumed that the phone was out of order. I decided to drive home without wasting any more time.

I arrived about eight o'clock in the evening, not to a loving welcome but to a furious wife. Why hadn't I told her where I was? Why did she have to hear about it from James M of L? Why hadn't I phoned him to tell him I was safe? And how did I escape the bomb? Didn't I realise she would think the worst? The questions came tumbling out of her, leaving me no time to answer.

I was dumbfounded.

'What bomb?' I asked.

'The one at the Loughgannon Castle Hotel. Where James told me you stayed last night. Where they are still sorting out the rubble. You didn't check out – so everyone thought you were under it.'

The hotel had been bombed at ten to nine that morning, five minutes after I had left. Happily, no one had been killed. It had gone off in a bedroom near mine, and all the staff and other guests had been busy with breakfasts, well away from the blast. There was just one person unaccounted for. Me. The only person I had spoken to, the receptionist, had concussion. She had been hit by a piece of falling ceiling, and couldn't remember me leaving. I hadn't seen the need to check out because the company had already paid the bill.

Naturally, the priests remembered my name and contacted Tom, who contacted James, who contacted Mairi to ask if I had phoned. From then on our home phone was ringing all day with press enquiries, and Mairi, distressed, had taken it off the hook.

I was very definitely in the doghouse, I suppose deservedly so. I telephoned first James, then Tom. By this time the driver had already told him I was safe, but he was still delighted to hear from me. I asked about the priests. He laughed.

'They are fine,' he said. 'You may even meet one of them again, if you dare to come back. He's one of the subjects on the trial.'

'You mean the one deafened by the bang?' I asked him.

'The very one,' he said. 'I thought you might be wondering about that. It wasn't a bomb, you know. It was an exploding still. These three guys are the best poteen-makers in the country. They supply me and a few more. Two years ago, one of the stills blew up – that was the bang. It was just a temporary setback: they soon got it up and running again. You tasted some of their stuff last night. Good, isn't it?'

'But what about the bomb this morning?' I asked.

His voice took on a more serious tone.

'We don't know about that one. It's more serious. Could be the Provos or the UDF, we don't know which yet. Maybe we never will. We think the stuff went off by accident. We hope so, because it could have killed plenty of people in the wrong place and time.'

It took a long time for Mairi to forgive me and for our relationship to return to an even keel. I did go back to Omagh a few months later, this time with her full knowledge, although not her approval. The trials went through their course without a hitch and were instrumental in getting the drug a licence for Menière's disease. Years later, Tom came to visit us in Scotland, only three hours by ferry and car from his home. He brought with him Dorothy, his charming wife, two large unlabelled bottles of clear liquid and a letter from a grateful priest. Our poteen-maker was no longer deaf. The drug trial had worked out especially well for him. He has been taking his pills ever since, and his deafness, dizziness and din have left him. And thankfully, now that Northern Ireland is peaceful, so has his despair.

ENSAY — BIG AND SMALL

Back home from Belfast, the marital atmosphere remained stormy. My doghouse stay was extending into its second week when we had a phone call late one evening. It was from an old colleague from my Collintrae days. He had been a neighbouring GP in Stranraer, and had given it up to return to his roots. I had always known of his homesickness for his birthplace in the Hebridean islands, but hadn't thought he would return there until he retired.

His homesickness had finally become too much. Hearing of a vacancy on the island of Ensay, he had jumped at the chance. Having been on it for a year, with no time off, he needed a break. Would I do his locum for him?

The call had come at exactly the right time. The job was in August, the children were on holiday, and I had no Huizens commitments that would clash with the dates. It would take Mairi back to her roots, too, and it might be just the thing to get us back on an even keel.

I was surprised when she expressed doubts about the job. After all, she had spent most of her summer holidays as a child on similar islands, and had always loved them. But she wasn't

99

sure about staying in someone else's house for two weeks, and about being the doctor's wife on call again. That was one of the reasons we had left practice in the first place.

Nevertheless, we decided to use Ensay as a trial run. Could we bear to be back in full-time practice, even if it was only for a fortnight? We had to know. So, about two months after the Belfast tiff, we drove to Oban, for the ferry to Ensay.

Ensay – or to be more correct, Ensay Mor, or Big Ensay – is about twelve miles wide. It is stuck out in the open Atlantic, north-west of Islay and Jura, and south-west of Mull and Iona. For those who know Scotland's west coast, it is set in a wild and windy area of sea with no protection to the west, except the coast of Labrador, about 3000 miles away. Labrador, we can vouch, is no protection. The ferry was an old MacBrayne's steamer, of about 2000 tons, built in the years either before stabilisers were invented or before they were considered necessary for the good health of passengers. I'm not sure which.

I'm a fairly good sailor, and the children are even better. While we were running around the deck watching the waves and the distant mountains disappearing from the stern, Mairi was lying sick on a couch in the lounge. If she had needed convincing that this was a good idea while we were still in Hampshire, she needed much more reassurance now.

As the ship went astern into the narrow harbour, up to the pier, we had our first glimpse of the island. There were a few pastel-coloured houses dotted around the small rocky bay, and a road disappearing into the centre. About 200 yards up this road was the hotel, and beside it the post office and shop. There were gently sloping hills to the right and left, and, it being August, they were covered with deep purple. Among the heather flowers were the odd sheep, a goat or two, and up on the hillside, our first red deer stag was looking imperiously down on us. Above the sea, hundreds of gulls were wheeling around some fishing boats to our left. Above the land were huge soaring birds: I couldn't make out, without binoculars, whether they were eagles or buzzards. It was staggeringly beautiful.

About a dozen cars were waiting to board: the resident doctor, Colin Shaw, was in one of them. We drove our Vauxhall up the ramp towards the road, and he met us at the top. He handed me a list of things to do, cheerfully told me that 'it would be a doddle' and looked forward to seeing me in two weeks. I watched him drive on to the ferry, and turned our car to his house, only a few hundred yards away. We weren't to know it then, but this was the first of many times we were to make this trip over the next ten years.

As Mairi settled into the kitchen, and Alasdair and Catriona settled into the seashore at the front of the house, I opened up the surgery. Colin had kept up his standards: the surgery was spotless and neat. Everything I needed was in place. I read the sheet of paper he had left me and got my first shock.

'Hi Tom,' he had written. 'I've left you a list of regular calls, and Judith, the island nurse and midwife, will fill you in on them. You will note that there are two garages. One has the short-base Land-Rover in it. That's for getting over to Ensay Beag (Wee Ensay to you). The other has the long-base one with the coffin. If you have any dentistry to do, you'll get all you need from the cupboard in the surgery. There are animal implements, too, for the vet stuff when you need it. Best of luck, Colin.'

Coffin? Dentistry? Vet stuff?

I opened the dental cupboard door. On its back surface was pasted a chart, divided into about 30 pictures, numbered in sequence. As I read it, my shock deepened. It was 'dentistry by numbers'. It showed me how to repair a lost filling, how to drain and pack an abscess, where to insert pain-killing injections for each tooth, how to mix the filling materials and how to pack and shape them into cavities. There was a helpful note pinned on the chart. 'To Locums,' it said. 'You probably will never need to use these materials: but I've found them invaluable on occasion. Please list any that you use and order replacements from Oban by phone.'

This was one cupboard I didn't want to open in earnest.

The surgery door opened and a young woman walked in. She introduced herself as Judith, and welcomed me to the island. She saw that I was closing the dental cupboard, and grinned.

'Not exactly what you expected, Doc?' she said. 'Don't worry, I'm on call to help you any time, and the workload isn't too bad.'

'Thanks, it's good to meet you,' I replied. 'Can you tell me about the coffin thing?'

'It's simple, really,' she said. 'There's no undertaker on the island, so we keep the coffin here. When someone dies, it's the doctor and nurse who go to the home and sort things out. The family of the deceased then have the job of ordering the next coffin to come on the first ferry from Oban, and we keep it. That's why we need the long-base Rover.'

'And the vet stuff?'

'There's no vet on the island, either, so you have to make things do in emergencies. It doesn't happen often: the crofters usually look after their animals themselves. We obviously keep the animal instruments separate from the human ones.'

'And the short-base Land-Rover, for Wee Ensay?'

'You'll see it on the map,' Judith replied. 'It's a small island, about two miles across, off the south-west corner. When the tide is at its farthest out, you can get across to it by Land-Rover over the sand. You need the short base for it to get over and through the rocks at the far end. At any other time, you need a boat. The stretch in between is a tide race at any time other than the hour around low tide, so you have to know what you are doing. You only have four patients on Wee Ensay, and none of them is likely to call you in the next two weeks.'

'So how many patients do we have?'

'One hundred and twenty in winter, and 600 now – about 450 visitors at this time of year. Most of them are islanders home to visit. There are a few tourists, and they are usually no bother. If they have managed to travel all the way here, they are usually fairly fit. You'll soon find out where everyone is. There's no main village: the houses are fairly evenly spaced around the roadside. Each has got its own croft, with two or three acres of land and a few animals. Some have jetties for their boats, and we all know each other. So there's no danger of getting lost on a call. You'll know from the map that there's just one circular road around the island, with a branch leading to the strand for Ensay Beag, and one up to the television mast on the hill in the centre. Everyone has a phone now, so you can't miss a call. And we will all know where you are, even if you have taken time off to go to the beach. There are no secrets on the Ensays.'

That has its plusses and minuses, I thought.

'So there isn't a heavy workload. That will be a change,' I said.

'All I can say is that there's not much at the moment. Colin has just done the morning surgery, so there's nothing official until four o'clock. I've just met your wife, and she is making a pot of coffee for us. Shall we go across to the house?'

We walked the few yards between the surgery and the house into the kitchen, where the smell of coffee and newly baked bread welcomed us. It turned out that the island bakery was next door and the baker, knowing I was coming, had made us a welcome loaf. Mairi, sickness over, was warming to the place. The children had already found friends to play with. The scene was tranquil and I was looking forward to an almost complete rest. The surgery records had been reassuring: an average of three patients a day over the last two months boded well for plenty of leisure time. The three of us watched from the window as the ferry slipped its mooring ropes and headed back to Oban. We wouldn't see it again for three days. It dawned on me that everyone on the island was now dependent on me for any medical emergency. I was back in Collintrae mode, but without the back-up I had had on the mainland.

Those first fourteen days on Ensay Mor were idyllic. We did have time together as a family. The children learned to fish in the sea, from boats and rocks, and we swam from the fabulous golden beaches on the sheltered north-east coast. We walked over hills together, watched eagles and buzzards soar over us and deer grazing unfazed by us. And I was called to the occasional emergencies.

The first was later that evening. It was 10.30, and the light hadn't yet faded from the western sky. The voice on the phone, female, southern English, high-pitched, in acute distress, sobbed her message at me.

'Can you come quickly, Doctor, I can hear a small child crying her eyes out somewhere on the hill, but I can't find her. I think she is lost.'

'Please talk more slowly,' I said to her. 'I realise you are upset, but I need more information. First of all, where are you?'

She mentioned a croft on the other side of the island, five miles away. I could get there in about ten minutes.

'Do you know the child?' I asked. 'And how did she get on to the hill?'

'I don't know anything about her,' she replied. 'I'm just a visitor, a holidaymaker. We arrived today on the ferry and we haven't met the neighbours yet. They are half a mile away. We don't understand how they could be so foolish as to let a child out at this time of night. But just listen to the noise, and you will see what we mean.'

She must have held the phone to the open door or window, because I could hear the wailing. Somewhere out on the hillside was a small child crying her heart out, without a break. It was getting cold: the stars were coming out, and even in August, a child could get hypothermia pretty quickly on an open hillside.

I told her I'd be there as soon as possible. There was a number for a special constable, so I phoned it, to tell him where I was and to ask him to join me there. His wife said she would pass on the message. I left a message for Judith, too, then went to the shorter Land-Rover. If I had to go off-road, I'd need it rather than the Vauxhall.

My caller met me at the door of her house and pointed across the road straight up the hill at the source of the noise. Whoever the child was, she was in great trouble. It sounded as if she was in considerable pain. In my Collintrae days, I had had to deal with a boy caught in a trap and I wondered if this might be what had happened. I started to walk up the hill, a torch in my hand, although in the gloaming I could see my way fairly easily.

Most of the hillside was covered with heather and bracken, but the crying was coming from an area of bushes and small trees, mostly birch and rowan, that ran alongside a stream. There was a drop of about five feet from the land into the channel that the stream had carved into it. As I got closer to the child, walking very warily, making sure that I didn't trip over a root or stump, it was clear that her crying was coming from the stream bed.

The torch picked up two eyes, staring back at me. The crying stopped. The eyes did belong to a kid, but not a human one. The noise creator was a baby goat. Its mother was roving up and down above it, trying to persuade it to climb out of its trap, but its little hooves couldn't get a grip on the peaty sides.

I slithered down to pick it up and delivered it unharmed to its mother, who showed her gratitude by biting a piece out of the sleeve of my jacket. I watched as the two animals pranced away into the night, looked down ruefully at my damaged jacket and made for the car.

Judith and Alec, the special constable, had been watching from afar, and were trying hard to look sympathetic. They didn't manage it. I could hear their hoots of laughter all the way home. The doctor had rescued a goat. What a way to introduce myself to the community.

The next morning's surgery started at nine sharp – or as sharp as any time in the islands. In Gaelic, the islanders' language, there isn't a word that expresses urgency in getting something done that even begins to approach the Spanish mañana. So the first of my three scheduled patients ambled in about a quarter of an hour late.

He was the harbour master, postman and school bus driver, Hamish McLeod.

'Hope I didn't get your goat, this morning, being a bit late,' he said, smiling innocently. The emphasis on 'goat' gave him away. 'It's just that I took a bit longer with the bus this morning, gathering the kids into school.' Did I hear an unnecessary emphasis on 'kids' too? Surely not.

We got down to business. All he needed was a blood pressure and lung check. Hamish had retired from a business career early to return to his island. Two years into his retirement, he welcomed the ferry three times a week, delivered the post, again three times a week, and delivered the fifteen children to the primary school every weekday during term. Three small salaries and a pension from his company allowed him to run a small fishing boat in the summer months for the holidaymakers.

The new lifestyle had done wonders for his blood pressure, which was now 50 points lower than before, and for his lung capacity. Years of asthma in the city had led his previous doctor to tell him he would be too breathless to walk by the time he was 60. Now, at 63, he could climb the hills as well as people 40 years younger.

I complimented him on his healthy lifestyle.

He rose to leave.

'Aye, Doc. I'm as fit as a mountain goat,' he said, and burst out laughing as he turned to go.

I groaned to myself. I could see what was coming.

Hugh Murdoch, a 50-something crofter, came in. I shook hands with him and beckoned him to his seat.

'I don't want to bleat – sorry – beat about the bush,' he said, his eyes twinkling. I had to grin, too. A pattern was emerging about the surgery that I knew I could do nothing about. He tugged at his goatee beard, then started to talk to me about his back.

'I'm a fencer and drainer,' he said, 'and I often have to lift things out of ditches. I'm sure you know what that's like, Doc.' He looked at me quizzically, seeking a reaction. I kept a straight face.

'I think I may have done my back in a few days ago humping a barrow full of stones out of a drain. My wife says it's my own fault. I get her goat, she says, with all the lifting I do.'

I still didn't react. I smiled politely and asked him to strip to the waist, so that I could examine him. Sure enough, he had pulled a muscle. I showed him some exercises to do, and that seemed to satisfy him.

Dressed again and heading for the door, he turned, and asked, 'How's your back, Doc? I hear you're pretty good at lifting things yourself. I could do with a hand: if you are free any time in the next couple of weeks, I'd be glad of your help.'

This time I couldn't help smiling myself. I gave in.

'You win,' I said. 'Is this going to go on all day?'

'Maybes aye, maybes no,' he replied, enigmatically. 'Thanks for your help, anyway, Doc. Should I ask the next patient to come in?'

I thanked him and waited.

The next patient was a girl in her late teens. I rose to meet her and shook her hand.

'Tom Smith,' I said.

'Mary Marshall,' she said. 'I'm a nanny.'

I sat back and roared with laughter.

'Not another one,' I said to her.

She was mystified.

'Another one?' she said, frowning. 'There's only me on the island.'

Had I made a mistake? Was the word nanny only a coincidence? If it was, I had been incredibly rude. I hoped she didn't have a serious problem. That laugh wasn't the best of starts to a consultation.

'I'm sorry,' I said. 'I shouldn't have laughed like that. It's just that I've had a tough time with the last two patients and I misunderstood you. What can I do for you?'

'Well, I'm looking after a three-year-old who has skin problems, and now I have a rash. Could I have caught something from him?'

The rash was mainly on her hands, though there were traces of it on her arms, too. It looked like an allergy, rather than an infection, so for the next few minutes we discussed what might have caused it, and how we might treat it with steroid creams. I dispensed a cream for her, and she got up to go.

As she opened the door, she turned and asked, 'If you think this is an allergy, Doctor, do you think I should go on to goat's milk?'

Then she laughed and quickly left the room.

I was left to ruminate on my first surgery. The jokes were certainly on me, but they were kindly meant. It was time for coffee.

The only call that day was to Wee Ensay. I knew that four people lived on the smaller of the two Ensays. There were three buildings on it. One was a large country house with an estate that covered nine-tenths of the land area. The owner, an American, only lived there for the month of July each year. The rest of the year it was kept clean and the grounds tended by an elderly couple who had grown up there. As far as I could see from their notes, neither had seen the doctor for more than twenty years. They were in their sixties, and nearing retirement.

The RSPB had a small cottage on the side of the island, where one of its officers lived, monitoring the wildlife for the society. Bill Forsyth, the birdman of Ensay Beag, was about as forthcoming as his counterpart on Alcatraz. He lived for his birds and for the solitude that the job gave him. It wasn't that he disliked his fellow man: it was just that he preferred avian society. I got to know him well over the years, and he became a good friend.

My caller that day, however, was Ensay Beag's fourth occupant. Brother Aloysius was a monk. He was the last remnant of the brothers who had lived there in a small abbey since Dolian, a follower of St Columba, had founded it in the seventh century. Iona's abbey had the great claim to fame, but Dolian's had never been sacked or burned in its 1300-year history. There was a continuing lineage of monks through all those years, and Brother Aloysius was the last of them. Vocations to the order had slumped, and when he died, that would be the end.

The thought hadn't made him miserable, though. Judith told me that he was a happy soul, never complaining and never needing company. Bill the birdman looked after him, bringing him his groceries and post and making sure he was well. He stuck strictly to the rules of his order, rising at dawn, spending most of the day in contemplation and prayer and sleeping in his habit at night, summer and winter, braving all the cold, wet and wind that the north Atlantic could throw at him.

When he could, however, he helped Bill with his birds. For a 60-year-old who had looked after himself since his last companion had died, ten years before, he was remarkably nimble.

He knew all the cliff faces around Ensay Beag, and it was rumoured that he had climbed them all in his youth. He hadn't always been a monk, he would say. As a teenager, he had collected young gannets, fulmars and kittiwakes for his mother's cooking pot, and that had involved abseiling down from clifftops long before anyone in Scotland knew the word for it.

The call had come in from Bill the birdman when I was in surgery, so during the coffee break I phoned him back to find out the reason for it.

Brother Aloysius had a really sore hand, he said. It might even be poisoned. Could I come to the island around 2.30 that afternoon, when the tide was lowest, so that he could guide me across the sand?

'Could the brother not come to the surgery?' I asked Bill. 'If the hand needs to be opened, it would be better to do it where everything could be easily prepared for it.'

'He hasn't been off Ensay Beag for 40 years, Doc,' Bill replied. 'When he needs doctors, they usually go to him. He is a monk, you know.'

I thought about it and was glad to agree. It would be an adventure, after all, to drive across the sands and into the abbey. I had never met a monk before and was curious about how he lived.

So at 2.30, I was waiting on the Big Ensay shore for Bill to come across from Wee Ensay to meet me. It was a fine, dry afternoon, the sands stretching for nearly two miles between the islands looked flat and easy to drive on, and the sea beyond was calm. Wee Ensay looked idyllic in the sunshine, the low hills having the same purple tinge of heather, the sea a deep turquoise, the sky a lighter blue and the sand a brilliant yellow. The pottery on the island uses exactly the same shades in its products and is world-renowned for them. I could understand why.

Bill was with me in minutes.

'Follow exactly in my tyre marks,' he said. 'Don't stray from them even by a foot. There are quicksands everywhere and we have lost a few visitors' cars to them. Happily, no visitors themselves, but I don't want you to be the first.'

With those unsettling words, we set off. I followed the marks as if my life depended on them, much as a soldier would follow the flags that showed the cleared path through a minefield. We reached the opposite shore in about five minutes, and then drove up through the rocks onto the machair – the grassy foreshore. It took us a further five minutes to reach the abbey.

No wonder it had never been sacked. It was tiny, no more than a stone cottage hidden in a copse of ancient oaks and other, wide-based, gnarled, older trees that I didn't recognise. The entrance was arched, like a tiny church would be, but the inside was a single room, comfortably furnished with a kitchen at one end, a single bed at the other, a table and a few wooden chairs in the middle. There was a roaring fire in the centre of the long wall to the left, and opposite, a small marble altar on which were a crucifix, a chalice and a bible. It wasn't as spartan as I had expected. In fact, I felt it could be quite comfortable.

Brother Aloysius welcomed me with a big hug and a smile. Then he held out his right hand.

'There's the damage,' he said, in a soft Highland accent. I looked down at his hand. The palm was like a football, and the fingers were swollen, stiff and red. Redness had spread up his forearm. That hug had made him wince, and it was obvious why. He had a severely poisoned right hand, and the poison was spreading up towards his armpit.

'You need surgery for that hand,' I said. 'It must be opened and drained, and you have to have the right antibiotics for it. It's dangerous for you to stay here. We need to get you off the island.'

'Sorry, Doc,' Brother Aloysius smiled. 'I won't go. I can't go. I have the duties of the order to perform. I'm the only one left and I can't leave this place untended. It would be 1300 years of constant service broken. It's not thinkable. Can't you open the hand here and give me an antibiotic from your bag?'

'You would need a general anaesthetic for it. The pain would be unbearable without it. And I couldn't guarantee that the antibiotics I have would touch the infection. How did it happen, by the way?'

The two men looked at each other, then Bill shrugged.

'I suppose doctors are like priests,' he said. 'You can keep a secret, can't you?'

I must have looked hurt, because he continued, 'Aye, I suppose you can. Brother Aloysius has been helping me with a particular bird. It's nesting on that cliff face opposite.'

I looked at the cliff through the window. There was a sheer drop of around 200 feet into the boiling sea below. No one could have climbed up from the bottom. There was a small hut on the flat ground above, beside which was a winch with a thick rope around it. The end of the rope was in a coil at the edge of the cliff-top: it was formed into a simple loop, big enough to go around a man's waist.

I was ahead of Bill's next statement, but I still didn't believe it when I heard it.

'There are two chicks in the nest, and we had to ring them if we could. I was at the top, and Aloysius went down to it. He managed the first chick well, but the second one dug her talons in to the palm of his hand.'

'How sore was that?' I asked the monk.

He smiled. 'I've had worse' he replied. 'And I got the chick back into the nest safely enough. I suppose she hadn't got very clean nails.'

'And all this just to ring a kittiwake or a gannet?' I asked.

The two men looked at each other again.

'It's not a gannet, or a kittiwake,' said Bill. 'It's a white-tailed sea eagle. It's the first to nest in Scotland for over a hundred years. Now do you see why you have to keep quiet?'

I sat down, thinking. The sea eagle nest had to be kept secret: if word got out, there would be egg-hunters crawling all over Wee Ensay. Their story would be safe with me. But if I left Brother Aloysius as he was, he could well die of septicaemia within days. At the very least, he would lose his hand if it were not decompressed within the next few hours. That meant opening it up, with a deep incision, to let the pus out and make the swelling go down. As for the antibiotic, simple penicillin might be enough, but I didn't know. It depended on what the chick had growing under its talons – did sea eagles eat only fish, or did they take rats and rabbits, too? Different prey carried different bacteria, and we had to make the right decision.

The Land-Rover came equipped for every eventuality, including emergency surgery, but not with an anaesthetic. There was a 'local' spray that might help a bit to numb the pain of the scalpel, but no way could I inject the area with anaesthetic and make everything numb.

Brother Aloysius was a mind-reader. He held his hand out to me again, and said, 'Get on with it, Doc. I'll bite the bullet for you.'

Five minutes later, everything had been done. With three parallel slits in the depth of his palm, packed with a dressing to drain them, and an injection of a broad-spectrum antibiotic into his thigh, Brother Aloysius had been given as much as we could.

'You had better get away now,' he said. 'The tide's coming in fast. It'll be over your axles if you wait any longer.'

I had forgotten about the sea crossing back to the big island. I followed Bill back to the water's edge. This time the sand couldn't be seen: the water was already about a foot deep and rising. I couldn't follow his tracks any more – just the centre of his wake. It was a terrifying rush from one rocky shore to the other. We made it safely, then Bill turned his car to make the crossing back to his home. He wasn't worried about it.

Half an hour later, I was back at the surgery. There was one patient to be seen. A Mrs McBride had brought her Jack Russell terrier to me. It had been over for an operation in Oban, at the vet's. The operation had been successful, but now the stitches had to be taken out. So that she didn't need to return to Oban, the doctor would do it, wouldn't he? I looked out the stitch removers from the animal instrument tray and started to do what I was asked. The dog, amazingly, lay still while I did it.

Bill phoned me the next morning. He had been to see Brother Aloysius. His hand was almost perfectly healed. The release of pressure and the antibiotic had done the trick, Bill said. I was staggered that he had recovered so fast. Maybe prayer had done its bit, too.

It's only now that I can tell Aloysius's story. Sea eagles came back to Mull twenty years later, and there are now dozens of them flying over the western isles. We have even seen them around the south Ayrshire coast. So I can write about the eyrie on Ensay Beag. And Brother Aloysius, now in his late eighties, has two younger men for company. They have taken on Bill's role, now that he has retired. The birds are flourishing, and so, for a short time, did the greenhouse next to the estate house. But that's a different story, to be kept for later.

Oh, and those trees I didn't recognise around the abbey? I found out what they were two days later. A bag of sweet chestnuts was left at the house: it had come from Brother Aloysius, along with a note that he had picked them from the abbey trees. They were the survivors of trees planted more than a thousand years before by the monks, as an everlasting source of food for them. I didn't know that sweet chestnuts could flourish so far north, and neither do any of the authors of books that I have read on trees. They were delicious.

The rest of that first locum stay on Ensay passed fairly quietly. I didn't have to use the coffin-carrier. Nor did I have to open the dental cupboard or attend to any more animals. There were a few walkers with tick bites, the odd fisherman who had hooked himself, a shepherd who had slipped while dipping his flock and ended up floundering about in the trough with them; and the usual numbers of people who needed blood pressures checked and their diabetes monitored.

There was plenty of time for us as a family to get to know the island and its people, and we loved them. By the time we had to take the ferry at the start of our 600-mile journey home to Hampshire, I had two children and a wife in tears. Did we really want to go back to the south? Why were we leaving such an idyllic place?

We were all standing on the deck, watching the island recede from us, when Alasdair pointed out a strange set of waves apparently coming towards us. As they got nearer, we saw that it was a school of porpoises, maybe 40 or 50 of them, rushing across our stern, making for the cliffs on the south side of Mull, about four miles away. We wondered what they were doing in such a rush.

It was only when they were disappearing towards the horizon that we caught sight of the reason for their panic. The huge black-and-white side of a killer whale appeared almost under our noses, streaking for them. It was marginally faster than its quarries: we were glad we weren't close enough to see the end of the chase. We were stunned at the sight, and fell silent for a while. Years later, we all admitted that this was a turning point regarding what we wanted to do, but then it was enough to convince us that there was much more to life than the rat race of the city.

The journey home took fourteen hours. Even on a Sunday, the motorway traffic between Blackpool and Birmingham was horrendous, and the road between Birmingham and Southampton, not yet up to dual-carriageway standard, was even worse. We arrived home after midnight, tired and sad, none of us wanting to face what the next few days might bring. There was a note in the letterbox, obviously hand-delivered (the rest of my mail was being kept by our neighbours). It had 'MOST URGENT' scrawled across it. I didn't want to open it that night, but felt compelled to do so.

By nine o'clock the next morning, I was in Heathrow Airport, about to board the KLM flight to Amsterdam.

THE PRESIDENTIAL DECISION

On the way to the airport I thought over and over again about the note. These were the days before mobile phones, so that no one could have contacted me on the journey down. One of the conditions of my being allowed to do locums was that I had to be available for any Huizens emergency, no matter where I was or what I was doing. On Ensay I had phoned in to the office every day, and anyone who might need me knew where I was. At around eleven that Sunday evening James M of L had dispatched the envelope by messenger to my house, knowing that it was the only way to make sure that I would get to Amsterdam the next day. Inside it was a terse message, and my airline ticket.

The message was to the point. James didn't use two words when one would do. 'Swine 'flu reported in the US. Be at the Hilversum office for the noon meeting. You'll know the score. Best of luck. James.'

I had phoned James when I read it, to let him know that I had received it. Even though it was the middle of the night, I knew he wouldn't be sleeping. The years as a guest of the Japanese Imperial Army had put paid to a normal sleeping pattern for him, and he was glad to hear from me. He thanked me for the call, and wished me luck with the 'woodentops' – his favourite name for the bosses in head office. James was more British, I mused, than he admitted.

I bought the *Guardian* and the *Times* at the airport, and scanned them for news about 'flu. It either hadn't broken yet, or the press hadn't understood its implications and hadn't bothered publicising it. I, and Huizens, understood its implications all too well.

To set the scene. By October 1918 the world was exhausted by the Great War. It was going to end all wars, although we all know now that it was only the first episode. Germany and her allies had lost around four million dead, and Britain, France and our allies had lost around three million, give or take a million or two. Everyone knew the end was coming, and the casualty numbers were falling as the will to fight on was ebbing away on both sides. At last, people thought, the daily obituaries in the press would return to the usual peacetime numbers, and normal living could start again.

Then people started dying from sudden overwhelming chest infections. It passed from person to person so quickly that the experts of the day estimated the time from catching the virus to its production of symptoms at only 24 to 36 hours. The illness didn't last long. It either killed you, or you survived. Between October 1918 and March 1919, it killed 22 million people worldwide: three times as many as the casualties on all sides in the war. Those obituary columns filled up once again.

The reports of the pandemic were stark. People got onto tramcars to go to work, apparently healthy, and died from torrential bleeding into their lungs before they reached their stop. The virus didn't respect geography or climate. Whole communities in Greenland were wiped out: the first boats to reach them after their isolated winter found no one alive. The young American GIs drafted to Europe died in their thousands – many more from 'flu than from wounds. In my old practice village of Collintrae, the records showed that the number of deaths from 'flu was twice that on the war memorial. The dead included the doctor and the district nurse, leaving the villagers with no medical, nursing or midwifery care.

At first, the illness was thought to have come from Spain, so it was called, naturally, the 'Spanish 'flu'. Which wasn't very fair, because its origins were in the Far East. It wasn't until years later, when researchers had the tools to identify its source more closely, that the name was changed: to swine 'flu. The first human cases had caught it from sick pigs.

In the 60 years that followed the pandemic that had killed more people than any other infection in human history, the swine 'flu virus had never returned. Yet everyone with knowledge of viruses was expecting it to do so. The World Health Organisation was eternally vigilant: it had 80 virus detection stations all around the world sending in reports to the headquarters – in Mill Hill in north London. Each year new viruses were identified. They showed slight variations in their make-up from the ones before them, and if the difference was enough to make the experts think they could cause new infections, and that the population was no longer immune to them, they were used in the new year's vaccines.

Occasionally, the virus changed so much that we had no protection against it, and it infected millions of people. Anyone who knew about influenza could name the years – 1933, 1957 and 1968 – in which it had killed hundreds of thousands. Most people who lived through them could name the Asian 'flu or the

Hong Kong 'flu as the one they caught in the bad years. But the deaths were an order of magnitude lower than from the swine 'flu. In '57 and '68 the winter deaths from influenza in Britain numbered around 100,000: the 1918 swine 'flu virus killed more than two million of us.

It was largely the fear of the return of that virus that had led to the WHO surveillance stations. We knew we would be hit from time to time by an unexpected change in the virus: the '57 and '68 changes were two examples. They were bad enough, but everyone knew that if the swine virus returned, only the people old enough to have caught it in 1918 and survived would be naturally immune to it. The instant it was identified again, we had to take immediate action against it or we might face mass deaths again.

Medical historians searched for clues as to whether the 1918 virus had ever hit us before. They had to go back to the Middle Ages – the fourteenth century to be precise – to find anything similar. That was the century of the great plagues, including the Black Death, which was spread by rats, and killed two-thirds of the population of Europe. The Black Death was well named, as its victims grew 'buboes' – large black blisters – in their armpits and groins before they died. But there was another plague, that came along with, or between outbreaks of, the bubonic plague. People who had been previously healthy died suddenly with bleeding from their lungs. They had no buboes: it was assumed that they had died so quickly from the plague infection that they hadn't had time to develop them. Historians concluded that this 'pneumonic plague' was simply a different version of the bubonic one, caused by the same bacterium, which has the rather attractive modern name of *Pasteurella pestis*.

But what if those 'pneumonic' pandemics hadn't been plague but influenza? Comparisons of what happened in the fourteenth century and the devastation in 1918-19 didn't bear thinking about, but the case histories were often identical. There were no trams in 1357, but records of the time showed that farm workers died, just like their modern counterparts, while walking from their villages to the fields.

Today we have effective antibiotics for *Pasteurella:* it is a bacterium. Bubonic plague will never devastate humans again, because we have simple antibiotics against it. Ordinary penicillin will take care of most cases. And we no longer have our ancestors' intimate contact with the rat fleas that carried the germ. It still causes deaths in the Far East, but it has disappeared from developed societies.

As an interesting aside on the plague, one of my medical historian friends told me, at a meeting on 'flu some years later, that the four-poster bed played some part in ending it. The cover above the four posts had a practical purpose. The thatched roofs and ceilings above bedrooms were favourite living places for rats. When they died – from *Pasteurella* infections, just like us – they would drop out of the roof space onto the unfortunate inhabitants below. The four-poster's cover would catch the bodies, preventing them from landing on the sleepers. If you were an ordinary peasant who couldn't afford a four-poster, you were much more likely to catch the plague than the more fortunate upper classes. This was just my friend's theory, but it's no coincidence, he believed, that four-posters came into fashion at around the time the Black Death died away.

That's a digression, however. The Huizens meeting was critical. We were one of the two biggest producers of influenza vaccine in Europe: the other was a company called Evans Medical, based in Liverpool. Between us, and the Pasteur Institute in Paris, we provided the world outside America with all its vaccines against the current strains of 'flu every year. In our factory near Amsterdam we made about ten million doses a year: Evans Medical made around the same number, and Pasteur a few less.

We grew the viruses in very carefully nurtured fertilised eggs taken from tens of thousands of hens that had been reared in a germ-free atmosphere. They had to be injected with the live virus, and then incubated at precisely the right temperature for several weeks. At the crucial moment, the viruses were 'harvested' from the eggs, immobilised so that they couldn't cause 'flu, then separated completely from the egg whites. All sorts of things could go wrong with the process from the time the relevant viruses were chosen for the vaccine to the packaging of each dose in each syringe. We were always on tenterhooks until we knew we had all the doses we needed for the next winter 'in the bag'.

The news of a swine 'flu outbreak couldn't have come at a worse time. In August, we were already well through our production schedule, and the factory was running at full capacity. Yet we knew that if the news was correct, and that swine 'flu had returned, all this would be for nothing. We would have to abandon everything we had done and switch to the production of a vaccine for the new virus. Travelling to Amsterdam that morning, I knew that I would have a heavy burden to bear at the meeting. My part was to play the medical man. I would be the only one there with front-line experience of a 'flu epidemic, and my clinical expertise, the Huizens people thought, would be crucial to the decisions made.

Willem, my faithful contact man, met me at Schiphol. On the way to the meeting, he told me all he knew, which wasn't very much. The American equivalent to Mill Hill had picked up a case of swine 'flu. The Huizens man in the US had been told about it the previous evening. There was to be an announcement later that day, and it wasn't going to be good news. We would know more about it at the meeting, where our American counterpart, who had flown across the Atlantic overnight, would tell us about it.

Half an hour later, twenty of us were seated around a long rectangular table, listening to him. The American authorities had had a meeting, the president presiding, at 9 pm: two in the morning our time.

'The president?' asked Willem, who being Belgian, the Dutch presumed, was slow on the uptake. 'The president of what?' he added.

'Of the United States,' came the reply. 'Gerald Ford. Who else?'

Like Willem, I was gobsmacked. The news must be terrible for the President himself to be involved. Dozens must already be dead, maybe hundreds. I wondered how the Americans had managed to keep the news out of the press. We were in terrible trouble. We would need to make millions of doses of vaccine as soon as possible. With all we knew about the previous pandemic, the virus would spread throughout the world in weeks. We didn't even have a sample of the virus to work on. We could never make enough in time to make the slightest dent in the number of deaths that were to come. A vision of tens of thousands of hens working overtime, laying eggs to save the human race, passed before my eyes.

'How many people are infected?' asked Professor Arendt. I

hadn't noticed him until then. He was several seats further up the table on the same side as me. He had a pad in front of him, on which there was a list of questions to be asked. 'And how far has it spread so far, in how long a time?'

We all sat a little further forward in our seats, craning to hear the answer.

'One', came the answer. 'Nowhere, and in two weeks.'

'ONE?' replied Professor Arendt. 'And it hasn't spread? In two weeks?'

'That's correct,' said the American. 'The virus has been isolated from just one man, he hasn't been particularly ill and he is now recovering. No one else seems to have caught it from him, but he was isolated fairly early in his illness.'

'Why was he isolated, if the case wasn't particularly severe? Surely that's unusual?' Willem asked. Belgians aren't so slow, I thought. There was a touch of Hercule Poirot about him.

'He was a new recruit to the US Army. He reported back to base two weeks ago with a 'flu-like illness, and he was put into quarantine as a routine, to stop any spread to the other soldiers in his unit. In the army every cough and cold gets investigated: the result was a huge surprise to everyone.'

'That's a relief,' said Arendt. 'So we don't have to bother about it. It's just a one-off. We can forget about it: he won't be infectious now, and it hasn't spread. We have brought everyone here for nothing.'

'Not so,' said the American. 'The president has made his decision. He wants 35 million doses of anti-swine 'flu vaccine made ASAP – within two months. The Americans can only make twenty million: he wants us to make the rest and send it. The expenses are on him. He can't take the risk of being the president who was in office when half the population died from a 'flu pandemic that could have been prevented.'

'It's insane,' said Arendt. 'We can't just set up a new factory out of the blue. Nor will the hens lay eggs to order. It isn't possible.'

'There's one small fact about the case that you should know. It may make you change your mind,' the American said.

'What's that?' Arendt asked.

'The patient worked on his father's pig farm. He may not have passed the virus onto anyone, but his pigs may have. They have been sold onto other farms and abattoirs, and there's no record of where most of them went. Farmers don't like 'snoopers', especially when they carry a closing-down warrant. They're not co-operating. We may be safe: but Gerald Ford isn't taking any chances.'

I wasn't needed. The president had spoken and the company had to take its decision on political, and not medical, grounds. The impossible became possible, and we started to make the vaccine. It wasn't a surprise to hear that our American friend had travelled across the Atlantic with a vial of the live virus in his hand luggage, in a diplomatic bag. My dead dogs of a year or two before were nothing compared with what he had brought through the customs.

That summer we made our ten million doses of the usual 'flu vaccine for the great European public. We made another five million doses of swine flu vaccine for the Americans. Along with contributions from Evans and Pasteur, the Americans got their shortfall of fifteen million doses and they gave the 35 million doses free of charge to their public. We didn't offer swine 'flu vaccine to the Europeans and Brits.

Which was just as well. The army recruit was the only person to catch swine 'flu. Since that year, 1976, there has never been another isolation of swine 'flu virus from any human being. All those doses of vaccine were made in vain, and several thousand Americans rue to this day the time that they were given it. I don't know if it was made in too much of a hurry, or if the virus itself was particularly nasty, but many thousands more Americans than expected developed serious complications after they were given it. There were even reports of deaths. It was a heavy price to pay for a president's decision to court popularity.

One result of those complications rebounded particularly on me. Huizens decided in their wisdom to appoint a 'flu troubleshooter. Whenever there was a serious adverse reaction to one of our 'flu injections, it would be reported to one responsible person, who would investigate it personally. That person would have to be medically qualified, so that he or she could discuss the facts on equal terms with the doctors involved. Preferably he would have to have a good command of English, as that would be the language in which the discussions would be held. The person they chose was me. Over the next year or so, I found out just how tricky reporting adverse reactions to medicines could be.

FIGHTING THE 'FLU

The 'flu vaccination season starts in earnest in September. That is the month the doses are packaged and distributed to pharmacies, health centres and hospitals. The 'shots' are given from late September to mid-November. It makes for six weeks of frantic energy and activity, and it concentrates the minds of those who have to organise it.

We had four million doses to give in Britain. To qualify for the 'jab' under the NHS rules, you had to be old, chronically ill, or in one of the emergency services. We had enough for all these categories, and a million or so doses left over for 'commercial' purposes. Factories, boarding schools, football teams and large businesses were all targets for our 'flu vaccination teams. From midsummer onwards our advertising and sales departments concentrated on getting our message across about the possibly devastating effect a bad 'flu epidemic might have on their production or on their staff. All they needed to protect them against the ravages of another '57 or '68 was a visit for a day of one of our ten teams, who would bring all the equipment and materials to vaccinate them. Sign up and be safe was the message.

Each team comprised a doctor and two nurses who travelled around the country with their supply of vaccine and their 'jet injection' guns. They were ingenious devices that used hydraulic power to squirt, without a needle, a very fine jet of vaccine through the skin of the upper arm. People would stand in queues with exposed arms and an experienced jet injector nurse could vaccinate at a rate of one per second. The pressure of the gun at right angles to the skin prevented any bleeding, and the jet of vaccine was so narrow that the hole it left was hardly visible. It was an extremely efficient way of vaccinating thousands of people in a day, until the advent of HIV and the possibility, no matter how remote, of transfer of fluid from one person's skin to another put paid to it.

Today, the use of 'flu vaccine is accepted. Government policy is to promote it every autumn, to protect as many of the 'at risk' people as possible from serious illness. So every year there is official backing for the campaign and we family doctors are even paid a fee for each injection.

It wasn't so in the 1970s. Health authorities were sceptical about how well the vaccine worked and didn't want to pay for it. There were even mutterings about interfering in the processes of 'natural' deaths in the elderly: vaccinating people in nursing homes would only keep the very elderly alive when it would be better for them, and presumably for the taxpayer, if winter pneumonias were allowed to take their lethal course. There's a quote in *A Christmas Carol* about curbing the excess population that is relevant. The health authorities obviously hadn't read the book to its end, where old Ebenezer changes his mind.

Our duty, we concluded, lay in changing the minds of officialdom, so we went to the highest in the land. I was deputed to take a team to the Houses of Parliament, to vaccinate the MPs and peers, and to push our research findings as much as I could. I'm no salesman, but I was genuinely enthusiastic about the project. I had suffered myself in the '57 outbreak and had to tend a busy practice in the '68 one, so I was happy to promote anything that would assign such experiences to history. And the trials of the vaccine had proved that it really did work. It was a good story.

We were lucky. The Wilson government wanted to back new technology, and we were seen to be at the 'cutting edge' of science. So four of us – another doctor, two nurses picked not just for their expertise but also for their spectacular appearance and their ability to wear nurses' uniforms in, shall we say, a pleasing way – arrived at the House one day in mid-September.

A room had been reserved for us somewhere in the corridors of power, well away from the chambers. We settled in, plugged in our 'gun' – imagine trying to take it through security today – and waited for our customers.

We had expected some opposition from Labour MPs, because they might see us as representatives of the evil pharmaceutical industry who were making money out of the sick. Not a bit of it. The Labour Party was enthusiastic to a man and woman. They lined up to get their 'shots' and were invariably polite and pleasant. I especially remember Joan Lester, known for her fairly extreme left-wing views. She was one of the MPs from whom I expected opposition to our scheme. Instead, she was charming and helpful. She offered to marshal her fairly large group of left-wingers into our room, and I was happy to accept her offer. She was as good as her word. Tony Benn, too, was impressive: he was friendly and well informed on all aspects of 'flu. Unexpectedly, the Tories were more stand-off-ish. We wondered if support from the government side had made them less likely to come forward. This was the time when the Liberals could famously have got into two taxicabs, so they weren't a significant presence in our queue.

After a few minutes, we heard a commotion outside the door. A steward had been posted outside to guide potential vaccinees to us. Someone was arguing vehemently with him. I walked into the corridor, to see Gerald Nabarro MP in full flow.

For those of you who don't remember him, he was an imposing sight, with ginger hair and a great handlebar moustache. He was famous for his eccentricity and his right-wing views, and he was determined to do us down. Seeing me, he asked me what on earth I was doing in the House, and he announced that we had three minutes to pack all our things and get out, before he made an official complaint to the Speaker about us. I tried to explain that we had been given permission to be there and were only trying to protect him and his colleagues from a potential 'flu attack in the winter to come.

'I've never had a cold in my life,' he barked at me. I gained the impression that he could only bark: he didn't seem to know how to lower his voice in normal conversation. 'I'll take vitamins and eat plenty of good food. That will sustain me through the winter and I advise you to do the same. Now I'll be obliged if you would leave this House.'

Prime Minister Harold Wilson arrived in the nick of time. He was avuncular, smiling, placatory and apologetic. To me, that is. Not to Mr Nabarro.

'I'm sorry you have had this harangue, Doctor,' he said. Then he turned to my would-be bouncer and spoke in low, slow, measured tones to him. I won't repeat what he said, because this is a wholesome book that children and elderly gentlemen and ladies of a delicate disposition might read, and the words would upset them. But they quietened Mr Nabarro.

Harold then turned to me, rolled up his sleeve and offered his arm for the first injection of the day. The rest of the Cabinet followed, as did the bulk of his party members. Give the Conservatives their due, they came in too, after it was explained that we were offering our services free of any charge as a way of helping to keep the House 'flu-free throughout the winter. Lords and Ladies followed, as did many of the staff of both Houses. Mr Nabarro stood outside the door throughout, trying to dissuade anyone from entering. The more he tried, it seemed, the more enthusiastic were our customers. At the end, I courteously offered him a dose. His face became even redder than usual, and I thought for a moment he was going to hit me. But he simply turned away and stomped down the corridor.

That winter the minister of health proclaimed that he supported 'flu vaccination, and we could have sold an extra two million doses or so, if we had been able to make them. We were on our way, and annual 'flu vaccination became a normal part of British health care. The Huizens profits from 'flu soared, but not without encountering a few hitches on the way.

Since the eighteenth century, when Dr Jenner demonstrated the success of his vaccine against smallpox, Britain has always had an anti-vaccination lobby. Whenever anyone falls ill after a vaccination, the lobbyists have always blamed the illness on the injection – regardless of any formal scientific analysis of the circumstances. In any group of four million people, a substantial proportion of them are going to fall ill in the next month, whether or not they have been given a 'shot'. How can you tell which cases are truly linked with the vaccine and which are coincidences?

The answer to that question fell to me. It was up to me to inquire into every case, and it didn't take long for me to be in the wars. Only a few days after our teams started their factory travels, our vaccine hit the headlines. Across the front page of a Scottish tabloid read by a million or more people a day, was a photograph of hundreds of young women lying unconscious on the floor of a clothing factory, accompanied by the following:

'Flu Jabs Did This to Workers –
Drugs Firm Condemned For Faulty Vaccine

The paper hadn't contacted me before they printed the story, or I would have given them the real one. But why let the facts get in the way of an opportunity to attack big business, particularly Big Pharma?

Our team in Scotland had phoned me that morning. They had been visiting a factory that made gents' suits. It had half a dozen production lines at the beginning of which were huge bales of cloth, and at the end of which were finished jackets and trousers. It employed more than a thousand women, each of whom had one skilled job to do. Chalking, cutting, sewing, cleaning, ironing all took place in order. I saw it in operation and was hugely impressed by the skill and the speed with which the suits were made – hundreds of them a day.

The vaccine team had organised things so that a few women could leave their production lines at appropriate moments, allowing the cloth to progress onwards as they took their minute or so away from them.

It was all going well when the first woman fainted, followed by a neighbour or two, followed by about a dozen more, then, as the number of horizontal ladies mounted, the whole factory joined in. Disaster. How could the vaccine have done this? I was despatched on the Southampton plane to Glasgow, where I was met by the Huizens area manager, and whisked to the factory.

The ladies had started to faint at 9.15. I had arrived at the factory at around 2 pm, by which time they had recovered enough for production to start again. The mass faints had stopped all work for three hours, and this had been enough time for the papers and the television news to get their photographs and to pile on the pressure to ban the vaccine. The factory management had forbidden all press interviews of employees, so that the news was based entirely on the pictures and on conjecture.

Within minutes of talking to the forewoman, I knew what had happened. Around a quarter of an hour into the 'gun' session, the storeman had joined the queue. He was no more than nineteen years old and was the only male employee. At the last second, just before our nurse pressed the gun trigger, he had panicked. He had pulled his arm away from the gun just as the jet of vaccine hit his skin. Instead of meeting the skin surface at a right angle, it hit the moving arm tangentially – slicing a neat thin horizontal cut across it. Naturally, it had started to bleed, copiously.

Instead of allowing the nurse to put a pressure pad over it, he ran up and down the line of ladies, showing off his bleeding arm. That's when the faints started. It was a chain reaction. Soon 200 ladies were lying on the floor, among the off-cuts of linen, wool and worsted. The vaccine had played no part in the fainting: only a handful of the prostrate women had actually had the injection. We had no need to check the batch for some awful contamination, as the press had claimed we must. The anti-vaccine story ran in the papers and the television all day, yet no one would let me explain. To this day people still think that getting a 'flu vaccination will make you faint. It was my first encounter with the bias of people with an agenda: it wasn't to be the last.

When Huizens started to manufacture 'flu vaccine, the medical team of the time predicted that there would be a steady incidence of allergic reactions to it. To make sure the company would not be held liable for the odd death, there were specific instructions about what to do if someone started to react to it. The worst predicted scenario was an 'anaphylactic' reaction in which the tongue and upper airways would suddenly swell up, causing the victim to choke and die within minutes. Everyone giving the vaccine had therefore to have nearby, preferably immediately to hand, a syringe of adrenaline to inject to stop the reaction. In fact, in the four years I was responsible for overseeing reactions to the vaccine, I was never notified of a single case of anaphylaxis. But there were deaths – and they were worrying.

My first call to a case of vaccine-related death came at 8 am one Wednesday morning. Two days before, a 67-year-old man had died suddenly just two hours after his doctor had given him a dose of our vaccine. The post-mortem was to be held in a Liverpool hospital that afternoon. As the responsible person, who might be able to give evidence to the coroner about the case, could I be there?

Seven hours later, I walked into the post-mortem room, having driven up the motorway as fast as I safely could. I hadn't eaten on the way. The pathologist looked at me curiously as I entered. He had just finished and was washing his hands at the metal sink on the opposite wall.

'I suppose you are the doc from Huizens?' he asked.

I nodded.

'You have come a long way for nothing,' he said. 'Have a look at what killed him. It's in his chest.'

I walked over to the metal table, where the assistant was cleaning up. The main artery from the heart had ruptured, and there was an awful amount of blood lying around in the man's chest. If a 'flu vaccine had done this, it was a very strange reaction.

'Did anyone tell you what happened?' the pathologist asked me.

This time I shook my head.

'I was simply told that death happened two hours after the vaccination,' I replied.

'You don't know about the wheelbarrow, then,' said the pathologist, who by now was removing his green overalls and putting on a white coat.

'Wheelbarrow?' I asked. 'No.'

'He had a long history of heart disease. His doctor called him in for a 'flu injection, and he walked out of the surgery happy as Larry.'

'Then,' continued the pathologist, 'he went to the shore. He lived in a bungalow in Southport, his back garden facing the beach, with a gate in his hedge through which he could get to it. He wanted to add some sand to a path and decided to help himself. With his wheelbarrow. Down he went, half filled the barrow, and he died while pushing it up the slope to the house. The strain ruptured his aorta. Must have died within seconds.'

'So it was nothing to do with his injection?'

'Absolutely nothing,' he replied. 'You can go home: the coroner doesn't want to see you after all.'

I took a lot longer on the way home, arriving back after midnight. The road from Liverpool to Birmingham and on-wards was the usual nightmare. It had been a long day.

On Friday of the same week, I was on my way up the motorway again. This time the call was to Clatterbridge Hospital on the Wirral. A woman had died on the bus home from her doctor's surgery, only a few minutes after her injec-tion. This time the link sounded foolproof. The local press had gone to town on the case, blaming the 'flu jab for the death and exhorting readers to steer well clear of it.

The journey to the Wirral was a little shorter than that to Liverpool. On the way I mused that I could possibly write a gazetteer of the mortuaries of Britain, but doubted that it would sell. When I arrived and walked in, I had déjà vu. Despite the different location, I was meeting the same patholo-gist. His normal base was Liverpool, but he was 'filling in' for his pal across the Mersey for a long weekend. He was having as busy a time as I was.

'You again,' we said to each other, with the faintest of grins.

'You didn't hear, then, about the ear syringe?' he said to me. The déjà vu strengthened.

'Not a wheelbarrow this time, then?' I asked him.

'No, but another wasted journey for you', he replied.

'Difficult one, this,' he said, 'but not for you. She went to her doctor because she had earache. He looked in the ear, saw what he thought was a lot of solid black wax and decided to syringe it away. He didn't get much out and stopped when the pain got worse. He saw from her notes that she had chronic lung disease, and was on the 'flu list, and gave her a shot before she went. He assumed that she had an ear infection, prescribed an antibiotic for her and some drops to soften the wax, and she left.'

'So it wasn't an ear infection?'

'Be my guest,' the pathologist said, gesturing towards the form on the slab. The head was opened: inside the skull was almost as much blood as I had seen in the chest two days before.

'The black mass wasn't wax but an aneurysm of the carotid artery. It had already eroded from the middle ear into the lower surface of the brain. The syringing burst it. When she got on her bus she had about four minutes to live.'

'So nothing to do with the vaccine, then.'

'Nothing at all.'

I had been looking forward to Friday evening: we had planned to go out as a family to the pictures. Instead, I spent almost all of it sitting in a jam around Birmingham while Mairi and the children enjoyed the film. The job was getting as busy as practice had been. I wondered, on the way, how the GP who had done the syringing felt. He might have a difficult time with the coroner. I was glad not to be in his shoes.

The Sunday papers didn't help me to relax. One of the health columns had picked up on the fact that there didn't seem to be a new 'flu virus around that autumn. In addition to this, the author mentioned reports from the provincial press that vaccine shots were causing mayhem in factories, killing poor unsuspecting people going about their normal business of gardening and the like, who furthermore had nothing wrong with them beyond earache. Pharmaceutical companies were no better than mass killers, wrote one alternative practitioner. Stick to Chinese herbs, acupuncture, echinacea, veganism, a macrobiotic diet and yoga and you will never succumb to influenza was his message. Defiling your body with a vaccine made from the very viruses you wished to avoid was preposterous and obviously dangerous, wrote another.

Take, for example, that last article continued, the poor guy who had been vaccinated at work in north London and who had died that same evening. Didn't the coroner there blame the vaccine? Surely it was time to stop the whole campaign and to sue the company that made the vaccine?

Wow. I hadn't heard about this north London case. I hoped it wasn't our vaccine, but I figured it must be. The first item on our agenda in the Monday morning meeting would have to be that report.

James M of L chaired it. On the surface things looked grim. There had been a coroner's inquest into the man's death on the previous Thursday. His wife had seen him off to work that morning, knowing that he was going to have a 'flu vaccination. He had been sent home from work in the afternoon with a headache. It had got progressively worse throughout the evening: he had hardly said a word to her, the pain had been so bad. Then, at around nine o'clock, he had suddenly died.

The post-mortem had shown a 'generalised inflammation of the brain' of unknown cause. The coroner stated that he had to consider that the 'flu vaccination had at least contributed to the death, and wished it to be referred to the Committee of Drugs as a serious adverse reaction.

Our 'flu vaccination manager had gone through our records over the weekend. We had indeed sold vaccine to the company. The gun team had vaccinated 40 employees there between nine and 9.30 in the morning, then left to visit another company in Hertfordshire, about 30 miles away. The team had not been told of the subsequent death, and this was the first they had heard of it. No one had notified us, either, as the vaccine manufacturer. That was a strange omission, as we should have been the first to know, so that we could check the vaccine batch used in his case.

One of the nurses from the vaccination team arrived a few minutes after we heard this brief explanation of events. She had with her the notes from that morning's session. We asked her if she remembered anything different about it. It had run like clockwork, she said. There were the usual one or two on the list who hadn't turned up, and she did remember one man that they decided not to 'do' because he wasn't feeling well.

Could we have his name? She looked it up.

You are probably ahead of me. He was, of course, the man who had died. He had spent the rest of the morning resting in the factory's canteen, nursing his headache, before taking the midday bus home. Everyone who had seen him that day, including his wife, assumed that he had had his injection. The coroner, too, had made the same assumption. No one had bothered to contact us or the 'flu team.

The coroner's verdict couldn't be overturned: the episode remained a 'vaccine-related death', and has been quoted as such in medical journals since then. At least his widow accepted our explanation and our condolences in good faith. The papers that slammed us weren't as pleasant: there were no rebuttals or apologies for the vaccine scare.

That hurt. Friends who knew what I did would ask how I could continue to associate myself with such a lethal product. It was as if I was endorsing cigarettes. Eventually, the fuss about the safety of the vaccines died down, and they became well accepted. In the meantime, we were pursuing the Holy Grail of 'flu vaccines – one that we could give by a nasal spray and avoid the dangers of injections. We nearly made it.

The First Steps Towards Home

I can't say the decision came to me in a flash. It was more like a deluge. There I was, dressed like a spaceman, in green surgical overalls, with a plastic see-through protector over my face, washing out nostrils. Not just one or two nostrils, but several thousand. The process, as described to me beforehand by my bosses, should have been straightforward. I would simply instil by syringe a quarter of a cupful of saline into one nostril. The subject obediently held the other closed with a finger while I did it, then blew the saline out again into the receiving sample pot. I was then to do the same for the other nostril. All I had to do was collect around 3000 of these pots in the next week or so, seal them, label them, and send them off to the lab in Amsterdam, 7000 miles away.

I could look on it as a holiday in the sun, they said. All I had to do, they said, was to appear at the minehead as the workers were going on or off shift, and do the business in a nice office the owners would provide for me. The rest of the day would be my own. Well, maybe I could deliver a lecture or two about the research in between times, but that would be OK, wouldn't it?

It sounded great. Oh yes, my bosses added. We would like

you to take blood samples, too – maybe a thousand or so – while you are at it. That wouldn't be much extra work, and there would be plenty of supporting staff to help me.

It was a far cry from my GP days in Collintrae, in both responsibilities and in distance. For the miners weren't into coal, but gold, and they were in Johannesburg. And they certainly weren't used to foreign, pink-skinned doctors asking them to donate their nasal mucus to research. It was a process as alien to them as it was to me.

After dealing with only six nostrils, I took off my mask. Doing so was essential for two reasons. One was that it was covered with sputum: the sort of messy film that you get on a windscreen on a really greasy day when you have just driven through a cloud of midges on a country road in an average west of Scotland summer. So I couldn't see a thing. The other was that plainly something was going wrong. It should have been simple for the men to direct their nasal streams into the pots provided. Somehow they found it difficult. The angle of spray was wide and the target small: and my face somehow kept getting in the way. The front of my green gown was covered, too. And this after I had dealt with only three men. I had another 2,997 men, and 5,994 nostrils to deal with.

That was when the decision began to form in my mind. What was I doing here, covered in other men's snot, when I could have been at home, in the bosom of my family? Tennyson M'Shombe, the nurse assigned to assist me by the resident mine doctor, was watching me. He grinned, widely, then spoke quickly in Xhosa to the next man in line. The clicks came thick and fast – first from Tennyson, then from the men as they passed whatever he had said down the line. About a dozen were waiting behind him. Suddenly, the atmosphere changed. The sullen line of men brightened up. They started smiling at me. One or two came forward to shake my hand. They started to talk, all at once, and through the general hubbub I could only manage to grasp the words 'Rangers' and 'Celtic'.

Tennyson turned back to me.

'I don't think you'll have any more trouble now, Doc', he said, laughing again.

From then on the nasal sprays were neatly concentrated. Not a drop hit my face or my chest. The pots filled up beautifully, and the collection started in earnest. The line seemed endless: three hours later, I was still filling the pots, and wondering why suddenly everyone coming off shift was keen to see me.

They even volunteered for the blood samples, without demur. It meant them exposing their forearms to a fairly large needle, and me taking about fifteen millilitres – a tablespoonful – of blood from them. I couldn't see the veins, but they were easy to feel, and I was good at hitting them the first time. That went smoothly, too.

When the last man had gone, Tennyson and I relaxed together.

'What did you say to them?' I asked him.

'They thought you were just another Afrikaaner doing tests,' he replied. 'They were jumping at the chance of spraying their mucus all over you and getting away with it. Can you imagine their feelings? To be able legitimately to spray their snotters over a white man? And not get jailed? You were in for a really rough time. Then I told them you were a Scotsman, seconded here.'

'Why did that make a difference?' I asked.

'They are all from Soweto. Most of the schools there were

set up by Scots, and they know all about Scotland. Once they knew that connection, they wouldn't let you down.'

It was my second day in South Africa. That night, in the Carlton Hotel, where I had been given a room for my stay, I made up my mind. Tennyson had gone back to his small house in the township, and I my life of luxury.

I ruminated over why I was sitting in a hotel room, so many thousands of miles away from home and family. The immediate reason, of course, was plain. It was my job to collect nasal mucus and blood because we had to know whether the recent varieties of influenza virus had hit this part of the world. The accepted knowledge was that they hadn't. Somehow the 'flu epidemics of '57 and '68 had passed by South Africa without infecting the indigenous population. When the rest of the world was falling ill in those years, the virus hadn't bothered the mineworkers at all. My job was to check if that was true: we could tell by gathering 'local' antibodies from the nose and 'circulating' antibodies from the blood. If they weren't there, this population was the ideal one on which to try out the world's first nasal 'flu vaccine – and I'd have to return in a month's time to give them their doses. In a further three weeks, I'd need to come back yet again, to repeat the whole 'wash and bleed' exercise, to see if the vaccine had caused the anti-'flu antibody levels to rise. That would prove that the vaccine worked.

But that wasn't the reason I was asking myself why I was there. Was this really the work I had been trained to do, as a doctor? Did I really see myself as a research pioneer, rather than seeing patients? It didn't take me long to answer. I picked up the phone beside my bed and dialled the number for home.

'How do you feel about going home?' I asked, when Mairi answered.

'But I am home,' she said. 'It's you that isn't. Are you feeling all right?'

'Never felt better,' I replied. 'Our real home, I mean. Ayrshire – the Stinchar Valley. Let's talk about it when I get back.'

The conversation did last longer, but what we said to each other after that remains private –after all, this is a book about medical practice, and what wives and husbands say to each other when thousands of miles apart isn't relevant. It's enough to say we were missing each other.

Over the next few days, I got to know Tennyson much better. Educated in Soweto, he had been brought up by devoted parents who loved poetry and literature. His brother was called Robert Burns M'Shombe, and his sister Elizabeth Barrett Browning M'Shombe. Evidently, his parents' teachers at the Missionary school were a healthy mix of English and Scots Victorians. Tennyson could recite the whole of 'The Charge of the Light Brigade' and that poem about the flower in the crannied wall. He was astonished at my lack of knowledge of great British literature. He also made it clear that we couldn't meet together after work. He had to go his way, and I mine: if we became friends my stay would be cut short, and he might even be arrested.

The study went well. It even finished a few days earlier than planned. That gave me time to visit Cape Town, Port Elizabeth and Durban, giving talks to the local doctors about 'flu and future developments in vaccines. On the way north-east from Cape Town to Port Elizabeth, I was driven along the Garden Route, which my driver called 'the most beautiful scene in Africa'. I scanned the unbroken horizon and the ribbon developments of houses along the side of the road, and looked in vain for my Scottish islands and mountains. I thought of the island of Ensay and the road from Ayr to Collintrae. They were a thousand times more beautiful, I told myself, and I resolved to return to them as soon as I could.

On my return to Johannesburg, the day before my flight home, I managed to spend the evening, surreptitiously, with Tennyson. He had arranged an elaborate charade, taking the place of his brother as a room steward at the hotel. There was no other way we could sit together with no one overseeing us. We spent an hour or so mulling over South African politics and how it might change. We also talked about Britain and how we might be able to fund him for a scholarship. He was highly intelligent and had a phenomenal memory – possibly the consequence of learning all those poems when he was a boy. When he had to leave, I was sorry to see him go into the Johannesburg night.

The next day, all samples collected and dispatched, I was packing up my belongings in the hotel and waiting for my taxi. The phone rang. It was Dr Eastwood, one of the doctors at the university's research centre whose company I had enjoyed, and whom I respected highly. Originally British, she was one of the 'good guys', having devoted her life to the tropical diseases that afflicted black Africans in the region.

'Tom, do you think you could help us out?' she asked. 'We have some curious cases in the hospital and we need your expertise in virus detection, fairly urgently. Four men have arrived from the north and they are pretty sick. One is certainly dying, and the others may not be far behind. Could you look at them for us – and maybe take some samples from them for your team in Europe to analyse?'

I had only half an hour left before checking in for my plane

– and I had a deadline to keep in Amsterdam the next day. If I went to the hospital, I wouldn't make the flight and would be delayed by at least a day. I really needed to go home.

'I have to make my plane, and I'm just leaving for the airport. Could someone else take the samples and send them on? I'm very sorry.'

Elizabeth was sorry too, but accepted that there was no other way. She might take them herself, or get someone else to do so. I then had what I thought was a brilliant idea.

'Elizabeth, why don't you ask Tennyson to do it? He would get a big boost from the extra responsibility, and he has seen the sampling done thousands of times. He would do it exactly as it should be done and he knows all about packaging and where they have to be sent.'

'Great idea,' she said. 'I'll be there to help him'.

We left it at that. Two hours later, I was in my BA plane on the tarmac at Johannesburg airport. Four hours later, I was still there. We had been told that there was a fault in one of the engines, and that it had to be fixed before take-off. We left half an hour after that.

In those days the route was Johannesburg – Nairobi – Zurich – London, with around a two-hour stop at each airport. Except that the stops at Nairobi and Zurich were extended to four hours, because of a fault in the same engine. Now seven hours late, with dawn breaking over the mountains in front of us, the plane started its take-off run from Zurich. We were at full speed, just before lift-off, when the engines suddenly cut out, the lights went off, and we were rushing, silently as the grave, towards the alpine foothills at the end of the runway.

Amazingly, there wasn't a sound from the inside of the cabin. No panic, not even the smell of fear, as the pilot put on the brakes. Everyone was pitched forward in their seatbelts. I only remember thinking that I would have been better off staying that extra day in Jo'burg, before the plane ploughed into the grass at the end of the runway. The tail slewed round, and the plane stopped, facing the way we had come.

There was still silence from all the passengers and crew. Then the pilot spoke to us. In clipped RAF tones he said, 'Jolly sorry about that. Nearly pranged, don't y'know. Dashed starboard engine caught fire as we reached flight speed, and had to shut everything down. Bit of a bother, but all's well now. Take your time getting off. You can see the busses coming to get you. Use the chutes and we'll all be OK.'

That broke the silence. To my surprise, everyone started to laugh. I even enjoyed my little trip down the chute.

Naturally, we faced more hours of delay as the plane and the runway were sorted out. Instead of going to Heathrow, getting home for a day, then travelling to my meeting in the Netherlands, I managed to get myself and my bags re-routed direct to Amsterdam. There I was debriefed on my work on the sample gathering, and had to spend the next three days discussing future projects with various managers and doctors in my equivalent position from other countries. Only then could I return home, to Hampshire.

Mairi, Catriona (now aged twelve) and Alasdair (now ten) greeted me warmly. They wanted me to tell them all about the people I had met and the places I had seen. I told the kids about the excitement on the plane (that worried them a little) and about the snotters (they loved that) and about Tennyson M'Shombe and Dr Eastwood. I saw Mairi frown at Elizabeth's name, and she got up out of the room.

She came back with the day's edition of the *Guardian* and

placed it beside her. I looked at her curiously, but she wagged her index finger at me discreetly. Whatever she wanted to say, it wasn't to be in front of the children. It was nearly eleven o'clock, and they wandered off to bed, happy that Dad was home again.

Back in the sitting room, Mairi poured a stiff whisky, and put it beside me.

'You are going to need this,' she said. She placed the paper in front of me and pointed to an item in the international news on page three.

'New virus kills researchers' was the headline. It told of the deaths of South African virologist Dr Elizabeth Eastwood and two of her assistants from a virulent new virus that they had caught from patients who had come from central Africa. They had died from fulminating pneumonia and massive bleeding from their lungs within 48 hours of treating the patients, all of whom had also died.

I couldn't speak, and could hardly breathe. I was dumb-struck by the tragedy that had befallen poor Elizabeth and possibly Tennyson, too. And by the thought that I had avoided their fate simply because I had to get on a plane. I phoned Dr Leo Rubenstein, the only person I knew in South Africa who could give me any information on what had happened. I waited a long time before he answered. Tennyson was still alive.

By the strangest of luck, a police agent, who had presumably been following me, had seen him coming out of my hotel that last evening, and he had been taken in for questioning. Dr Eastwood hadn't been able to contact him and had recruited other staff to help her. They had died and Tennyson had lived to fight the system for another day.

He had to wait for the Mandela era to fulfil his potential, but he now has a top job in the Baragwanath Hospital in Soweto, and we still correspond from time to time. They gave him a tough time in detention, but he looks back on it as his lucky break.

We didn't know it then, but the four men, and Dr Eastwood and her team, turned out to be the first people in southern Africa to have caught Ebola fever. It is still devastating many rural areas of sub-Saharan Africa.

That night, Mairi and I decided on our future. We were going back to our beloved Stinchar Valley, as soon as we knew how.

My Decision

Two weeks after my return from South Africa, James asked me to come to his office. He sounded serious. It was just him and me. I had been in Huizens' employ for nearly five years now, and we knew, liked and trusted each other. He was one of those rare chief executives who was completely honest and who cared more for his colleagues and employees than for his company's bare financial and market figures. By this time Vivian had left the company for a promotion elsewhere: his fiery Welsh character made him too independent for the wood-entops, and I was now the medical director. It was a director-ship in name only: I didn't have shares in the company and I had no real power over any decision except where medical expertise was needed. So I hadn't seen the bombshell coming.

'I've bad news for you,' said James. 'The main Huizens Board in Huizenhoven wants to sell us off. They want to concentrate on electrical and white goods: they don't understand the medical business, and they think we are leaking too much money in our research.'

Things had been uneasy between Huizens Pharma and Huizens Electrical for a long time. The bosses in Huizenhoven didn't appreciate the need for huge investment if new drugs were to be brought to the market. But to sell us off? I was astonished.

'Who are they selling us to?' I asked.

'Anyone who wants to buy us,' was the reply. 'So we have to make the books balance.'

'Meaning?' I asked, with a bad feeling about what was coming next.

'That we have to shut down most of your medical research trials. We have to show a better balance sheet, and the most expensive items on it are your trials. Huizenhoven never really forgave us for the quarter of a billion those dogs cost us.'

'But the trials are just bearing fruit. And think of how the investigators will feel. How do we explain things to them?' I asked.

'We just have to. We are funded by Huizenhoven, and the funds are being withdrawn. We can't argue.'

I walked out of the room dazed. It wasn't just the ending of so much promising research, but how I could deal with my little group of trial co-ordinators. We had built up a brilliant team over a few years, and it would have to go. Jobs would be lost, and I would have to make the transition as painless as possible.

I didn't agree with the Huizens decisions, and said so. We would be a much better prospect for a take-over if we kept our trials alive, and with good drugs still in the pipeline. I began to understand why James called his bosses the woodentops. But I had no choice. I had to visit all my universities and hospitals in turn, to explain, face to face, what was happening. It wouldn't be pleasant, but it would be fair to my investigators. And maybe some of them had the prestige to force Huizenhoven to change its mind.

I wouldn't travel alone: I would ask Willem, also promoted in the Netherlands to a much higher position in the hierarchy, to come with me. We met at Heathrow and set out on our round-Britain voyage. The itinerary took in university hospitals in Aberdeen, Edinburgh, Glasgow, Belfast, Birmingham, Manchester, Leeds and London. We would finish up in Bart's, where we would meet again my friend and mentor Professor Mawson.

Willem was brilliant. He knew the fine details of every trial and of every drug, and he was a great travelling companion. That turned out to be my last formal meeting with Willem and Arendt. When I got back to work in Southampton the next day, James called me into his office.

'It's about your return trip to South Africa,' he said. He was in serious mode again.

I was due to return there for the follow-up tests of the nasal vaccine. The tests of the bloods and nasal mucus had shown that the miners were the perfect population for trials. I had heard from Dr Rubenstein that Tennyson was out of detention and had been allowed back to work, so I was looking forward to seeing him again.

'You aren't going back,' James added.

'Why not?' I asked him.

He pushed a letter over his desk towards me. I picked it up and read it.

It was from the South African authorities. I was no longer acceptable to them and would be refused entry if I tried to return. It didn't give a reason.

'You want to know why you can't go back?' James asked me.

'Naturally.'

'I have a friend in the Dutch consulate, who has a friend in government circles, who has a friend... You know how it goes. When I received this I did a bit of digging around. You were marked down as trouble on the first day. Do you remember an incident with a hospital porter in the Baragwanath? That's when you were put under supervision.'

I remembered it only too well. I was being shown around the hospital – the biggest in Africa, and devoted only to the welfare of the '*niet blankes*' – when my Afrikaaner guide and I came across a young porter in difficulties.

It was nearly lunchtime, and the man had been trying to push a huge metal trolley full of trays of food through the doors opening into one of the women's wards. The doors were made of thick rubber with perspex see-through portholes in them at eye level. They could be pushed from either side and overlapped in the middle when they were closed, so that they needed a fair amount of power to open them.

The porter didn't have enough strength to push the trolley all the way through them. They had stuck on the sides of the trolley, so that he could neither push it through them nor pull it back. He was having a bad time.

I did what I thought anyone would do. I stepped forward, pulled one door away from the trolley, and he was able to walk through with ease. He looked at me, astonished, then carried on.

Two things happened simultaneously at that point. The ward full of ladies waiting for their meals, which had been up to then full of loud chatter and laughter, fell completely silent. They were all looking at me, amazed. The other was that I had a sudden pain in my left elbow – the arm that wasn't holding the door open.

I looked down at it, hearing at the same time a voice close to my ear. My elbow was held in the vice of my guide's thumb and forefinger. He was squeezing very hard on the nerve that runs around the inside of the joint – the one that gives you pain when you have tennis elbow. It was intense: a professional's pressure. The pain ran down to my hand and fingers.

'Don't you dare do anything like that again,' hissed my guide. 'You are a white man – you don't help these people: you let them get on with their own business. You aren't in Britain now.' Only then did he release the grip. I couldn't move my fingers for several minutes.

I should have known better, I suppose. I had been fore-warned that I should watch my step, and that I had to follow the rules. Petty apartheid, my friends who had visited before me had told me, was a real pain, but it had to be adhered to by out-siders, or they would be made *persona non grata* faster than they could say Jacobus van der Merwe. Jack Robinson isn't a com-mon name among Afrikaaners.

Naturally, from that moment on, I was suspected of being unsupportive of the regimen. I had been tailed wherever I went: my friendship with Tennyson and the good relationships I had struck up with the miners had been red flags to them. The proof of my undesirability was the evening I thought I had spent undetected with Tennyson. Why should I prefer the com-pany of a '*niet blanke*' man when there were plenty of '*blankes*' to have fun with?

No, I was obviously subversive: South Africa could manage perfectly well without me, thanks.

'So who is going in my place?' I asked James.

'No one,' he replied. 'We are stopping the nasal vaccine research. It's too far from the market, and costing too much.'

The company seemed to be piling up the straws on my back. The one that broke it followed in James's next sentence.

'It's not the only news I have for you,' he said. 'I have tickets for you to go to Copenhagen on Friday.'

This was Wednesday. I had been in Amsterdam over Monday night: it looked as if I was to be spending another night away from home on Friday. I hadn't left Collintrae to spend so much time away from my family. The children were beginning to wonder who the stranger was who spent a few evenings with them once in a while.

'What's on in Copenhagen?' I asked him.

'It seems you are,' was the reply. 'You have to listen to Professor Hans Larsson present a paper at a meeting in Copenhagen University, then you have to demolish him with a few chosen remarks.'

'Demolish him?'

'We have had a problem, I'm told, with a trial Professor Larsson conducted with one of our drugs. Something to do with the way it was set up and then analysed. It shows the drug in a bad light – not sufficiently effective and too many side effects. Problem is that the controls weren't tight enough. And the analysis isn't correct. Here is the dossier. You have a few hours to bone up on it, then put together a question or two that will blow his research wide open. If we don't do it, we lose yet another drug. Huizenhoven said you will be perfect. They think Monday's meeting proved that.'

I looked at the folder on the table. It was on our new drug for high blood pressure and heart failure – a step onwards from betablockers. So far all the trials had been without problems: the Copenhagen trial was news to me. That wasn't surprising, as the professor was known to be anti-pharmaceutical industry:

he had been the death knell of other promising drugs.

I thanked James for the information, and went to my office to read the dossier. One of Willem's colleagues in Hilversum had written a résumé of it and pointed out where the planning and analysis had gone wrong. He had also managed to get hold of Professor Larsson's proposed speech and slides. He had marked areas of the slides that had mistakes in them, and where the analysis could best be criticised. As I read on, I realised that Huizens had a point. The data had been collected in a biased way and the analysis had been made with the obviously specific purpose of destroying the drug – and Huizens' reputation.

The conference was hugely prestigious: it was the Annual World Congress on Hypertension and Heart Failure. It was Copenhagen's turn to be the hosts, and all presentations had to be available in advance to its delegates. Professor Larsson was not just a speaker but, being from the host university, he was the congress chairman. He had to show an example to the other speakers, and as a matter of courtesy, because it was about a Huizens drug, he had sent his presentation in full to Hilversum. Big mistake. We weren't going to show him courtesy in return.

I travelled to Copenhagen on the Thursday evening. I tossed around, sleepless and anxious, all night in the unfamiliar hotel bed. The next morning, I went to the Congress armed with a few slides of my own. At eleven, Professor Larsson started his talk. At 11.20 he finished it and the session chairperson asked for questions. By 11.25 his paper was in shreds, all credibility destroyed. The chastened professor agreed that it would be withdrawn from the congress publication. Huizens' drug was saved.

But what about me? Four hundred people had heard me savage the professor's work. When I sat down, there was not a sound. No one smiled; no one approached me afterwards to say that I had been right. I felt the wave of hostility: the professor was their local hero, and no matter the rights and wrongs of the trials, I had humiliated him in front of them.

I had been invited to the congress dinner that evening. I didn't stay for it. I took the first plane back to London and managed to have dinner with the family. That night I wrote out my resignation: it was on James's desk on the following Monday.

I had to give three months' notice. James understood, but tried to make me reconsider. He even offered me a substantial rise in pay, but he knew, of course, that it wouldn't make me change my mind. We had a family discussion on what we would do. Three of us voted for a return to the west of Scotland. Catriona, by this time thirteen years old, was the dissenter. We had moved from Basingstoke to Lyndhurst, in the New Forest, three years before, and she had fallen in love with horses. She would never find a similar riding school in Scotland. She was overruled by the rest of us.

How would I earn a living? By this time, I had a regular column in *Pulse*, thanks to Hertzel. I had commissions to report one or two conferences, with the promise of more; and old doctor friends from my Collintrae days would give me locums on their days off and holidays. We would probably make ends meet. We could sell our house at a profit and build one on a plot of land next to the Stinchar that was for sale, and still probably have money to spare. In the meantime, one of our farmer friends near Collintrae would be happy to rent us a cottage until the new house was ready. Asked what rent he would like us to pay, he said 'fifteen pounds a month'. It was a bargain, even more so when, after a few weeks, he refused any rent at all.

On July 1st, 1977 we said goodbye to our Huizens colleagues and did our last minute packing before travelling north. That evening, at around 7.30, I had a phone call from Malcolm Maxwell, director of a headhunting firm. He had heard that I was leaving Huizens. Would I be interested in living in Paris?

'What would I be doing in Paris?' I asked him.

'Heading a research team of an international company. You would run the European division, have all the support you would need, have free education for your children at the international school and an apartment in the centre of the city. We could offer you 60,000 dollars a year.'

I didn't reply immediately. My Huizens salary was around 7000 pounds a year – which was high in the late seventies. Malcolm obviously thought the line had been cut off.

'Hello, hello. Are you still there?' I could hear him ask.

'Yes,' I said. 'Can I phone you back in a few minutes? I need to think this over.'

'Sure,' he replied. He gave me his number.

My conversation with Mairi took about two minutes. No, we weren't going to Paris, vast sum of money or not. We were going to South Ayrshire, and that was that.

I dialled Malcolm's number.

'Sorry, but no thanks,' I said. 'But I do have a name for you: a man who would do the job exceptionally well. And he has the advantage of speaking five languages fluently.'

'Great,' came the answer. 'What's his name?'

We drove to Collintrae the next day and settled into our farm cottage. The farmer happened to have three horses that weren't being ridden enough – Catriona was suddenly in heaven. She and Alasdair, aged eleven, lost their southern accents within a week of starting school. Mairi and I set about starting up our writing business.

Oh yes, and Willem Brand moved to Paris. In 2005, 25 years later, he retired from the chairmanship of the second-largest pharmaceutical company in the world. In the *Financial Times* his retiring bonuses were reported as in excess of 30 million pounds and his pension as more than two million a year. We still see him from time to time. He has visited the Stinchar Valley many times and he says he envies me my life of peace and tranquillity in my beautiful valley. We don't talk about our relative bank accounts. When we walk over the hills together, I still wear his boots.

Settling Back

We had been seven years away from our beloved Stinchar Valley and we were returning to a very different role in the community. There was a new doctor in our old house in Collintrae, and etiquette, as well as common sense, required that I mustn't in any way come between him and his patients. Happily, it wasn't hard. David was an older man, well aware of my previous role in the district, and was happy to welcome me back: he asked me to do the odd surgery and few days of locum for him; the old practice was in very sound hands, and I was privileged to help him out from time to time.

My former patients, too, recognised that things were different, and were savvy enough to avoid medical subjects when we met in the street or in the shops. I was now just the 'locum' and not 'the doctor' and they quickly adjusted to the new relationship.

Some things, however, remained the same. Like the weather. During our first winter back, I was asked to 'do a week' to let David step off the GP treadmill for a while. It wasn't a good week. The snow and I started together on the Monday, and it didn't stop for four days. By Thursday Collintrae was cut off from Girvan to the north and from Stranraer to the south by drifts. We could only be reached by boat, of the life or the fishing variety.

That was awkward: I had enough drugs in the dispensary to last for several weeks, but there were patients who needed specialist opinions, some of them fairly urgently. In those days, consultants were happy to do 'domiciliary visits' for their country colleagues, and Dr David had arranged, before he had gone off duty, to bring down one of them to see three patients in and around the village. I was to meet him and take him to them. It was a part of country general practice I hugely enjoyed, especially as Dr Slessor, the consultant who was coming, was a good friend and an excellent heart and lung man. On a normal Thursday we would have given him lunch, then seen him off on the road to Stranraer, where he had an afternoon clinic.

Except this week there was no road to Stranraer, and no road from Girvan. That was no problem for Alec Slessor. He wasn't letting a little snow get in the way of seeing his patients. A keen sailor, he phoned the previous evening to say that he would take a boat from Girvan (the road from Ayr was still open), call in at Collintrae harbour, and then carry on to Stranraer. He might not get home to Ayr that evening, but a good meal, a glass or two of Scotland's finest and a warm comfortable bed in the best hotel wouldn't come amiss.

That's how it came about that half the population of Collintrae, when they heard the news that the good doctor was coming, was lined up at the top of the beach, well wrapped up against the cold, waiting for his arrival. Naturally, the *Annabel*, our most prestigious fishing boat, had been detailed to go to Girvan – around twelve miles to the north – to look after him for the day.

Alec arrived early, at around 10.30, when I was still finishing morning surgery, or I would have gone to meet him. The tides weren't right: Collintrae harbour is dry for about two hours around low tide, so that any boat trying to land has to run up onto the shingle beach to its south side. It is an art catching the right wave and keeping the boat upright as it does so, because the waves come straight from the open Atlantic at that point – almost the only place on the Clyde coast where they do.

McIlwraiths and McWhirters fear no Atlantic rollers or shingle beaches. They fearlessly surfed the *Annabel* in from about 50 yards out, and she ploughed high into the shingle. I wasn't there to see the arrival, but by all accounts of that day it was magnificent, the boat lying high and perfectly upright, the bow well above the low-tide mark. A ladder was propped up against her, and one of the fishermen lifted Alec over his shoulder and carried him down, depositing him dry as a bone on the shingle. The two then struggled up the steep and unstable bank of stones to the grass beyond them.

A few minutes later, they both appeared at my surgery door. I was surprised to see the fisherman with him, but said nothing for the time being. I was saying goodbye to my last patient as I saw them approach. Alec and I shook hands, and he welcomed me back to the area with a beaming smile. Seven years before, he had counselled against my move south, and he was pleased to see me back 'home'. Mairi placed a steaming cup of coffee in front of him, with two solid slices of the ginger cake that we knew he liked from his visits in the past. He fell on them with his old enthusiasm. Our seven years away seemed like minutes.

Then he lifted the first set of notes from the little pile I had on the desk. 'These your lot for today?' he asked.

'Yes,' I said, still a little puzzled.

'Well, let's go and visit the first one,' he said.

'We don't have to,' I said. 'He's here.'

'Here? That's odd. Are they not domiciliaries, then?'

The rules for domiciliaries were strict. The consultant was asked to visit only if the patients couldn't travel, and there were problems in the management of their illnesses. That was the cause of my frown.

For our first patient, whom David suspected of being at risk from severe heart failure, was standing beside Alec. He was Big Rab, about six feet six tall and twenty stone of muscle and bone.

'What are you doing here, Rab?' I asked. 'We were coming to see you at home. You are supposed to be in bed, relaxing.'

Rab shrugged. 'I knew the doctor would need some help off the boat,' he said, 'and I'm the strongest man in Collintrae. I couldn't let anyone else do it'.

Alec had one of his famous grins on his face. He had been thumbing through Rab's notes. 'Supposed to be in heart failure, yet he is running up ladders, carrying thirteen-stone men down them and crunching up a stony beach? Doesn't seem likely, does it?'

'You never know in Collintrae,' I murmured.

Rab laid himself down on the couch, and Alec started his routine of history-taking and examination. Slowly, the grin on his face faded: after ten minutes his face was as concerned as mine.

'Rab,' he said, 'you need to be in.'

'In?' asked Rab.

'In hospital,' Alec replied. 'I think one of your main arteries is thinning and it could burst fairly soon. We need to take you into Ayr and sort it for you.'

He beckoned me over to examine Rab's chest. Sure enough, there were the swelling of the chest wall and the constant rushing sound of blood through an aortic aneurysm. It was astounding that his earlier exertion hadn't caused it to rupture completely. If it had, he would have died on the beach.

'How will you get me there?' asked Rab. 'The road's set to be closed all day.'

'We are going to have to get you on that boat,' Alec said. 'And take you by sea.'

'Can it wait an hour or two?' the big man asked. 'The tide will be in then, and we could board the usual way, from the harbour.'

'That's fine by me' said Alec. 'You've managed so far; an hour or two's delay shouldn't make much difference. Tom, can you keep him here comfortably for the moment, while we see the other patients?'

I called through to Mairi, and she took Rab away into a downstairs bedroom to rest, while Alec and I went out to the car to visit our next 'domiciliary'. Although the main roads were impassable, the roads around the village had been diligently cleared by gangs of children, who had built impressive snowmen and the odd igloo with the material they had shovelled up.

Joan MacRae had been a favourite patient of mine in my Collintrae years: we had come through many of her stormy illnesses together. She was only 40 now, but she looked much older, with a thin, lined face, greying hair and a hunched back – the result of many years of being unable to expand her chest properly. She had had whooping cough as a child, and it had left her with scarred lungs that were now more fibre than elastic. To breathe, she had to hold onto something solid – a chair back, a door, a banister, anything with which she could 'fix' her chest muscles so that she could breathe through the only muscle that would expand her lungs – her diaphragm.

David had done his best, but was now running out of options for helping her take every next breath. He had asked Alec along more in despair than in real expectation that she could be helped.

When we walked through the front door of her tiny cottage, I immediately saw that she was much worse than at any time I had seen her before. She was struggling for every little bubble of air, blue with lack of oxygen, and near death. She gasped that she had just been like this for a few minutes – she had felt 'something go' in her lungs.

Alec sprang to her side and placed his stethoscope on her for no more than two or three seconds.

He turned towards me. 'Have you got a big syringe with a wide-bore needle?' he asked. I opened the emergency bag and pulled out several for him.

He fixed the needle onto the syringe and stabbed Joan with it in between two of her ribs on the right side of her chest. The inside of the syringe rocketed out of its barrel, hitting the newly plastered wall beyond. It hit with such force that it entered the plaster like a dart on a board and stuck there. There was a loud hiss from the now empty syringe shell, and Joan was pink and breathing again.

Joan had developed a 'tension pneumothorax', in which a bleb or cyst on the surface of the lung had burst, allowing air to flow around the outside of the lung, between it and her chest wall. The problem with this is that the air can't flow back out again, so with each breath, more air formed around the lung, collapsing it. If we had arrived any more than a minute or two later, she would certainly have died. Alec's instant action had certainly saved her, although it might have been safer if he had removed the cylinder from the barrel of the syringe first before plunging the needle into the chest. The hiss, of course, was the air escaping from the hole in the chest wall.

Joan looked at us as if we were miracle workers, then across at the plunger of the syringe still sticking in the plaster of the wall behind her chair.

'Sorry about the wall,' Alec said. 'Send me the bill for the repair.'

Joan laughed. 'Repair?' she said. 'I'll not repair that – I'll leave it sticking there, just to remember you.'

Alec's face turned serious.

'You are going to have to come with us,' he told her, gently. 'I can't guarantee this won't happen again in the next few hours. You need to be admitted to our unit for a few days, to seal that hole properly.'

'How will you do that?' she asked him.

'We blow a little talc onto the surface of your lung, to make it stick to your chest wall. That stops the collapse.'

'Then get on with it here,' Joan answered. 'I've got plenty of talc in that jar, and you surely know where to put it.'

For a moment, I believed that Alec might try just that, but he demurred.

'We need to do it under X-ray control, Mrs MacRae, and it needs to be surgical talc – proven sterile. If we can get you back with me to Ayr this afternoon, we can sort you.'

'How will you do that with the roads closed?' Joan asked, curious and a little fearful. 'I can't go by helicopter: my lungs wouldn't take it.'

'By boat,' said Alec.

I closed my eyes for a minute, imagining Big Rab and Joan sharing the *Annabel*'s tiny cabin, and each in immediate danger of catastrophe. At least our third domiciliary wouldn't be so dramatic. Margaret Duncan was as well known to me as Joan. In her seventies, she lived with her husband Bert in a beautiful cottage beside the river. Bert was famous for growing the earliest and tastiest tatties in Ayrshire, and Margaret had the most amazing greenhouse, heated throughout the winter, in which she grew exotic fruits like lemons and apricots. Nobody else could produce fruit like Margaret, and her dried or crystallised fruits always won first prize at the Ayr Horticultural Show.

Sadly, she was getting older, was less sharp than she had been, and more importantly, had lost her teeth. Her 'wallies' didn't work very well, so she had to be content to suck her precious fruit, rather than chew it. That wasn't what had worried Dr David, however. He had asked for a 'domiciliary' because he wanted a second opinion about her fairly rapid onset of mental slowness. Was she depressed, becoming demented, or did she have a physical reason for her poor general health? She was a little anaemic, and her thyroid tests weren't quite right, but not quite off the range enough to state that thyroid was the problem. Her heart was a bit ropey, but no more than expected for her age. Could Dr Slessor take a look at her and suggest some way of managing her better?

Alec was renowned for such cases: his bunch of extremely loyal GPs would send him a referral letter two pages long and receive a ten-pager in reply, always courteous and always to the point. Many people had much for which to thank him.

When we arrived at the cottage, Bert was waiting for us, agitated and frightened.

169

'I've never seen Margaret like this before,' he told us. 'She has pains in her tummy, and she can't pass anything. She is just lying around holding herself, in agony. It started only an hour ago, about two hours after breakfast. Could you help her?'

I left it to Alec to see her first. He felt her abdomen, listened to it intently with his stethoscope and straightened up.

'We have another one for the boat,' he said. 'It's going to be crowded. Her bowel is obstructed. We can't leave her here.'

'Boat?' asked Bert. 'What boat?'

'The *Annabel*,' I told him. 'It's OK, she will have plenty of company.'

Luckily, the back seat of the car allowed her to lie down almost flat, and we drove her to the harbour. Rab and Joan were waiting by the *Annabel*, looking a bit fearful about the twelve-mile journey over a reasonably calm sea. The snow was still falling: there was now doubt about the road north of Girvan, so we had no time to waste. Mairi phoned Stranraer to tell the clinic that Alec couldn't make it that day. The Stranraer doctors understood, and forgave him his lapse, and the *Annabel*, with her four passengers in the tiny for'ard cabin, made her way over the now flat-calm sea towards Girvan and Ayr.

All three of our patients recovered. Rab had corrective surgery to strengthen his artery and survived another twenty years. Joan had her lungs covered with a dusting of talc and managed to survive without another bout of pneumothorax. A few years later, the syringe plunger fell out of the wall. She glued it back again and it is there to this day.

As for Margaret, it turned out she did have significant thyroid underactivity, and when that was treated she returned almost to her old self. She got new dentures and started to chew again. And the cause of her obstruction? A dried apricot that she had swallowed whole. In her small intestine, it had absorbed water and swollen to a phenomenal size – her apricot was as big as a peach. When the surgeons who removed it saw it, they could not believe how fresh it looked, and put it at her bedside, for interest, so that she would see it when she came round.

Naturally, seeing it there, she thought it was for eating. So she ate it. The first time in history, I think, that the same piece of fruit has been eaten twice.

HAVE STETHOSCOPE AND PEN — WILL TRAVEL

The move back to Ayrshire was a calculated risk. I would have no regular income, except what I would make as a locum and from writing. I had left a secure, well-paid job in industry for the unknown, and had a wife and two children to support somehow. On the plus side, we had few outgoings. The money we had made on our house sale in Hampshire was more than we needed to buy the site and build our new house, and we had no school fees to pay. I was still writing for *Pulse*, thanks to Hertzel's generosity and friendship, but over the next year or so, I would have to find other sources of income. Mairi and I worried a little about that for a while, but we needn't have.

The plot of land we had bought lay beside the road from Kilminnel to Braehill and led down to the banks of the Stinchar. We hadn't known when we bought it, but somehow the fishing rights for our 35-metre frontage onto the river had never been assigned. On our side of the river, to the east and west of us, and the south bank opposite us, were famously expensive and excellent salmon-fishing stretches. But I could stand on my very small stretch of shingle on a late summer's evening and drop a fly on to the surface of the water. Around me, anglers paid £200 a day for the privilege; I could catch the odd salmon and sea trout for free. I wasn't good at it, but the fish seemed keen to swallow my fly, and they tasted delicious. The fact that I had the local bobby as a teacher and gillie helped to fend off criticisms and even downright opposition from across the water. It began to feel like heaven.

The idyll didn't last for long. Telephone calls and letters – these were the days before the Internet – began to offer us a new way of life. One of the first was from Hertzel. He asked if I could come down to London for a chat: he wanted me to expand my role at *Pulse*, and he needed to see me personally about it. I didn't like the address he gave. It was a ward in a London teaching hospital. Could I come fairly quickly, he added, as he needed to sort things out in a hurry?

This was the late seventies: there were still night trains from Stranraer to Euston, and the first stop was the small station at Braehill, four miles from my new home. I got on the train there at ten at night, and was in Euston by 6.30 the next morning, in time to have a shower and shave in the station's Superloo before facing the city of London's early-morning rush hour.

Hertzel was a deep yellow, almost green. He grinned at me as I walked in. His terminal liver failure hadn't dampened his enthusiasm for life. After congratulating me on moving back to Scotland and out of the clutches of the Pharma industry, he got down to business. One of his jobs was to report medical meetings, not just for *Pulse*, but also for other journals. He did it anonymously, as he didn't want the *Pulse* management to know the full extent of his writings. Could I take them over? He had trained me, he said, his grin widening as he did so, for the job.

He pulled out a box file from his locker, and opened it. On

the top was a diary, and the dates inside were covered with the details of meetings up to a year ahead.

'I'm not going to make them,' he told me, 'but you can. This is all yours. I've already told the journals I would be speaking to you. They know your background in the industry, and that you won't let the bullies wear you down.'

'Bullies?' I said.

'You will know when you meet them,' Hertzel replied. I wasn't sure what he meant, but let it go at that: I had tears in my eyes and was too upset at seeing him in this state to carry on the conversation. Hertzel put his hand over mine. Amazingly, he was comforting me.

'I've had a great life,' he said. 'And I'm a lot older than any of my colleagues think. So don't be sad over me. It's my time, and that's it.'

We talked for another hour, about all sorts of subjects, and then he sank back on his pillow, exhausted by the effort. I got up to leave, and he thanked me for coming, still with his impish grin. I carried his diary away with me and took a tube back into central London, where I spent the afternoon reading it and making phone calls. I ate at an Indian restaurant in a street behind Euston Station, and by 8.30 that evening I was back on the night train to Stranraer. At 4.30 the next morning, I crawled into bed at home.

Mairi woke up as I climbed into the bed beside her.

'The hospital phoned,' she said. 'Hertzel died at around nine last night. Oh, and could you take a shower?'

'Pardon?'

'You smell of garlic and curry, sweat and train. It would be good if you could wash it all off before you come to bed.'

There wasn't much left to say, except to ruminate that I'd

174

have to be better prepared for 'executive travel' if I were going to follow Hertzel's path. I dutifully showered, thinking of poor Hertzel as I did so. He had always been neat and immaculately dressed: I wondered if his long-suffering wife had ever had to tell him to shower. I dried myself, walked through into the bedroom, collapsed onto the bed and fell immediately into a deep, dreamless sleep.

Three days later, I was on my way to the first of Hertzel's appointments, in Montreux, on the shores of Lake Leman. The occasion was the Annual Conference of the European Respiratory Society. Chest physicians obviously didn't do things by halves. I was booked into the best hotel, the Montreux Palace, with a room overlooking the lake and the Castle of Chillon, famed for Lord Byron's tragic prisoner. The whole floor above me was taken up by the entourage of a Middle Eastern sheikh, and there were ominous-looking guards posted at the stairs and lifts to make sure the hoi polloi didn't stray onto it.

My brief was an odd one. I wasn't there to attend the whole conference, but to report on a special session. Its subject was a new drug for asthma in children and teenagers, and my job was to make a four-page tabloid-style newspaper about the eight presentations – five in the morning and three in the afternoon. It seemed simple enough. The American manufacturers of the drug had given me summaries of the presentations beforehand and photographs of the speakers, with a few copies of relevant slides. They were paying for my travel and hotel expenses on top of my fee: they would print the newspaper and distribute it to chest physicians and paediatricians all round the world. All I had to do was to provide the text. I didn't foresee any problems.

I had been preparing for this type of work. Over the previous few years, I had learned to type. I had used a Pitman typing manual that Mairi had kept from her schooldays. When I had started to write for *Pulse*, I had written my articles longhand, and she had typed them. That wouldn't be efficient if I were going to be a full-time writer and journalist. It wouldn't even be possible, because my speedwriting at meetings was indecipherable to anyone but myself. I couldn't return home with shoals of hand-written sheets of paper and expect Mairi to type from them. I had found, too, that taping meetings wasn't viable. It meant listening to what was said twice over – once in the lecture hall and once on the tape. It took a day to transcribe an hour of speech from a tape, and that would take far too long. I would have deadlines of no more than two days after the end of a meeting: my reports would have to be typed up and delivered by then.

So in my two years or so of learning to type I struggled. I spent several hours a day with the manual, becoming faster and more accurate until I could type as fast as I could think – probably even faster. I used oceans of Tippex to begin with, but as newer typewriter technology developed, it got easier. Eventually, I bought a small electronic machine, the kind that showed a full line of print before transferring it to the paper. There were no desktop computers, far less laptops, then. So along with my fabulous machine, I simply carried several pens, a notepad and a ream of paper. I was determined to travel light.

My employers had met me at the Montreux hotel entrance. They were suave, fresh, Ivy League Americans, smiling and ingratiatingly glad to see me. They reminded me of the Mormon missionaries at home, earnest with eyes shining in their enthusiasm for their new product. I was welcome to whatever the hotel had to offer in the way of food and drinks: all I had to do was put them on the bill.

They left me the list of participants in the congress. I recognised many of the British names, including two of my old classmates who were now distinguished physicians. I saw that they were in much more modest hotels than mine and felt a little guilty. I mulled over the possibility of strolling along the magnificent lakeside esplanade to their hotel and having an evening drink with them, but thought the better of it. I needed to do my homework for tomorrow's meeting: there would be plenty of time afterwards.

The meeting went well. The speakers were mostly American, interspersed with the odd European – a German, a Frenchman and a Swiss – and they were all hugely enthusiastic about the drug. I was convinced, too, by the quality of their presentations and the detail of their researches. It seemed that this was a brilliant addition to fast and safe treatment of severe asthma in young children. One intravenous injection of the drug, and the breathlessness would disappear, with no serious side effects.

By the time speaker number eight, the most distinguished of them all, had made his summary of all the presentations, I was feeling good about the job. They had all spoken clearly and succinctly, and I had been able to speedwrite in time with them. I didn't think I had missed anything of importance, and was confident that I could produce the newspaper text that evening and hand it to my employers before leaving Montreux.

Then Dr Sheila Dawson stood up. I knew of her from her work in Great Ormond Street.

'Could I make a comment, please?' she asked, innocently.

'Of course, Dr Dawson,' the chairman replied. 'We would

be happy to have your opinion.'

'Frankly,' she said, 'I'm waiting for our first death from this drug.'

Suddenly, the atmosphere chilled. The whole audience leaned forward. Everyone knew Sheila, and they were well aware that what was coming was very much to the point. I looked across at my two mentors: they were frowning and pale. One had taken a pocket-sized tape recorder out of his conference folder and had switched it on. I knew I had to get what followed word for word. I started a new page on my notepad.

'We have obtained your drug from the National Institutes of Health in Maryland, since you did not see fit to choose us for your trials. We have attempted to use it in seven children aged between eight and twelve years old admitted to our casualty department in acute lung failure due to asthma. In four of them, the recommended dose caused heart arrhythmias that we considered life-threatening. It turned out that the children had been using theophylline at home: your drug interacts with theophylline to give a toxic effect. Why did you not mention this in the meeting? Surely other investigators have had similar findings. It is only a matter of time before some child doesn't recover from this potentially lethal side effect. We advise our colleagues in Britain not to use this drug.'

Sheila sat down. There was total silence for a few seconds, then heads started to come together, and the sound of whispers all around the auditorium grew to a crescendo.

The chairman spoke.

'This is the first time I have heard of this complication. Can I ask any of the other speakers if they have met it in practice?'

None of them had – or at least none of them spoke.

One of my hosts stood up.

'As this is completely new to us, I think we should talk privately with Dr Dawson afterwards about it. Perhaps there were some irregularities in the dose. In the meantime, we see no reason not to recommend the drug to you.'

He sat down again. What a mistake, I thought. To suggest that the blame might be Sheila's, or her department's, for a dosage error, wouldn't endear him to the audience. One hundred and fifty British chest physicians wouldn't take the same view.

The chairman brought the meeting to a hurried close and invited the whole audience to a conference dinner later that evening. I wondered how many would attend.

I packed up my things and walked to the exit. I wanted desperately to speak to Sheila, but she was surrounded by a crowd of doctors who were as keen to know more as I was. The American who had made the somewhat controversial statement to end proceedings buttonholed me.

'You don't need to put that last comment into your report. It is completely unsubstantiated. We need to know more about her data before we can make any judgment.'

I was stunned.

'I can't do that,' I replied. 'There were over a hundred British doctors here today. If I make a report without Dr Dawson's contribution in it, they will think I'm a paid industry hack. In any case, we owe it to the children to take this very seriously.'

He moved his face up to mine, almost touching me.

'If you do put it in, we will certainly edit it out, so you have no choice. We are paying you to produce it and we have the say on what goes in it and what stays out.'

'But I do have a choice,' I said. 'Send me the bills for the hotel and airfare, and I'll pay them. I'm not writing the report.

You will have to find someone else to do it.'

It was his turn to be stunned. I left the hall, walked to my room, packed my things, made my way past the guards on the stairs down to the reception desk. I watched as about a dozen women in full black hijabs filed past me, never glancing to one side or another, on their way to their third-floor retreat, then I asked for a taxi. I remembered Hertzel's warning about the bullies and reflected that it hadn't been long before I had met a prime example. As the cab passed the Castle of Chillon, I felt some sympathy for Byron's prisoner and the women I had just seen: in a way, in the last two days, I had had something in common with them, but I could escape.

I arrived home a day early, much the poorer. I couldn't believe how much the room and the business class airfare had cost. I wasn't too sure how Mairi was going to take the loss of income and the huge cost of my trip, but she simply shrugged it off. We were due for another week on Ensay, and that always made us feel better.

The drug was never given a licence in Europe. Dr Dawson published her results in the *Lancet* shortly afterwards, and that killed it. Memories last a long time in the pharmaceutical industry. Twenty-five years later, I was approached by a representative of the same American company. He had read one of my self-help books on chronic chest disease and asked me if I would like to talk to their representatives about it. I said I would be delighted, but that I had a 'history' with the company. He might find that I wouldn't be flavour of the month with the hierarchy.

Sure enough, he phoned me a few days later. He was sorry, but he had to withdraw the invitation. Somewhere on the company files my name was blacklisted – he didn't know why. I didn't enlighten him, but I wasn't sorry.

The first evening back home, Mairi and I had a crisis meeting. My first venture into conference reporting as a freelance had gone horribly wrong. We couldn't afford a repeat. We had to get our responsibilities clarified before we entered into any contract with our employers. That wouldn't be difficult, we felt, if they were learned medical societies or peer-reviewed journals, but we were not going to repeat the Montreux experience with anyone organising a drug-company-sponsored meeting. We had to make it clear from the start that my report was to be honest, and that everything, however detrimental to the sponsors, had to be printed.

Mairi made another suggestion. I wasn't to travel alone. We would be a team: she would organise the interviews, the photography, and the business contracts, and I would provide the text. She would help with layout and the keyboard skills. And she would also be a support if I needed to argue my case with Hertzel's 'bullies'. My parents now lived next door, having retired to the Stinchar Valley, and they would keep an eye on the children, now in their teens, while we were away. The benefit turned out to be mutual: grandparents and grandchildren got to know each other well, and they all cared for each other on the few days in each month that we were away.

That's how T & M Smith, Medical Writers, came into being. From then on we didn't look back. Not that the new partnership was of any relevance to our next few days on Ensay.

RETURN TO ENSAY

Our previous journey to Ensay had taken eleven hours from Southampton, and we had had two children to keep sweet on the way. From our new home beside the river Stinchar it was much shorter, and we were just two. We were fairly quiet for the first part of the journey. We had originally estimated that our earnings from Montreux would keep us for the next two months, and that what we were about to earn from our week's stint in Ensay would be a bonus, perhaps to be put away for a holiday. However, refusing the Montreux fee, and paying for the trip over and above the loss, made a big hole in our accounts. The locum on Ensay now became our bread and butter. It had to go well.

Happily, the fates were good to us. We drove up the Ayrshire coast to meet the ferry that would carry us across the Clyde to the beautiful Cowal peninsula. It was a fabulous sunny day, the sea glassy calm, and as the buildings of Gourock shrank into the distance behind us, our money worries faded with them.

The road from the Holy Loch over the Rest and Be Thankful to Inveraray, and then on to Oban, past Loch Fyne and Loch

Etive, was quiet and an easy drive. We were in plenty of time to board the boat to Ensay, and as we turned down the hill towards Oban harbour, I reflected how much more beautiful it was than the road to, and from, Montreux. Maybe I was biased, but the Swiss mountains didn't hold a candle to the smoother outlines of the hills of Mull just a few miles away, across the sea.

Mairi wasn't seasick, and I was itching to get back to real medicine, and meeting old friends again, on Ensay and Little Ensay. It would be a haven of peace and serenity for the next few days.

As usual, I met Colin Shaw at the pier. He had little to report: there were two older patients who needed home visits, but weren't expected to be a problem. Oh, and there were new folks on Little Ensay. They had been there for seven months now, but they hadn't troubled him much. At which he grinned. I knew Colin, and that grin. I wondered why he had used the word 'much', but let it pass. He got into his car and drove into the hold of the ferry, and we turned to drive on to his house. I had a surgery to do that afternoon, and I wanted to shower and change before it. And I wanted to check on the tide times. I was keen to find the best time to return to Wee Ensay, to chew over the fat with Bill Forsyth and Brother Aloysius again. Had the sea eagles bred? Were there more of them flying above the cliffs of the small island? I had so much to catch up on.

The surgery began well. Two old friends dropped in just to say hello, and another brought some eggs for Mairi. In half an hour I had accepted two crabs and a lobster from the postie – he had had a good day at the creels – and a freshly baked loaf and a sultana cake from our next-door neighbour. I was being paid to do this, I thought. Was there ever a luckier man than me?

Just before the scheduled end of the surgery, a Mrs Williams, a holidaymaker from South Wales, walked in. She was holding a handkerchief to the left side of her jaw and was obviously in some discomfort: the portion of her face that I could see was pale and drawn, her forehead wrinkled in a frown. I guessed she was around 50. I invited her to sit down.

'I've lost a filling from one of my back teeth,' she said. My heart sank. The dental cupboard beckoned, ominously. 'It doesn't hurt all the time, but it's very painful when any food goes near it. Can you do anything? I hear you are a dentist, as well as a doctor.'

'I'm afraid I'm not,' I replied, 'but I do have dental material here, and I may be able to help.' Her frown deepened, and I sympathised. I stood up, walked over to the dental cupboard, and opened the door. The instructions for replacing a filling were there, as plain as could be, along with precise identification of all the tools I would need. I swallowed, then asked Mrs Williams to open her mouth. The cavity was plain to see: the tooth was her second premolar, two behind her left lower canine. The base of the cavity looked clean enough. It looked as if I could make do with a temporary filling without having to drill further. I could then leave her own dentist in Cardiff to clear up the mess I was bound to make.

'When do you go home?' I asked her.

'We are off on the next ferry,' she said. Today was Wednesday: the next boat was on Friday at noon. I had to keep her going and pain-free if possible for the next three days, given that the journey to Cardiff would take the rest of Friday and much of Saturday morning, too. I hoped her dentist worked on Saturdays.

The artwork behind the dental cupboard door was very

184

specific. It showed exactly how to clean out a cavity left by a missing filling, how to mix the materials to make a paste and how to get it into the tooth before it set. There were even instructions on how to smooth any rough edges with dental spatulas, to leave a very professional-looking job. I had absolutely no confidence that what poor Mrs Williams would end up with would bear any resemblance to the finished product in the picture.

Luckily, she was my last patient that day, so I could take my time. She obligingly lay back in the chair, tilted her head back and opened her mouth. I hoped she didn't notice my shaking hand as I 'puffed' the cavity clean and then stuffed the rapidly solidifying paste into the hole in her tooth. I smoothed it all down with the correct spatula, removed the little redundant pieces of filling material with my gloved finger and a small piece of gauze, and stepped back to admire my work. It didn't look bad, I thought.

Mrs Williams pushed her tongue against the offending tooth and smiled.

'That feels all right,' she said. I don't know which of us was the more astonished.

She thanked me and asked me what she had to pay. That set me slightly aback, as I hadn't considered the possibility that dental services, unlike medical ones, came at a price. I told her it was free, and she thanked me again. She left happy. I wiped a film of sweat from my forehead, closed the surgery door and walked up to the house with my presents and a dental story to tell Mairi.

The tide was high that evening so I had to abandon my plan of a quick trip to the wee island: we settled for a walk to the pier before dark. It was late summer, near the end of August, so it was still light until nine o'clock. We watched two small boats with outboard motors putt-putting their way into the harbour, and waved to their happy occupants, holidaymakers who were making for the pub after an afternoon's successful fishing.

About 40 yards out from the head of the pier, there was a disturbance on the surface of the water. At first, we didn't see what had caused it, but when it happened again, we were transfixed. A large grey seal's head popped up and stayed above the surface, staring straight at us. Or so we thought. Because a second or two later up popped another head, only five or so yards away from it, directly in the seal's line of vision. The seal hadn't been staring at us, but was looking for its playmate. Except that the 'playmate' wasn't another seal, but a dolphin. It held its head about a foot above the water, steadily gazing back at the seal. It was like a scene from a circus, except it was in the wild ocean.

The two animals then ducked down under the water at the same time, only to rise again a few moments later, in a slightly different spot a few yards to the west. Slowly, they started to circle around each other, keeping eye-to-eye contact all the time their heads were above water. The dolphin's head bobbed a little, perhaps to gulp some air: the seal's head remained steady. Mairi and I watched them for a full twenty minutes as they rose and submerged together, sometimes approaching as close as a few feet. As it grew dark, we had to leave them to walk the 200 yards to the house, the Milky Way, a brilliant broad band across the blackest of night skies, lighting us home.

At 8.30 the next morning, Mrs Williams came to our front door. She had two big jars of homemade honey with her.

'We keep bees at home,' she said 'and we always bring a few

jars of honey with us. Please take these with our thanks. Oh, and the filling is doing fine, thanks.'

I thanked her and took the honey jars into the kitchen. The golden spread went well with the bread that was left from the feast of lobster the night before. I walked across the short path from the house to the surgery in good fettle, thinking that all was right with the world.

In the surgery, an elderly couple was sitting waiting for me, quietly. I guessed they were in their mid-seventies. They looked careworn and thin. I didn't recognise them as locals, but they didn't look like the average holidaymaker. The man had on a grey suit, a white shirt and an old school tie. His shoes were polished and neat, his fingernails clean and cut to the right length. He had a carefully folded white handkerchief in his breast pocket. The lady was a female version of him, with a faded blue suit, crisp white blouse buttoned to the neck and an ivory cameo brooch fastening it. Her skirt hem was just below the knee, and her shoes, like his, were expensive but formal, rather than fancy. They both sat with their hands clasped in their laps, looking up at me.

Just one thing marked the difference between the two. The man was wearing a top hat. It was old, so that it was shiny in places, and there was just the suggestion of fraying at the rim, but it had been well cared for. It sat straight up on his head, and he showed no sign of wanting to remove it.

'Hello,' I said to them both, cheerfully. 'Beautiful day, isn't it? Please come in.'

I opened the door of the consulting room and stood beside it, letting the lady, then the gentleman, enter before me.

They sat down in the two chairs beside my desk. I sat down, too, and introduced myself. Still they hadn't spoken. They looked at each other, obviously embarrassed, each waiting for the other to speak.

I decided to break the silence.

'Would you like to tell me who you are? I think that might be a good start. Then I could get your notes out.'

'They may not be here yet,' the lady said. 'We have just returned to the island after 40 years in London. I'm Euphemia Campbell, and this is Hector McNeil. We are brother and sister, brought up here, and we're both widowed now, so we decided to spend our old age together. It's been good so far, but we have run into a wee problem and we would like your help.'

'That's what I'm here for,' I said brightly. I felt bright, too, as the sun was shining over the harbour, and the Paps of Jura, fifteen miles away, were glowing a golden yellow. I was ready for any problem, especially a wee one.

'Tell me about it,' I said, settling back in my chair.

'You will have to take off your hat, Hector,' said the lady to her brother.

I watched him slowly divest himself of his topper. He had pepper-and-salt hair, quite a lot of it, well styled and neatly combed. The only unusual thing about his head was that there was a kitchen knife sticking out of the top of it, embedded up to the hilt. The wee problem had suddenly become rather bigger.

At times like this, memories of our training flood back. As students we had been regaled in our psychiatric lectures with stories of the oddest patients. One day, our professor had brought into the tutorial room a man who had also been wearing a hat, although in my memory it was a bowler. When his hat came off, it revealed the handle of a screwdriver that he had hammered into the top of his skull, bit by bit, over several years. He had had headaches, apparently, and decided to treat himself after the manner of the ancient Celts, who were skilled in making holes in their skulls from which, on the evidence of the healing around the holes, they had usually recovered.

I recalled that the problem in that man's case had been what to do with the screwdriver. Should it be removed, and if so, how should it be done? Having been in situ for some years, it wouldn't be a simple matter to pull it out. That might cause bleeding into the brain: so returning the poor man's head to normal would require a neurosurgeon's skill, in full theatre.

I remembered, too, that he hadn't wanted it removed. It had cured his headaches, and he didn't want them to return. Wearing the bowler was a small price to pay for his headache-free life – naturally in a long-stay ward in the psychiatric hospital.

My man, Hector, didn't seem in the least abnormal mentally, apart from his 'wee problem', but he still hadn't spoken.

I felt I had reacted suitably to the topper-doffing, showing little emotion or surprise, as if this was an everyday case for me. I stood up, looked closely at the wound and noted that the knife was embedded in the collapsed remains of what must have been a large cyst. It was still oozing a small amount of a colourless fluid around it. I didn't touch the knife, preferring to know a little more about it before I took any action.

I asked Hector how the knife happened to be stuck there.

'I've had this cyst for a few months,' he said. 'I've had them before, and I've always been able to deal with them myself. I've just punctured them, and they have usually gone down. This was the biggest one, I suppose about the size of a hen's egg. It was getting a bit tight, and I thought it would be easy just to burst it with a sharp knife. But the knife seemed to slide in a bit deeper than usual – it didn't hit the bone like it usually did – and I was frightened to pull it out myself.'

I had to come to the crunch question.

'How long is the blade?' I asked him.

'About four inches,' he answered.

The wee problem, which had been growing, was now huge. Where was the tip of the knife? The Ensay surgery was a bit short of tools, the requisite anaesthetic apparatus, and, frankly, the expertise, for delicate brain surgery, and that was what he needed. I took comfort in that he had put his knife in exactly the same place as the man at medical school – the midline. With luck, the blade would have slid in between the two halves of his brain, stopping short of hitting the brain itself. Four inches was just about short enough and the lack of blood was encouraging. But was that clear fluid coming from the sebaceous cyst, or was it cerebrospinal fluid? It looked too runny and clear to be the first, so I was fairly sure it was the second. If that were the case, a helicopter flight was next on the agenda. The nearest neuro-surgical unit was at the Southern General in Glasgow, and top-hat man would have to be there pronto.

'How did you manage to get the knife in the right place? You surely couldn't see the top of your head?' I asked Hector, who was still sitting calmly, if glumly, on his chair.

'We used two mirrors,' he replied. 'I sat with my back to the mirror on the wall and Euphemia held up her hand mirror in front of my face. It was easy to see, although difficult to press the point of the knife exactly into the top of the cyst. The skin seemed tougher than the others had been, so I suppose I used too much pressure. Once it broke through the surface, the knife just slid into my head. It was a bit scary, and once it was in I didn't want to pull it out. I thought that might be foolhardy.'

'Foolhardy?' I thought to myself. Wasn't it foolhardy enough in the first place?

'Why didn't you come to me about it? What made you try this yourself?'

'We have always been independent of doctors,' said Euphemia. 'Our father taught us basic medical care, and we didn't want to bother you while Dr Shaw was away. We didn't think this cyst would be any different from the others.'

'How many others have you attacked like this?' I asked her.

'About six of them,' she replied. 'You can feel the scars in his scalp. They all healed well.'

I felt his head, being very careful to keep my probing fingers well away from the knife. Sure enough, there were small red slightly raised lines above his ears, at the back of his head and above his left temple. They had been fairly good self-surgeons. Until now.

I picked up the phone and dialled the number for the neuro-surgical unit at the Southern General.

Two hours later, Hector was on his way by helicopter to Glasgow. Later that evening, I heard that the 'cyst' had in fact been a meningocele – a pocket of the covering of his brain that had poked itself through a gap in the top of his skull. He had always had the defect in his skull, and it had only been a matter of time and age for the 'cyst' to find its way through it. The other self-operations had been on sebaceous cysts – simply blocked sweat glands in the skin – so it wasn't surprising that he had thought this one would be treatable in the same way. I should have picked up on the clue he had given me. The 'skin' of a sebaceous cyst is much less tough than the *dura mater*, the membrane inside the skull that covers the brain and which forms the surface of a meningocele. That was why he had found it initially so hard to push the knife into it.

The rest of that Thursday passed without incident. I did my scheduled two home visits, chatted to old friends on the way, held an evening surgery to which no one came, and shut up shop at around seven.

On the kitchen table was a newly baked loaf of brown bread, still warm. Colin had bought a bread-maker since we had last 'locumed' and he was happy for us to use it. I cut a thick slice, ladled a lump of Mrs Williams's honey on to it and took a healthy bite. It was delicious. The honey still had bits of comb in it, and its combination with the rough texture of the bread was perfect. I took another bite, then another. While chewing the third bite, I felt something hard against my tongue: it didn't feel like seeds from the loaf, so I picked it out of my mouth.

It was a filling. I ran my tongue around my teeth in turn, and found the gap. I wasn't going to be able to see my dentist for ten days: could I last that long without treatment? It quickly became clear that I couldn't. A gulp of hot tea produced a spike of pain. The dental cupboard beckoned for the second time that day.

I had to ask Mairi to help. Like Euphemia and Hector, we found ourselves trying to perform surgery with the aid of a mirror. Mairi held it up to my face while I tried to fill the hole in my own lower right premolar with the dental goo. I began to appreciate Hector's skill in self-trepanning as I made a thorough mess of the inside of my own mouth. Once the bulk of the filling material was in the hole, Mairi took over, cleaning up all the bits and rough edges with the spatula I had used earlier in the day with Mrs Williams.

My dental patient arrived at the surgery next morning to

wish me goodbye. We swapped notes about our fillings and how comfortable they were.

'Odd that you should have lost one when eating my honey,' she said. 'That's how I lost mine.'

I reflected as she left that she might have warned me. I watched as she walked down the single track road towards the pier. The ferry would be leaving in around two hours, and someone else would take over her dentistry. I wondered what her dentist would say when he saw my amateur dabblings in his speciality, then turned my attention to three people stepping out of a Land-Rover parked in the lay-by next to the surgery. A man and woman, and a teenage boy. They were coming my way. There was no one else in the waiting room so I went to the front door to welcome them.

A Quiet Weekend on Ensay

I recognised the Land-Rover. It was Bill Forsyth's. He had brought the threesome, I assumed, from Wee Ensay, and was waiting in the car while I saw his passengers. I remembered Colin's parting words about the new folks not troubling him 'much', but let the thought pass.

The man was in his early fifties, I thought. He was just a little overweight, sleek and well dressed. The boy, thinner and solemn, was in a brown school uniform, one that I didn't know, but I guessed, from his kilt, that it was a private school, probably in Edinburgh. My first thought looking at the woman was 'hedge backwards'. That wasn't just her hair but her whole outfit. A woolly hat over her ears, from which her straggly and unkempt hair sprayed out like a halo, was matched by a similar woolly sweater several sizes too big for her. Below that was a denim skirt, also shapeless, thick woollen stockings and dirty brown brogue shoes. She was gaunt and wild-eyed, and seemed reluctant to come into the surgery. I couldn't guess at her age – she could have been an old 35 or a reasonably young 50. She wasn't wearing make-up, and her face was wrinkled and dry.

Her two companions seemed to drag her up the path from

the road, then round the corner of the custom-made surgery building to the shelter of the door. The two males helped her – I thought even pushed her, one at each elbow – up the two steps into the hallway, and into my consulting room. She looked entirely out of place in their company.

I shook hands first with the man, then the boy. When I offered my hand to her, she shrank back. I brought an extra seat in from the waiting room, lined it up with the two already beside mine and asked them to sit down. Man and boy ushered her into the middle one, and flanked her, as if to prevent her escaping.

I introduced myself as the locum and asked what I could do for them.

'You can't do anything for me,' she muttered, so quietly I only just heard her. She was speaking to herself, not me. She said nothing more.

'Can I speak for her?' the man asked me.

'Go ahead,' I said. 'I assume the lady wants me to see her.' I was becoming uneasy. Was she here against her will? If so, I would have to see her on my own, without the two obvious restraints on her.

I looked at her, with what I hoped she would interpret as a sympathetic, and not a condescending, smile. She stared back, thought for a moment, then nodded her head. There was no hint of a smile in return.

'My name is Anderson,' said the man. 'James Anderson.' 007 flitted through my mind for a moment, then disappeared. This wasn't a time for humour: I had a feeling this wasn't going to go well.

'This is my wife, Alberta, and my son, Robert. Robert and I are only here for two days – we are taking the ferry this morning. We came to the island just to make sure that Alberta was all right, and she patently isn't. She has been having terrible stomach pains, but she wouldn't come to see the doctor. We couldn't leave the island without making sure she did. Could you look at her for us? Please?'

This was getting odder by the minute, I thought.

'Are you happy with that?' I asked her. 'I won't go any further without your permission. But I'd like you to tell me what's wrong.'

'I have been having a lot of stomach pains in the last few days, that's all,' she said, almost whispering the words, looking at the floor as she spoke. 'Sometimes I have to curl up with the pain, it is so severe. But I can manage it with plenty of painkillers. I'd like to go home now.'

'I wouldn't like you to leave without me at least feeling your tummy,' I replied. 'Would you mind?'

She shook her head, and I asked her to lie down on the examination couch. She did so very slowly and reluctantly. She was obviously afraid of something: I hoped it wasn't me. I asked the two men to go into the waiting room while I looked at her, and they did so, the boy going over to his mother and squeezing her hand before leaving. Her husband didn't go near her as he walked out.

Her abdomen was swollen and very tender, especially lower down towards her pelvis. She winced as the flat of my hand pressed the region below her navel. I was getting unhappier by the minute.

'When did you last have a period?' I asked her.

'I haven't had periods for months,' she said. 'I assume I've stopped them. I am 44, after all.'

I have delivered plenty of babies in 44-year-olds, and older, I thought. She wouldn't have been the first to mistake a pregnancy for the menopause. I'd have to be very careful in what to do, and say, next.

The ferry was due in just over an hour. There would be a day-trip boat from Oban the next day, but if she needed hospital treatment she would have to be on her way before that. Standing there with my hand on her abdomen, I was thinking of at least a fairly severe pelvic infection or even an ectopic pregnancy. I had to know. A urinary infection I could cope with; a pelvic organ infection would be more difficult; an ectopic, lethal. She needed an internal examination for me to be sure of the diagnosis.

'Could you possibly be pregnant?' I asked her, as coolly and reassuringly as I could.

'Do you mean am I having sex? That's none of your business.' She had raised her voice for the first time.

'I'm not trying to pry into your private life,' I said, 'but I need to know. If there's a possibility of you being pregnant, then you have to be admitted to hospital. You may have an ectopic pregnancy, and if you have, you can't stay here. Especially on Wee Ensay. You are too far away from immediate help.'

'I'll do as I please,' she said, shouting now.

'At least let me do an internal. I'll call my wife over, to make you feel more comfortable about it.'

'I'm having no internal examination,' she shouted.

At that, she sprang up from the couch and ran out of the door, along the short corridor to the outside door. I heard it slam, and then a key turning in the lock. I followed her, and peering through the window in the door, saw her running around the corner towards the road, and out of my sight. I crossed over to the window that looked onto the shore, just in time to see her throw the key across the road towards the sea. It disappeared beyond the band of bracken and reeds onto what I hoped was the foreshore, and not into the sea itself. She carried on running towards the harbour, in the direction of Wee Ensay. As there was only one road, and the slipway for the track across the sands to Wee Ensay was seven miles along it from the surgery, I didn't have any fear that she would disappear into the blue.

My immediate worry was how I would get out of the surgery. I made a mental note never to leave the key in the door in the future. Luckily, James and Robert Anderson had managed to open the window in the waiting room, and were outside it, talking to Bill. Bill hadn't seen the key thrown, but luckily, young Robert had, and was guiding him towards where it might lie. While we waited, I asked the boy's father a little more about their background.

His wife had left them both, he said, a year before, to live the 'alternative life' in the islands. She had become bored with being an Edinburgh wife in the coffee morning set, and run off with a 'new man'. He had been left to look after Robert, but they still cared for her, and they had wanted to see her before the school term started. They had stayed in the Ensay hotel, of course, as they didn't want to intrude on her new 'arrangements'. When they had discovered how much she had changed, they insisted on bringing her to see me – and Jake, her boyfriend, hadn't objected. That was mainly, James told me, because he was a 'bit out of it himself'.

'Who is Jake?' I asked him.

'The new gardener at Wee Ensay house. He used to work in Edinburgh – that's where Alberta met him. He had been a jobbing gardener. Except he was doing more than the garden at our house. Cheeky bugger even got Alberta to write a reference for him to the owners – that's how he got the cottage here.'

I was going to ask more, but at that point, Bill appeared back from the shore, waving the key in his hand. He wasn't wet, so I assumed it hadn't reached the sea. He brought it round to the door, opened it for us, and the chase began. We didn't have much time. The ferry was approaching the harbour and would only take half an hour, if that, to unload, load up and be away again. We all climbed into the Land-Rover and made for the road to Wee Ensay.

We found her a full mile away, still running. I was beginning to change my differential diagnosis. She wouldn't have managed that with a bursting ectopic pregnancy inside her, unless she was being driven by the excess energy that serious mental illness can sometimes confer on people. Yet I couldn't take the risk. She still had to go to Oban by that ferry, somehow.

We stopped beside her, and she looked at us, hard.

I got out and returned her stare. She was exhausted, drooping, beaten. She fell against me, and we lifted her into the back of the Land-Rover, beside Robert, who started to cradle her in his arms. Bill drove on to the next passing place, turned the Rover and made for the boat. I phoned the hospital from the harbour master's office and spoke to the doctor on duty. He was happy to help, but I warned him that she might not be too co-operative, and that I didn't know how stable she was mentally. I knew the hospital had no way of keeping her in against her will, but she was in no shape to argue.

An ambulance would be waiting for her at the Oban pier. James and Robert couldn't go to the hospital because they were catching the train back to Glasgow, and on to Edinburgh that evening. Apparently, Robert had to be back at school the next morning. I wondered about that, because it was a Saturday, and I would have preferred them to stay at least overnight.

'She doesn't want us near her, anyway,' James said. 'So there's no point in us staying. She would only get angry again. Her boyfriend is responsible for her now.'

I wasn't sure about that, but left them to it. As I was standing on the pier watching the ferry make its way back to Oban, I saw the movement in the water that Mairi and I had seen on the previous evening. This time it was the seal on its own. Bill was standing beside me. He had three hours to wait before he could catch the low tide again for his journey back to Wee Ensay. I told him about the seal and the dolphin and he smiled.

'They're well known to the locals,' he told me. 'We're not sure if it's the same dolphin every time, but it's certainly the same seal. We know it from the white scars on its head – maybe the result of an attack from an orca. The two are often seen together out in the bay. They never hurt each other – it looks as if they just enjoy playing. Staggering, isn't it?'

I agreed that it was, and invited Bill to the house for a cup of tea, some bread and honey (I asked him if he had any doubtful fillings) and a chat. It turned out that Brother Aloysius was still on the island, and the sea eagles had bred. There were now four above the cliffs. I was keen to see them again and told Bill that I would try to get across the sand some day in the next week.

'You might be there sooner than you think,' he said. 'My bet is that you haven't seen the last of Mrs Anderson. And when you do come across again, have a look at the greenhouse she and her friend are tending. Their tomato plants are quite special.'

I hadn't a clue what he was talking about.

Three hours later, I had a call from the hospital. The

ambulance transfer had gone well, Mrs Anderson had been examined, had an ultrasound, wasn't pregnant, and probably had nothing more than a severe urinary infection. That was the good news. The bad news was that she had done a runner. She had told them that she 'wouldn't take any artificial chemicals into her body' and was not staying in the hospital a minute longer. She picked up her handbag and disappeared into the darkening Oban evening.

Of course, she was perfectly at liberty to go her own way, but I doubted whether she had enough money to afford a place for the night. That worried me, as she now seemed to be on her own in the town with no one to look after her.

At midnight, the phone rang beside my bed. It was the Oban police. The first part of the call went something like this: *Did I know a Mrs Anderson, who lived on Wee Ensay?* Yes I did. *Is it all right for her to stay in the cells overnight? She's refused to go back to the hospital.* As far as I know it is. I don't think she will come to any harm. *That's all right then, thanks.*

I sensed that he was about to put the phone down.

'Wait a minute,' I said. 'Why is she with you?'

'For her own protection,' he answered. 'She has just trashed a public house in the main street, and been very rude to the barman. We thinks she needs a bit of peace and quiet. She's a bit odd, isn't she? We don't want to charge her, but we can keep her in overnight and see what we can do for her in the morning.'

I thanked him for calling me and put the phone down. I lay back on the pillow, drifting into dreams of massive man-size tooth cavities into which I was falling, naked, reaching the bottom only to be covered by a mixture of dental filling and honey. I needed to find a key to get out of the hole, but it was far away, hidden among seaweed and bracken.

I was shaken awake. Mairi was leaning over me, worried.

'Are you all right?' she asked. 'You were screaming in your sleep.'

'I'm not surprised,' I replied. 'It's just the day I've had. It will be better tomorrow.'

I got up and walked around the room. The window faced the bay: there was a full moon, and its light was reflecting on the glassy calm sea. I wondered about the full moon and Mrs Anderson's behaviour, then thought it was unworthy of me. I banished the mental turmoil of the nightmare from my mind, went back to bed and slept deeply and dreamlessly for the rest of the night.

The next morning was another of those beautiful days in the islands when you are acutely aware that there is nowhere else in the world you would rather be. The blue sky was only troubled by the odd cloud sitting on top of a mountain on the far horizon. I had breakfast and started on my pre-surgery walk down to the harbour and back: it was a great way to start the day. In the distance a ship was approaching. I surmised that it would take another hour or so to reach us, the timing of it confirming it as the 'day-tripper'. From June to September, on Saturdays, the ferryboats were often put into use for the tourists who relished a day out 'on the water', travelling from island to island. Ensay was on a route that included Islay, Jura, Mull and Iona, and today the trippers would have an hour or so on each of them before steaming back to Oban, happy and well fed and watered. Rumour had it that the bar was the best stocked in the Highlands, and that the return journey was considerably noisier than the morning's sail away from Oban.

Ensay being the first stop, I didn't think that this would be a bother for me. By the time they reached us, the trippers were only full of tea, porridge and bacon and eggs, nothing stronger. Today's calm seas would guarantee that they kept them down, although the *Lochinvar*, the ferry that was approaching, was known as the 'vomit comet' to the locals. Built long before stabilisers, it pitched and yawed with every small ripple.

So it was a surprise to see Mairi waving to me from the front door. I broke into a steady run to reach her.

'The captain of the *Lochinvar* wants to speak to you,' she said, handing me the telephone.

'Doctor Smith here,' I said. 'How can I help you, Captain?'

'By meeting me at the pier and getting a passenger off my ship,' he answered. 'She tried to throw herself overboard into Corryvreckan.'

Everyone in the West Highlands knows Corryvreckan. It is a permanent whirlpool, a maelstrom, even, to the north of Jura, caused by the meeting of several currents. Small boats have been lost in it: a person wouldn't survive more than a few minutes. A woman contemplating jumping into it wasn't making a cry for help: she was seriously suicidal.

'Can you not keep her until you return to Oban?' I asked him. 'There isn't much sense leaving a tripper on the island whe`n she will need to get back.'

'She isn't a tripper – she is one of yours. She lives on Wee Ensay. We only took her on board at the request of the police. She would be better at home, in your care,' said the captain.

Mrs Anderson. What next?

The tide was in. She wouldn't be able to cross to Wee Ensay for another five hours or so. In the meantime, I'd have to look after her.

I walked back down to the pier and watched as the

passengers stepped carefully down the steep gangway. I walked up it, deciding to play things by ear. I didn't know what to expect. Hamish the harbour master followed me.

She was lashed to a seat on the deck, with two burly and serious-looking seamen beside her. She didn't look aggressive at all, just exhausted and pitiful. Hamish and I undid the ropes and lifted her gently to her feet. She was almost asleep. We half carried her off the ship and gently eased her into Hamish's car. I had phoned the hotel a few hundred yards up the road to expect her, and there was a warm room ready for her. We laid her, still in the clothes she had been in two days before, on the bed.

I told her that we would arrange for her to get back home that afternoon, and left her to sleep. Her room was on the ground floor, and the landlady assured us that she would look in on her every few minutes.

I walked back to the surgery and phoned our consultant in psychiatry. He was in Lochgilphead, 40 or so miles away on the winding country road from Oban. I told him the whole story and asked him what I might prescribe to prevent her from harming herself, at least for the next few days until I knew more about her. In her present state there was no point in conducting a full psychiatric interview.

He couldn't suggest anything from afar, he said: could I send her to his hospital on the following Tuesday or Wednesday? If she was aggressive and agitated, I might prescribe a tranquilliser, like Valium, in the meantime. I didn't think that was a good idea. She was already zonked enough: a sedative would simply make her worse. And she probably wouldn't take it anyway.

I dialled the number given me for her partner Jake. He

sounded slow and slurred, as if he had just woken up. When I explained what had happened, he became more lively. He agreed to come across with Bill that afternoon at low tide and bring her home. He would look after her, he said. He had some remedies of his own he could give her.

The rest of Saturday passed without incident. Mairi and I went to the hotel for our evening meal, and our host said that Mrs Anderson had gone off 'meek as a lamb'.

Sunday morning started too early. At seven. This time the voice on the other end of the phone was Jake's.

'Could you meet Bill at the slipway for Wee Ensay?' he asked. 'We have a crisis here. I can't waken Alberta. I don't think it's just sleep. The tide's OK for the next two hours if you can make it.'

I jumped out of bed, dressed quickly, climbed into the practice Land-Rover and made my way to the slipway. Bill was waiting for me. The sand was dry and I could easily follow the path his tyres had made. We drove up to the big house in convoy: the gardener's cottage was beside it, across an old stable yard. It looked untidy and shabby. He hadn't done much with it in his seven months.

Jake was waiting at the cottage door and led me in. Alberta was lying on a couch in the main room, deeply asleep. I raised one eyelid and shone my pen torch onto the pupil: she stirred, but not enough to waken her. Her eye reacted only very slowly to the light. There was a strange, sweet smell in the stale air of the room. I didn't at first recognise it. Then I remembered my days in Amsterdam. I looked around the room. There was a pot on the stove, blackened with smoke on the outside. I got up from beside Alberta, crossed over to it and looked inside. There was the congealed, half-burnt mess of a mushroom stew in the bottom. There were more mushrooms, uncooked, in a basket beside the stove.

I glanced across at Jake. He was sitting on the sofa, half-dazed himself, his legs sprawled in front of him. Either he didn't care much that Alberta was so ill, or more likely he was ill himself. Bill was standing in the doorway. He beckoned to me and nodded his head to his right. I went to the door and saw that he was looking at the greenhouse to my left.

They were strange tomato plants. For a start, there was not a tomato on them, and no sign that any trusses had developed, which was odd for the end of August. The leaves had jagged edges, unlike any tomato plants I had seen. I walked back in to rouse Jake.

'What did you eat last night?' I asked him.

'Only some mushrooms. I've picked them before,' he said. 'They are quite safe.'

'Not these ones,' I said, 'and especially not when you've been using pot.'

'You've seen them, then?' he asked. 'The plants, I mean?'

'Yes. How many has she been smoking a day?'

'About a dozen roll-ups, and we bake with it too. I've tried to cut her down, but she won't.'

'We've got to admit her: I don't know what these mushrooms have done to her liver or kidneys, or what the cannabis has done to her brain, but she needs to be looked after. I'm calling for a chopper, and once the hospital finds what she has had, someone's likely to be calling here to search the place. I'll leave it to you to sort things. Perhaps weedkiller might be a good place to start?'

He didn't have to reply. I guessed he had been in similar spots before. He was taking the loss of his crop very calmly.

The flattest place for the helicopter to land was around the other side of the house, from which the offending plants couldn't be seen. The crew congratulated me on ordering two helicopters in the space of a few days. It was unheard of for Ensay. Alberta was away to Glasgow within an hour. Five minutes later, Bill was round with a spray. We took the remains of the mushrooms to Brother Aloysius, who was delighted to see us. He identified two of them as poisonous and one as powerfully hallucinogenic.

The mixture of cannabis and wild mushrooms explained Alberta's irritability and erratic behaviour, her abdominal pains and then her near-comatose state. I should have guessed that she was a 'user', but admit that it had not crossed my mind until I walked into the cottage. I would love to write a happy ending, but I can't. I've followed Alberta's progress over the years, from a distance, and she hasn't done well. She and her husband didn't get back together, and Jake disappeared out of her life soon after he had to destroy his cannabis plants. She lives in sheltered accommodation near Oban, where a team of carers looks after her. Her kidneys, liver and brain are all damaged. Robert, now a young doctor, visits as often as he can. She still refuses, even when he tries to help, to take prescribed medication. For her, 'natural' medicines are 'the only way to go'. The irony is not lost on her son.

VIENNA

Home again in South Ayrshire, a message was waiting for us from Willem. Would we like a trip to Vienna? If so, could we contact him urgently? He had left a Paris phone number. It was good to hear from him, but I kept in mind my experience in Montreux. Would Willem be a bully, now that he was in charge of a huge budget that encompassed marketing, as well as research?

My fears were groundless. Willem wanted a straight report on the forthcoming World Congress on the Heart and Diabetes. He proposed that I attend, pick out the most important talks, report them and produce a short news sheet, no more than four pages, every day. He would arrange for the printing and the distribution of the paper to the delegates each morning before breakfast at their hotels. The cost was to be shared between several pharmaceutical companies, none of which would have any influence on what I wrote. His company, of course, was one of them. The report was acceptable to the European societies of both diabetes and cardiology, so that I was in the clear. All we needed to do was produce the text.

I explained to him that he would have to employ two of us,

Mairi and me, as a team. To our astonishment, he agreed at once. Then he asked the crucial question.

'How much do you charge for this type of report?'

Mairi was listening in. I cupped my hand over the mouthpiece and raised my eyebrows at her.

'What about fifteen hundred?' I whispered to her.

She shook her head.

'Three thousand,' she whispered back.

'That's far too much,' I replied.

'No, it isn't,' she said.

I took my hand from the mouthpiece.

'Three thousand pounds,' I said, fearfully.

'Done,' said Willem, immediately.

From then on, Mairi negotiated all our fees and contracts.

A week later, Mairi and I arrived at Glasgow Airport to join the line of people waiting for the early KLM Amsterdam flight. I had checked beforehand: the route was now Fokker-free. We didn't need furry boots. There was a familiar figure in the queue just ahead of us. Pat English was the reader in diabetes at Glasgow's Western Infirmary. He was going to Vienna, too, and his travel agent, like mine, had routed him through Amsterdam rather than Heathrow. All I had to carry was a case that was small enough to be cabin baggage and our portable electronic typewriter. Mairi had a similar case for her things. Willem would provide all the other necessities on site. Pat was trailing with him a foldaway bicycle with small wheels.

He saw us looking at it, and smiled.

'I've been to one of these conferences before' he said. 'The Austrians use the old imperial palaces, and if you want to get to different sessions you have to take a bus or tram. I can just hop on my bike – it's a lot faster.'

I'm on a steep learning curve here, I thought. Maybe Pat is right. I had seen the programme, and two of the reports we had to make were on subjects in different conference halls. I had planned to take taxis and charge for them. It was a pity, I thought, that Pat's bike didn't carry three.

It was our first visit to Vienna. The traffic problem wasn't so bad. The organisers had laid on coaches to take us between meeting sites, and they worked well. While Mairi set about organising our place in the room set aside for the press, began planning interviews and photo opportunities, and started talks with our printers, my first scheduled reporting session was on '*The prevention of sudden death from the cardiovascular complications of diabetes*'. It was billed as a 'plenary' session – one which most of the thousand or so delegates would attend – and would be chaired by the famous Professor Muller of Berlin.

I got to the great hall of the Hofburg Palace early and sat in the front row, pen in hand, pad on knee, dragging up as much eagerness and enthusiasm as I could for a rookie journalist, and watching as the great and the good of diabetes and cardiology started to fill up the seats behind and around me.

At nine o'clock, Professor Muller entered from the back of the hall, walked down the central aisle, turned left where it met the stage and passed immediately in front of me on his way to climbing the six or so steps at the side onto the stage. He was an imposing figure, immaculately dressed, well over six feet tall and fatter than I would have expected of a diabetician and cardiologist. He was used to eating well, I mused: the colour of his well-rounded cheeks was closer to mauve than to pink. Was he a bit breathless, I wondered, as he puffed up the steps? He stood behind the lectern at one side of the stage, opened a small sheaf of papers and spoke.

'Good morning, ladies and …'

He stopped, threw his arms up in the air and pitched forward over the lectern. His large bulk seemed to be fixed there, his arms now hanging down, his head to one side.

It was a brilliant demonstration of 'sudden death from the cardiovascular complications of diabetes'. What a fascinating way to get your audience's attention from the word go. Applause broke out from around the hall. I must admit to being tempted to clap myself, but I was closer to him than most and I wasn't sure he was acting.

Professor Muller didn't respond to the applause. He wasn't acting. He had, in fact, died in front of 600 of his peers, none of whom could help him.

Once the penny dropped there were plenty of volunteers to try to revive him, but it was useless.

The conference did go ahead later, after a respectful break: there were another three days to come, and the thousand attendees still had presentations to make and to hear.

Mairi and I set about making notes, gathering photographs, typing up reports, interviewing the great and the good and hoping that, after such an inauspicious start, nothing more would go wrong. Luckily, we had Willem's organisational expertise behind us, so that we planned to give the proposed texts and layouts to the printers at around nine o'clock each evening, after which we could relax over a late meal and a glass of wine. The next morning, the news sheets would appear, and hopefully be appreciated.

The production came at a price. We had a room on the sixth floor of an old hotel, built as a palace for minor nobility in the nineteenth century. It was September, and stiflingly hot. There was no air conditioning, and the rising heat turned the top floor into an oven. It was impossible to sleep without opening the window. Sadly, the Viennese roads authority had chosen just that week to refurbish the cobblestones. They couldn't stop the trams during the daytime, so they chose to do it between midnight and six in the morning. With the window closed, we were suffocated: with it open, we were bombarded by the noise of steam hammers and pneumatic drills. We eventually slept with the window open, pillows around our heads and cotton wool balls stuffed into our ear canals.

The next morning, our bus arrived promptly at 7.45 to take us to the main conference hall. It was scheduled to start at our hotel, pick us and two or three others up, then go on to pick up more delegates at each of the five other hotels, before eventually arriving at the conference centre. On our way out, we passed a pile of our news sheets at the reception desk. They hadn't been slipped under the room doors as arranged, but left for guests to pick up if they wished. It wasn't a good start, but we lifted them up and took some of them to the bus, intending to pass them on to others when they boarded.

There we met Rosa Kleb. Remember the poisoned-stiletto-toed SMERSH agent in *From Russia With Love*? The nasty woman who eventually got her just deserts for failing her bosses? She was guarding our bus. She asked us, in an accent that would have been perfect for the Eastern Bloc's worst spy, what we were doing carrying leaflets aboard her bus.

'This is not allowed,' she said. 'You cannot distribute advertising material in this vehicle. You must take it back to the hotel.'

No amount of discussion would change her mind. The newsletters had to be returned to reception. We walked disconsolately back to the reception desk and asked if someone would see that all the delegates to the conference got one.

'Hurry up,' she shouted at us. 'We are late already. We have many other hotels to visit, and your delays are making us behind schedule.'

Mairi and I looked around the bus. There was no one else on board. The others – and we knew of at least four – hadn't risen in time. Rosa didn't like it at all. There were names to be ticked off or underlined on a list on her clipboard, and she definitely did not like disorder. I had a close look at the front of her clumpy black shoes. I couldn't see room for a spring-loaded stiletto, but I was sure it was there.

Finally, the bus left, with only the driver, Rosa and us on it. We arrived at the next hotel. No one was ready there – another twelve names were absent. At hotel three, four and five, it was the same story. Everyone had enjoyed the previous evening too well, and no one, except us, felt like attending the earliest lectures. The bus arrived at the conference hall with only us, a raging mad Rosa and a driver with a broad grin on his face on board.

She went off in a hurry to find a telephone, and we chatted to the driver. He was a medical student hired to drive us around: the bonus for him was that it got him entry to the conference. He spoke perfect English.

'I loved that,' he said. 'She takes the biscuit – is that what you say in English? She has been driving us insane with her nitpicking and over-organising. Now she will have to find out what to do about all the other delegates. My scheduled run is over: I'm going into the meeting hall. Someone else can deal with her.'

Off the three of us went, thinking we had seen the last of her.

The next two days went well. Willem's team did us proud, and the news sheets were well received. Rosa was not in evidence on the following mornings. We heard she was creating havoc on another bus. On the last day, we had to prepare a summary of the whole conference, based on interviews with the session leaders. We got the photographs and the texts sorted, and planned to finish at seven. One of the pharmaceutical companies that supported our newsletter was holding a magnificent bash at a castle in the Vienna Woods that evening, and we were invited. It wasn't exclusive: around 600 others were going too.

We arrived back at our hotel room from the conference at around five, and plugged in the typewriter for what we hoped would be the last time. Down went the switch, and off went all the lights and electricity on the whole sixth floor. Somehow we had shorted the power supply. The hotel wiring looked as if it hadn't been renewed since the war, but to this day we are mystified about how it could have happened.

I had to go down to the ground floor, by the stairs, as the lift wasn't working, and try to arrange some way by which we could complete our job. The receptionist was helpful and directed us to an office that still had electricity. The manager, however, didn't trust our 'electronic machine'. Fearing that if we plugged it in again, the rest of the hotel would be left without power, he gave us two old Remingtons to thump away on. It meant we were slower than planned. At seven sharp, the bus arrived to take us to the dinner. Rosa was there to marshal us on to it.

We hadn't finished. We needed ten minutes more. We pleaded with her to wait. She wouldn't.

'If we have the courtesy to arrive on time, you should respect us by being ready. You will have to make your way to the castle on your own,' she snarled at us.

The four other delegates didn't want to leave without us, but she ordered them into the bus. We told them to go, that we would catch up with them later. Off the bus sped on its travels to the other hotels, leaving us behind.

We shrugged our shoulders, got on with finishing our task, handed the package over to our printer contact and dressed at a fairly leisurely pace. We couldn't be bothered seeking out the castle by ourselves. We would just eat around the corner, at a local café. The *sacher torte* in the window looked sumptuous.

So it was half an hour later when we sauntered out of the hotel, to see the bus returning, full of passengers. In the front seat was Willem. If Rosa was thunderous before, she was positively volcanic now. Willem had been in the last hotel and had been looking out for us. When he heard that Rosa had left us behind, he had made it clear what he thought of her attitude to her guests. We sat beside him, and Frau Kleb was told that there was no seat for her now. She would have to stand all the way to the castle, or find some other transport. She stood.

Wow. This wasn't a good way to make friends.

The Vienna Woods are on the outskirts of the city. Riding through them, on a late summer evening is a once-in-a-lifetime experience. The whole population seems to be strolling about enjoying the ambience of the sculptured landscape, the magnificent trees and the palaces and castles. Our bus was one of around twenty carrying people to the castle. It joined a long line of others parked by the side of a road deep inside the woods. A small gravel pathway made of led off it into the trees. We walked along it in the muggy heat, men in lounge suits, ladies in summer dresses and high heels, for about a quarter of a mile, where it ended at a moat.

Across the moat was a magnificent castle. To reach it we had to step onto a small wooden raft that was pulled across the moat by ropes fixed to its sides. A man at either end kept it straight by hauling on wheels around which the ropes were wound. It was a slow journey, and as it could only take around 30 people at a time, a small queue had formed, waiting to cross. No one minded. The evening was still hot, there were drinks to be had from a stall beside the queue, and we could hear the strains of one of Strauss's waltzes drifting across from the castle. A full orchestra was there to help us enjoy the evening to the full.

And so we did. At least until we got to the main course. The castle looked great from across the moat. We imagined a great dining hall with long wooden tables groaning with roast beef, suckling pig and all the trimmings of a mediaeval banquet, under a Gothic vaulted ceiling with rafters and paintings of past worthies and emperors.

It wasn't so. There was no ceiling. We were in the open air, at small modern tables covered in pristine white cloths. The castle was a ruin, only a shell of a building.

Which is why we only enjoyed the evening up to the main course. It was being served when there was a brilliant flash, followed by a deafening bang. Then came the rain. I've since been in New Zealand when a foot of rain fell in eight hours. The rain that night in Vienna was of that order. It was like being in a massive cold shower with the tap on full. Within seconds, everyone was drenched. The meal was ruined. No one had thought of bringing umbrellas.

Our only course of action was to pack up and get back to our buses. There was no shelter on the way, except the thin foliage of the trees. So we all became quickly saturated with water. The men were sorted out from the boys, as the better-quality suits kept their shape: other jackets and trousers became baggy and shapeless as the poorer material took up the water. The ladies became interesting too. Hairdos were ruined, and most of them, in summer blouses, became entries in the Vienna Woods wet T-shirt contest.

It was as we were waiting our turn to board the raft that I noticed Rosa. She and the other bus managers had been sitting at a table of their own, near the moat. She was jumping up and down close to the water's edge, screeching orders at the men operating the ropes, telling them to go faster. I suppose the deluge had weakened the earth beneath her, and her jumping may, in retrospect, have been a tad foolish. Because suddenly the edge crumbled, and she sailed over it into the water. You are not meant to make much of a splash when you dive: I wouldn't have given her more than 0.1 out of 10 for style, and I certainly wouldn't have given her more than 1 for her technical skill, although she did enter the water head first. Nor was she elegant when she climbed out. The hot summer had caused a green algal bloom, a thick film of which clung to her as she climbed out onto the bank.

I will draw a veil over the distressing scene that followed. Rosa was helped away, not in the best of moods, but she definitely lightened ours.

Once back over the moat, it soon became apparent that the gravel path we had walked on from the buses was only one or two pebbles deep. It had turned into a quagmire: ladies were losing their shoes in it. Mairi, country-wise, took hers off and walked on the grass. The return to the hotels was a shambles: some of the buses had parked just off the road. They were stuck, the wheels spinning uselessly on the soft ground. Their would-be occupants were coerced into getting behind them and pushing. As most of them were in their fifties, and prided themselves, probably over-optimistically, on their cardiovascular fitness (they were experts in the subject, after all), I feared that we were about to witness yet another sudden death. Two in one week would be a first. Mairi and I climbed into our coach: the driver had switched on the heating full blast to dry us out. There was no sign of Rosa. We wrung out what we could, and endured the long and slow journey back to our hotel.

We were leaving the next morning. The hotel had given us free use of a drying room, where we hung our wet clothes for the night. Our bus was due at nine o'clock, and Willem was coming to have breakfast with us at eight, to tidy up various odds and ends, to pay us and to join us on the journey to the airport.

Packing up took more time than we had anticipated. To start with, someone had locked the drying room, with our clothes still in it. The receptionist didn't have the key: when it was eventually found, we had to rush our packing and it made us late, yet again, for the bus. Only a few minutes, but still enough to create a stir, because the redoubtable Rosa had recovered from her near-drowning experience and was back in position as bus manager.

When she found that yet again she had to wait for us, she exploded, this time in Austrian German. Mairi and I heard only one word that we recognised – Englanders. We gathered that the rest was not complimentary. I considered correcting her: we were Britishers or Scottishers (what is the word for Scots in German?), not Englanders. But discretion took over. We just shrugged our shoulders and climbed onto the bus.

Willem had heard it all, and of course, could speak fluent German. He opened his document case and rumbled about in it for a few seconds, before taking out a slim sheet. Speaking to her in German, he handed it to Rosa, then sat down. She looked at it and her face, already red, darkened to full purple. She sat down and stayed there, silent, all the way to the airport. As we got off, she made a point of saying goodbye to all the other passengers, but maintained her stony silence with the three of us.

Sitting in the airport, waiting for our planes, I asked Willem what he had given Rosa.

'There was a meeting yesterday on anger management and its prevention of heart attacks and strokes. I thought the German version of it would be a perfect leaving present for her. She didn't appreciate it, or, apparently, you two.'

As we sat there, Pat English joined us, without his bicycle. I asked him where it was.

He smiled ruefully.

'In some scrap-metal yard,' he replied.

In his rush between two palaces, the bike's front wheel had got caught in a tramline, and with a tram bearing down on him, he had had to dismount in a hurry, leaving his bike to its fate. The tram couldn't stop in time, and his precious transport had been mangled.

We arrived home, the daily reports completed and paid for. Willem had done us proud. We had two more commissions to write about the Vienna meeting from specialist diabetes and heart journals, thanks to him. We had turned the corner. Our four eventful days in Vienna had given us plenty to write about for the journals.

The Vienna experience gave us ideas on how to expand our services. There was scope for much more than simple reporting. Representatives of medical societies, journals and drug companies hinted that they would welcome interviews with, and comments from, experts, both on paper and on video. The computer age was beginning, and it wasn't long before developments in portable computers, and in slide and video presentations, would let us put proposals like this into practice.

In the meantime, we still had the locum work.

KENYA

Over the next few years, our writing business expanded. People saw us at meetings, diligently writing away, and wondered what we were doing. They would come up to us afterwards and ask if we could send them reports, too. Our portfolio of clients expanded from these occasions, without us ever having to advertise or promote ourselves. We would receive phone calls at any time of day or night, from such countries as the United States, Australia or Japan.

One call came in just before Christmas, 1978. It was altogether different, and wasn't a proposal for a job. It came from Manu Tailor, my old mate from medical school. We had gone through our five student years together, then two more years as junior hospital doctors. He had shared a flat with Mairi and me when he was between jobs, and in return taught me real Gujarati cuisine, a taste for which has stayed and flourished with the enlarging Smith family ever since.

His house jobs over, Manu had returned to his native Kenya to set up practice in the town of his birth – Eldoret, in the highlands on the road to Uganda. It was a thriving market town catering for the wheat, tea, coffee, beef and dairy farmers in the surrounding area. Six thousand feet up and just north of the equator, it enjoyed a wonderful warm climate and rich soil, and Manu was able to practise modern medicine for all the community, African, Asian and European.

The call was more a demand than a request. We had never been to Kenya to see him, he complained, although we had always promised that we would. Could we make it next autumn? If we didn't come fairly soon, he added, we might miss our window of opportunity. I wasn't sure what he meant by that, but assumed that the politics of Kenya were worsening for people of Asian origin like him. Close by, in Uganda, Idi Amin had expelled his population of Asians, and we knew that the pressures in Kenya were building, too.

Our bank balance had been the stumbling block to distant travel until then. The conference payments and locums, and our much-reduced living expenses, now made the journey feasible. Without hesitating, I said we would come, all four of us, to Kenya. In August 1979, we arrived, tired but happy, at Nairobi airport, delighted to see him again.

Eldoret is 200 miles north-west of Nairobi, and it takes three to four hours of hard driving to get there. David, one of Manu's friends, had a large minibus and offered to meet us off the plane, so that we could enjoy the journey in comfort. Ila, Manu's wife, had stayed at home, to prepare what we knew would be a marvellous welcoming meal. I was given the front seat: Manu explained that this was the correct seat for me as the head of the family in the eyes of a Kikuyu like David.

Only a few miles into our journey, I saw a brilliantly coloured bird, about the same size as a starling. It was perched on the branch of an acacia tree near the roadside.

'What do you call that?' I asked David.

'In Kenya,' he replied, 'we call that' – he paused for effect – 'a bird.'

I didn't know what to say. David had been correct in his answer, but not very informative. I heard the children's muffled laughs in the back.

Then David laughed, too.

'It is a purple-breasted roller,' he said. Except, because Kikuyu doesn't have the letter 'l', it came over as 'purpur-breasted rorrer.'

We got on fine after that. On the way we saw gazelles, giraffes, baboons, eagles and masses of birds, including pink flamingos at Lake Naivasha, 30 miles from Nairobi. David knew the names of them all: not just 'giraffe' but the type of giraffe. He explained the differences between them by the size and number of their spots. He turned out to be a natural David Attenborough, with a wealth of fascinating information for us all. He stopped to show us a white-tailed eagle by a lake: it looked identical to those that fly over the cliffs of Wee Ensay.

We stopped at the equator, 8000 feet above sea level, and we all got out to straddle it. The temperature was perfect, the sky was cloudless and we were in the middle of a fertile plain, with wheatfields around us that stretched for miles. Half an hour later, we were 2000 feet lower, in Eldoret, being hugged and kissed by Ila and Bharti, Manu's wife and ten-year-old daughter. They had a beautiful bungalow on the outskirts of the town, with a small garden filled with tropical plants, shrubs, herbs and vegetables.

The plan was for me to work with Manu for a week, and then the seven of us would take off for a holiday around the country, visiting Mount Kenya, the Masai Mara, Keekorok and finally Mombasa, where we would stay for a week in a beach hotel before flying home. It sounded wonderful, and it was.

I suppose this chapter could have been a travelogue about the wonders of Kenya, its geography and its animals, but plenty of people have written about them. It was the people of Kenya, meeting them in their normal environment, who really impressed me. I gathered they might be different when we passed, on our way to Eldoret, an African couple, probably in their forties, walking along the road. The man, proud, elegant and upright, strode along in front, flourishing his walking stick with every step. His wife was staggering a few yards behind him, bent almost double by the wardrobe lashed to her back and the load of firewood tied to the top of it. Yes, a wardrobe. I don't know if it was full of possessions, but it was heavy enough by itself.

'Won't he help his wife?' I asked David.

'No,' he replied. 'A man has to think, and he can't do that with a burden on his back.' And he laughed again.

The morning after our arrival, Manu took me to his surgery. Uganda Road, the main road through Eldoret is wide and straight. It is lined by shops outside which are wooden walkways and shades against the sun. On the road from Manu's house to his surgery I was struck by the mass of healthy-looking, laughing people, colourfully dressed, going about their businesses of selling and trading. There was a central marketplace where the farmers, mostly women, had spread their fruit and vegetables over cloths and blankets. Business was brisk, with plenty of traders and customers arguing good-naturedly about prices and quality. It had a good feel about it, with no obvious stresses on the surface. Manu told me that the population was a mixture of tribes, the Kikuyu, the Kalenjin, the Luo and the Luhya, but that the tribal differences that had led to bloodshed in the past had long been resolved.

We passed by a church: there were cars outside, cheery village notices about meetings and signs proclaiming 'everyone welcome'. Writing about my time there so many years ago, I still can't believe that in 2008 the town was the scene of terrible inter-tribal killings, culminating in many Kikuyu women and children being burned to death in that very same church.

In 1979, there was little sign of the political strife that was to come. We walked into Manu's rooms in the main street, to be welcomed by his smart and smiling nurse-receptionist, Michael. Manu had told him about me, and he was delighted, he said, to meet me at last. The waiting room and surgery were, as I expected, spotless. Manu had fitted his consulting room to the highest standards, and had trained his staff to follow them, too.

The waiting room had around a dozen people waiting to see Manu or his nurse. He looked in on them, smiled, said 'good morning' and introduced me to them as one of his colleagues from Great Britain. They stood up and offered me their hands. I shook each one in turn and told them how glad I was to be there with my old friend and colleague Dr Tailor, then turned to follow Manu into his consulting room.

He stopped at the door and hesitated for a minute. He was looking at a small boy in a corner, who was busy reading a comic, and who was the only one in the room who hadn't greeted me.

'I'll take the lad first,' he said to the nurse. 'I think he needs me the most.'

The boy smiled shyly, rose from his seat and walked slowly after us into the consulting room. As he did so, Michael told us that when he had arrived at school that morning, his teacher had thought 'he wasn't quite right' and had brought him along to see the doctor. She had had to leave him at the surgery to attend to his classmates, but she would be happy to hear from the doctor about him.

'It's Raphael, isn't it?' Manu asked him.

'Yes, Doctor,' Raphael replied.

'You are usually full of energy, aren't you?' Manu asked. 'I've often seen you playing football, haven't I?'

'Yes, Doctor.'

I couldn't see what it was that had worried both his teacher and Manu about him. To me he was simply a normal, shy little boy. He didn't look or behave as if he were ill, except perhaps that he might be a little listless.

Manu asked Raphael if he could take a little blood from his finger. He nodded, unconcerned. He had probably endured such tests many times before.

The little bubble of blood was quickly smeared across a slide and put under a microscope. Manu had a glance at it, then asked me to look. I was looking at a phenomenon that I had only seen before in books and lectures – the invasion of red blood cells by millions of malaria parasites. A substantial proportion of his red cells had tiny black dots inside them. This puzzled me. He had no symptoms, as far as I could see. He wasn't shaking or shivering; he had no fever, pains or headache. He was just a quiet little boy.

Manu picked up the phone and rang the local hospital. A bed was quickly arranged for him, and his anti-malarial drugs ordered to be started as an emergency. That was another thing that puzzled me. Why was this so urgent, when he was obviously tolerating the infection so well? Couldn't he be sent home with his treatment and take it there?

Raphael's teacher arrived quickly in her car and whisked him away to the hospital, and Manu began to explain.

'Malaria,' he told me, 'doesn't often follow the textbook description. Most people here have it chronically, and they get on with their lives. But you have to watch out. Even a small change in normal behaviour – like a little boy normally full of energy deciding just to sit down and read a comic instead of playing games – can be a significant sign of a storm to come. My bet is he is sickening for a bout of cerebral malaria – and the blood film confirmed that. So we have got him into hospital and under treatment just in time.'

'And if his teacher and you hadn't seen the warning signs?' I asked.

'He could be in a coma by the morning, and maybe dead in a few days.'

I was shocked. Our training in Birmingham together hadn't ever touched on the management of tropical diseases in Africa. We had been taught about the indications of infection when people arrived back in Britain, but I didn't remember one lecture about the realities of life in the tropics.

Raphael recovered quickly, and within days, he was back to his normal self. The rest of the day was spent dealing with exactly the same problems that I faced in Britain, such as high blood pressure, heart disease, diabetes, obesity and arthritis. But each time, Manu also wrote out a repeat prescription for malaria prevention. We talked about it over a mid-afternoon coffee break. Malaria, he said, had almost been wiped out in Kenya before DDT had been banned. Now everyone had it: the ponds and stagnant water that were the breeding places for the mosquitoes were left untreated, and the disease had returned with a vengeance. He was fighting a losing battle, but at least he was still fighting.

As we finished our coffee, there was a commotion outside the consulting room, and Michael popped his head round the door.

'It's Ambrose,' he said. 'He seems very angry. Can you come out to see him, Doctor?'

Manu grinned at me and whispered, 'You have to meet this guy,' and we both went to the outside office.

There was Ambrose, easily six feet six tall, muscular, with a massive Afro haircut and no teeth. He was chewing on a stick, but still managed to keep it in his mouth while he spoke. He looked menacing, fierce, dangerous – and angry.

'Why were you not at home yesterday?' he asked Manu. 'I had a present for you.'

Manu explained that he had been away to Nairobi to meet me, a doctor colleague from Britain. That mollified Ambrose a little.

'Well, I have it here, and would like to give it to you.' He gestured to a pick-up truck parked outside the surgery. In the back was a very large dejected sheep. I'm a fairly good judge of sheep, and this would have been a contender for a prize at the annual Kilminnel Show.

Manu stared at it.

'What do you think I can do with that?' he asked Ambrose.

'Eat it.'

There followed a long conversation between the two men, debating the whys and wherefores of killing, butchering and eating a sheep, not to mention that Manu, being Hindu, was vegetarian.

Eventually, Ambrose stomped off.

'I will sort things,' he shouted. 'I will be back.'

We watched the pick-up with angry driver and depressed passenger disappear down the street, kicking up red dust as it did so.

As we drove home to his house, Manu explained the background. Ambrose had quite a history. He had been interned as a Mau Mau in the troubles, although Manu doubted very much that he had been an active member. The Kikuyu were forced to join, but most of them, Manu explained, wanted nothing to do with violence. Ambrose certainly looked the part, but there was a softer side to him.

The problem was that he didn't always keep to his softer side. The result was that his wife had borne him eleven children, before being sterilised. Then she had come to Manu with yet another pregnancy: somehow the operation hadn't worked. So in the next pregnancy, Manu had made sure by sending her to Nairobi for the confinement, after which she was well and truly 'done'. The baby girl was as welcome as her eleven siblings, and had been thriving until she became very ill with diarrhoea and vomiting. Manu had had to admit her to hospital for drips and antibiotics, and after a fraught time, she had recovered. Ambrose had wanted to reward his favourite doctor with his best sheep. It was a Kikuyu thing, Manu said, and very difficult to refuse.

Half an hour after we arrived home, there was a ring at the door. Ambrose was there, with his pick-up. This time the sheep wasn't depressed. It was in bits. Ambrose had had it killed, butchered, and it was ready for cooking.

'Now you can't refuse it,' he told us.

Manu could only thank him and take in the vast amount of meat. After Ambrose had gone, he phoned the hospital, asking the staff to come and pick it up. The sheep fed the patients and the staff for days. Nearly 30 years later, the baby girl is a successful lawyer in Canada. Ambrose, Manu told me, was always a generous and kind man, who cared a lot about all his children. He had made sure they were all educated. He obviously cared about his doctor, too, but it wasn't the Kikuyu way to display such 'soft' emotions. Under that hard, aggressive exterior was hidden a heart of gold.

Over the next week, I learned a lot about medicine in Africa. Eldoret is at 6000 feet, which explains its constant temperate climate, but Manu was also the industrial medical officer to an opencast fluorspar mine. To get to it we had to drive to the top of the Kerio Valley, a less well-known canyon than the Rift Valley, but no less impressive. From there we drove down the hairpin cliff-edge road to the valley floor. There the temperature was well above 40 degrees: stepping out of his Peugeot felt like stepping into an oven.

As we did so, a young woman passed us. She had come from the small market area around the mine entrance, and was heading for the base of the cliffs. She was wearing a striking floral-patterned long dress, and had a huge bundle on her head, wrapped in a brightly coloured cloth. There wasn't a scrap of fat on her. At home I would have judged her to be an athlete. She smiled at us, and we smiled back. I was curious: there didn't seem to be any houses in the direction she was taking.

Manu saw me and grinned.

'She's going home with her early morning shopping', he said.

'Where is her home?' I asked him.

'Up there,' he replied, pointing to the top of the cliff, 5000 feet above.

'But that's higher than Ben Nevis,' I said.

'She will do that every day,' Manu replied. 'And she will go straight up that path, not on the road we came down on. It's twenty miles up the road, with all its bends: it's only a mile straight up. All the people who work down here use the path.'

We saw her disappear into the shrubs near the bottom of the cliff and appear again, after only a few seconds, around twenty metres up, walking straight upward. The path was only just discernable, a narrow vertical streak of less-dense vegetation.

'How long will she take to get to the top?' I asked Manu.

'Three or four hours,' he replied. 'It is nothing to her.'

I was fairly fit myself, I thought, but in the 40-plus degree heat at nine o'clock in the morning, I reckoned I would last about ten minutes on a gentle upward slope. I wasn't going to try.

This was Friday, Manu's day for medical examination of new recruits and for the sick parade. His patients were happy to allow me to sit in the room while he attended to them. There were around a dozen to be seen, most of them for routine examinations. One man, however, had been brought under protest by his brother. Their home was in northern Kenya, near Lake Turkana, where the rest of their family were fishermen. The two brothers had decided some years before that there was not enough income in the fishing for them all, and had sought their fortune elsewhere. They had ended up in the mine. Every year they had some time off to go home: they had been at the lake three months before, and they had both returned to the mine in their normal healthy state. Lately, however, one of them, in his brother's words, was 'going off'.

Simon, the patient, was a man of few words, it seemed. He sat there, listless, and a little confused about why he was there. His brother, Peter, did the talking for him.

Manu listened patiently. Simon had always been a happy, active man. Even at work he had been happy, and considering how hard it was, that was unusual. In the last week or so, that had changed. He had lost all interest in his work, his friends, and even in going to the drinking house. When Peter tried to cajole him out of his lethargy, he had become irritated and had even cried. That was the most odd change in behaviour of all, and was why he had been brought to the doctor.

Manu looked at me and raised an eyebrow.

'Any ideas?' he asked.

I shook my head. I hadn't yet got enough information.

I asked Peter if Simon might be depressed about something.

'What's that?' he replied.

'Depression isn't a diagnosis we consider here,' Manu said. Then turning to his patient, he asked, 'Can I look at your neck?'

Simon nodded.

Manu felt his neck, then his armpits, groins and stomach. He was obviously testing for enlarged lymph glands.

'Do you mind if Doctor Smith examines you, too?' he asked. Again the nod.

Simon had small raised lumps in all the areas Manu had felt, plus a slightly enlarged liver and spleen.

'Any ideas yet?' Manu asked me.

I shook my head. This was something outside my experience and knowledge.

Manu asked the brothers if they had noticed any unusual insect bites on Simon when they had been fishing at the lake.

'There was one,' said Peter. 'While he was bringing the boat on to land. He had been stung by something on the back of the neck. He said it hurt at the time, and it raised a big lump there. But it went down by the next day.'

'What happened then?' Manu asked him.

'About a week later, another lump came up, at the same spot, and he was sick for about a week with it. But that went down, too. We don't have any doctors near our village, so when he got better, we thought nothing more of it. It's only now that he seems to have got sick again.'

Manu turned to me.

'Right, Tom, now you have the whole story. What do you think?'

'Is this another form of malaria?' I asked him. 'Like Raphael?'

'Wrong insect and wrong parasite,' Manu said, then turning to Simon, asked, 'Can I take a blood sample?'

Simon spoke for the first time.

'Sure, Doctor, anything you want.'

Manu spun down the sample in a centrifuge, used a pipette to take off the top layer of clear plasma, then put a drop under the microscope on a worktop nearby. He looked at it briefly, then asked me to do the same. There were dozens of long, thin worm-like creatures in it. I had no idea what they were, but they were surely abnormal. I straightened up and looked at Manu.

'Trypanosomes,' he said. 'The bite was from a tsetse fly. There are loads of them around Lake Turkana: happily, we are too dry for them in this part of Kenya. They need a lot of mois-ture to survive.'

He turned back to Peter and Simon.

'You have an infection from that insect bite and you need treatment for it. We will organise it for you.'

The two brothers were delighted that the doctor had solved their problem so quickly, and they left, thanking Manu profusely.

'So he has sleeping sickness,' I said. 'I'm impressed. I'd never have made that diagnosis without specialist referral.'

'You have to be the specialist yourself here,' Manu replied. 'The nearest ones are in Nairobi, 200 miles away.'

'How did you know the bite was from a tsetse, and not a mosquito?' I asked him.

'Tsetse bites are painful – they sting like a bee – and mosquito bites are painless. That was the first clue. The second was the timing of the lump, its disappearance and its return. That's a typical trypanosome history.'

'Will he recover?' I asked.

'He has around a 50-per-cent chance. We use a drug called melarsoprol, and cure rates at this stage, when the infection has begun to reach the brain, are not as high as we would like.'

By around two o'clock, Manu's responsibilities had ended, and we made the winding journey up the road towards home. It took us an hour to reach the top and to drive through the small group of houses that made up the village. Understandably, many people working at the mine preferred to live in the better temperatures there than in the cauldron below. In the centre of the village was a small square, and a few ladies were selling vegetables. We recognised the floral dress and the bright cloth spread out in front of the intrepid climber whom we had seen only hours before at the mine. She looked at us, smiled and waved. We waved back.

While we were on the way back to Eldoret, I asked Manu what he meant when he said that he didn't consider depression as a diagnosis.

'It's simple,' he said. 'People are naturally at ease with themselves here, naturally happy, if you like. Maybe it's the amount of sun we get. There's no seasonal affective disorder, perhaps because we don't have seasons. So we only get down in mood when we fall physically ill. That's why I don't look for depression as a cause of illness until I've ruled out absolutely everything else first. I can't remember when I last diagnosed it in an African. Ex-pats and fellow Indians, yes, but not in indigenous Kenyans.'

I had to admit, thinking over my last few days, I hadn't seen any grumpy faces, only smiley ones.

The following day we packed up our things into the boot of Manu's Peugeot and started our travels – seven of us in one car, but it was never a problem. We took a detour into the highlands to see a tea plantation, where the estate manager, one of Manu's friends (as everyone seemed to be), presented me with a quarter-sized chest of his best leaf. We then travelled to Lake Victoria (we left before nightfall to avoid the mosquitoes) before moving on via Naivasha again to Nairobi. The next night we spent at Treetops, on Mount Kenya, where Princess Elizabeth had heard that she was now queen. We watched, transfixed, almost till dawn, the animals coming to the watering hole just below us. Then on to Keekorok, where rock hyraxes and ground squirrels came within touching distance of us in our tents. In the middle of the night, Mairi wakened me up, cross that I had left the shower on. I didn't think I had, but wandered through to the toilet part of our tent. As I thought, I had turned it off, but the noise of the shower continued.

I looked out of the flap that served as a window in the side of the tent. The noise was coming from three zebra that had chosen our tent wall for a latrine. It's amazing how much urine a zebra produces at night. As I climbed back into my bed, I ruminated on the fact that our human kidneys shut down at night, presumably to avoid disturbing our sleep. Zebras, as prey animals, keep awake all night, and so don't need that fluid-conserving property. I wondered if anyone had written it up in a journal: next morning I put the thought aside. I had better things to do – watching elephants walking trunk-to-tail across the road in front of us; marvelling at the amazing wildebeest migration; spotting the odd ostrich or cheetah in the distance; and standing beside a pool and trying to count the hippo as they rose and sank again.

On our way back from Keekorok, we met a car that skidded to a halt when it reached us. Five Japanese gentlemen jumped out, terrified. One spoke English. The African driver sat still at the wheel, looking bemused.

'How far is it to this Keekorok place?' the English speaker asked, obviously in great distress.

'Only another four miles,' Manu replied.

'Thank you,' said the Japanese gentleman, climbing back into the car.

Their driver leaned out of his window and looked hard at Manu.

'Aren't you Doctor Tailor?' he said.

'Yes,' said Manu, 'and you used to live in Eldoret, didn't you?'

'Yes, Doc,' said the driver. 'I'm really glad to see you here. These men from Japan were thinking I was kidnapping them, and leading them to a gang that would put them up for ransom. I was starting to get scared that they would run off into the bush.'

236

Manu got out of our car and spoke to the tourists. He explained that Kenya was a big country, and that they would be on the road for much longer than on any journey in their country. Their driver was completely trustworthy, he added. There was no fear of kidnapping.

That seemed to settle the Japanese, and their car sped on its way.

That evening we spent near Nairobi, in a hotel that Manu had booked in advance for us. There were courtesy local papers in the hall. The headlines were full of an incident in the south of Kenya, near the Tanzanian border. Some tourists from the Far East had indeed been kidnapped, taken over the border and held to ransom. It left us wondering, but Manu reassured us that it was an isolated incident, far away from the normal tourist areas, and that we were in no danger. And nor, he assured us, were the five Japanese gentlemen we had met on the road that day.

That was our first hint of trouble in Kenya. It wasn't to be the last.

The next day, we drove along the main road from Nairobi to Mombasa. It is straight and runs very gently downhill for 300 miles: it seems completely flat, but it drops 5000 feet from the capital to the coast. Halfway along it there is a Sikh temple, where Manu pulled in for a rest and refreshment. It is tradition there that the priest offers each visitor a lump of what I can only describe as sweet goo. I think the main ingredients were semolina and ghee, but there were spices in it, too. To put it kindly, it was a little too greasy for our western European taste, but we couldn't refuse it. We stood in line, and our Sikh host dropped a golf-ball-sized piece of it into each hand in turn.

Within a few minutes, I had all four of ours in my hand.

Surreptitiously, Catriona, Alasdair and Mairi had each passed their lump to me. I had no choice but to swallow all four. They remained like a lead ball in my stomach for the rest of the journey to our hotel in a beach resort just a few miles south of Mombasa. That afternoon we walked on the beach, just in time to be soaked by the daily rains at four, ate a pretty good evening meal, then returned to our rooms to sleep. Except that three of us didn't. My children and wife had their first attack of the runs: I was unaffected. I put my immunity down to eating my Sikh sweet, and slept through the night like a baby.

On our last day, Manu took us to see Charlie Patel, another of our medical school colleagues. Charlie had been three years above us, but we knew him well, and he and his wife made us very welcome. As we were chatting to him about his practice, he mentioned that he had recently had to care for two patients whose immune systems had failed, for no obvious reason. They simply became thinner and thinner until they died of minor infections. Manu hadn't had any such cases, and nor had I. We couldn't offer him any diagnosis.

It turned out that he was talking about the first people with AIDS in Kenya: nearly 30 years later, there are around 10,000 cases in Mombasa alone. Charlie has become an unwilling expert in the disease. We still exchange Christmas cards. He is despondent about the way Africa is going, and sad about Kenya and its troubles.

Manu, on the other hand, didn't stay. Shortly after we visited him, the pressures on him to leave built up to an intolerable level. There were people in very high places in the Kenyan government who wanted African doctors to take over practices like his, and they didn't care about the methods they used. It soon became clear that if Manu and his family didn't leave, practice there would become very difficult. By 1985, they were settled in practice in rural England, never to visit Africa again. It was Kenya's very considerable loss, but our great gain.

Manu and I heard from time to time from David, but have had no contact since the 2008 riots. We fear that he, as a Kikuyu, didn't make it through them. We still have the presents he forced on us when he met us to say goodbye at Nairobi airport. Somehow we carried back to Scotland that quarter-chest of tea, a Zanzibar box, a large mis-shaped gourd that he had himself made into a lamp for us, and a crate of fresh fruit. We would also have accepted a cow, several goats and a whole flock of hens, but as these would have been in exchange for our daughter Catriona, an offer she declined, we reluctantly refused them.

FREEZING IN FINLAND

Taking a month off in Kenya had worried me a little, as I was acutely aware that for the greater part of that month no one could contact me urgently. That could have meant loss of income, something our newborn business might not have been able to stand. I needn't have worried. There was plenty of work to be done.

I hadn't realised it at the time, but *Human Potential*, the book I had written with Wendy Cooper that had been published in early 1980, was about to provide me with a whole new career as a lecturer.

I had better explain about *Human Potential* first. Our publishers sent Wendy and me all around Britain on newspaper, radio and television interviews to talk about it. We covered more than 2000 miles in my own car – me driving, Wendy navigating – in a week. The interviews were hugely successful, with everyone fascinated by the book's contents.

Wendy had done her homework. We wrote about the people we had interviewed, including the survivors of the rugby team that had crashed in the Andes, and who had to eat their fallen comrades to survive. We described the ordeal of the Robertson family, adrift for 38 days in an open rubber dinghy in the Pacific after a killer whale had sunk their yacht. The family of five had survived by grabbing turtles that had tried to mate with the dinghy, mistaking it for a giant and available female. A Japanese fishing boat picked them up in the nick of time: the sexual activities of the turtles had worn the rubber so thin that the Robinsons watched their dinghy burst and sink within minutes of their rescue.

Wendy had interviewed Odette Churchill, the British secret agent in Nazi-occupied France, who, caught by the Gestapo, had managed to hold out against torture without betraying her colleagues for 48 hours – plenty of time for them to disappear. While her torturers were pulling out her fingernails and drilling her teeth, she had brought down before her eyes an imaginary cinema screen, on which she projected happy scenes with her children in her garden at home. It was my first encounter with successful self-hypnosis.

Then there was Sir Douglas Mawson, the Antarctic explorer, who was left to travel back to his base 315 miles across the ice cap with no food and only his dogs to eat. His food-bearing sledge plus one companion, a Lieutenant Ninnis, had disappeared into a crevasse, leaving him and his colleague, Dr Xavier Mertz, with one team of dogs. One by one, six of the dogs were eaten. Mawson didn't like the livers: Mertz was grateful that Mawson had left him with a double ration of them. Mawson survived, albeit without skin on his hands and feet. Mertz found out the hard way that dog livers are poisonous. He died of overdosage of vitamin A after only two weeks. This was the first inkling for doctors that vitamins could be too much of a good thing.

The Mawson story was an epic of survival, yet hardly

anyone knows his story. Could that be due to the fact that while he was struggling across the ice cap, the bodies of Captain Scott and his team were found only a few miles away from their base? Perhaps Mawson was too modest about his achievements. A man who later could describe hauling sledges over iceridges, crevasses and through high winds in sub-zero temperatures as 'a breeze' was no self-publicist.

Human Potential was full of such anecdotes, and on the basis of the feedback we had about our around-Britain tour, it should have been a great success. Unfortunately, a glitch in the publisher's relationship with the printer meant that there were no books in the shops for at least a month afterwards. By then the listening, viewing and reading public had forgotten about it, and it didn't sell. A few copies got into libraries. It was a hard lesson in publishing, one that neither Wendy nor I forgot.

However, it did bring 'extras'. A reporter on the Scottish *Mail on Sunday* heard one of the radio interviews when having a haircut. He thought it might be worthwhile serialising in his paper, and invited me to do so. The result was a contract to write the paper's doctor page that lasted for twenty years, through five editors. I got on well with the first four, only to be sacked by the fifth in the first week of the new century. I will gloss over the reason for the sacking, mainly for fear of litigation, but it was at a time when all the media was into alternative medicine in a big way, and I didn't want to go down that route in my column. I didn't burst into tears when the man who sacked me also disappeared from the newspaper not long afterwards.

The other 'extra' was also a spin-off from working with Wendy. She was on the women's hormones lecture circuit, talking to doctors about HRT, so she was still in contact with the old Huizens team. A week or so after our fruitless charge around Britain for *Human Potential*, Arendt, my old contact from Huizens, rang me. He, unlike Willem, had stayed with the company through its change of owners, and was keen to get the lectures to doctors going again. Wendy had suggested to him that I might be interested.

I agreed immediately, and then was told the first meetings would be in Finland. In February.

Arendt arranged my travel, from Glasgow to Copenhagen, then to Helsinki. We would be 'travelling around' he said, from then on. I looked out my Fokker boots and splashed out on some Arctic clothing. February in Glasgow is cold and wet. A half-inch of slush on the runway delayed my plane for an hour, which meant a run from one end of Copenhagen airport to the other to catch the plane to Helsinki. It was, of course, on time taking off, and landed at Helsinki fifteen minutes early.

Most of the disembarking passengers, being Finns or Danes, didn't seem to worry about the snowdrifts piled up around the runways and the compacted snow underfoot. They, sure-footed, left me behind picking my way carefully over the frozen surface. The journey by car from airport to hotel was conducted at the usual speed for Finns: at the highest possible speed on the straight, and a controlled skid at each bend, hoping that the studded tyres would grip perfectly on the foot-thick ice that masqueraded as a surface. At the hotel, I met the other speakers, Wendy included, who had checked in an hour before, from the London plane. They had been well looked after, having swallowed in one gulp the traditional antidote to the cold and to carsickness – a large slug of deep-frozen vodka.

Vodka doesn't solidify in a deep freeze: it becomes an oily, almost tasteless, dense liquid, that is cold inside the mouth and halfway down the gullet, but very hot when it reaches the stomach. The vodka tray was still full of glasses, from which we were invited to drink freely. While I got stuck into my first, the others were enjoying their second or third. Or was it their fourth? No one, least of all our Finnish hosts, was counting.

Our first session was to be that evening in Turku, a seaport and university city on the Baltic coast, a two-hour coach drive from Helsinki. I sat in the middle of the coach, as the back had a tendency to swing violently from side to side at each corner. It was like choosing a cabin in the middle of a ship to avoid seasickness.

The evening went well. The audience was small, polite and attentive. We speakers knew we hadn't set the heather on fire, but we hadn't bombed, either. After all, '*The biochemistry, pharmacology and use of female sex hormones in clinical practice*' wouldn't attract a large fan base in capital cities, far less a small provincial city in Finland. The meeting ended at about eleven, and, like my companions, I was glad eventually to tumble into bed.

The next morning, Arendt and a few friends had arranged a treat for us. We were to go cross-country skiing in the woods near Turku. It would be a 'bonding' experience, putting us in a good mood for the next evening's talks. The temperature of minus twenty degrees Celsius would make the experience all the more memorable. As a Scot would say – 'Aye right'.

Dawn breaks in southern Finland at around ten o'clock in February. At around that time, our hangover-ridden six speakers, including the intrepid Wendy, who was all of 60 years old, were standing in the snow, our nostrils hanging with tiny icicles from the instant freezing of our exhaled breath. Ahead of us was what seemed a fairly flat plain of snow, dotted with clumps of fir trees, and old ski tracks, presumably from the previous day, running towards them, and eventually disappearing into them. In precisely the opposite direction were other ski tracks, leading into a small, gentle upward slope and over a rise. The lights of a small town, about three miles away I guessed, were going out as the rising sun made them redundant.

We struggled into our ski clothes, thoughtfully provided by an impossibly healthy looking guide, and then strapped the skis onto the fronts of our boots. Having only attempted downhill skiing once before, I was faintly surprised that the heels were left free, so that we could stand almost on tiptoe yet leave the ski in contact with the ground. As soon as we started, it was clear why: we needed pushing power, and we couldn't do that with foot and ski bound together as a single unit. It was also clear that the slopes weren't gentle. Even the smallest uphill gradient was a mountain. It was no 'breeze' and I was no Douglas Mawson.

Wendy and the others glided off on the track towards the woods: I was tail-end Charlie. I only fell a few times, then got the hang of it. It began to feel like sliding on the ice on my old school playground, and I thought I was coping fairly well. Then the children passed me, going like trains. The local kindergarten was having a day out. About 30 children steamed past me, none of them older than six, and some as young as three. They had all been born on skis.

Only then did I find out that the course on which we had started out was six kilometres long. It took the form of a wide circle: the two tracks I had seen at the start were its outward and inward paths. Out through the woods we went, and in over the 'gentle' slope we came back. The five-year-olds passed me three times, and I was even overtaken by the three-year-olds twice. Needless to say, I only completed one circuit. By halfway through, I felt as if I had been walking on my arms for an hour. At the end, Wendy, who had also 'lapped' me, came out to help me in.

We warmed ourselves up with more of the vodka laced with a lot of sugar and a little strong coffee at the end. Except that I couldn't raise the cup to my lips because all the muscles in my forearms had stiffened. The rest of the speakers took turns to help me: I was being fed like a baby when the kindergarten kids waltzed in. By my reckoning they had all completed at least twenty kilometres. They crowded around to watch this strange man being fed, and looked worried and sympathetic, chattering to each other in Finnish about me.

Finnish sounds beautiful, but it bears no resemblance to any other European language, except, the Finns told me afterwards, to tenth-century Hungarian. I wasn't fluent in either of them, so I wondered what the kids were saying. My host eavesdropped for a while, then informed me that they thought I was a poor sick man, out from some final care home, enjoying a last few days of ski-ing before succumbing to what must be a terrible terminal illness. They were all very sorry for me. I still have a photograph of me somewhere at home, taken that day. It isn't in the family album: it lies beside old passport photographs and is convincing proof that the kids were right.

After lunch, we boarded the plane to Oulu, a university city on the Gulf of Bothnia, just 100 miles south of the Arctic Circle. Naturally, the Finnair plane left on time, and landed at around three in a surreal landscape. It was just getting dark, but we could see that the countryside around the city was under about twenty feet of snow. I'm fairly certain about its depth, because the plane landed in a chasm, the walls of which were hard-packed snow, and the floor perfectly cleared tarmac. Looking out from the airport lounge to the runway, the only part of a landing plane we could see was the tip of its tail.

The roads in Oulu were even deeper in the white stuff than those around Helsinki, and the drivers, thankfully, were equally skilled at controlled skids. Professors Nieminen and Nurmi, our hosts from the university Faculty of Obstetrics, met us and guided us to our hotel, to book in for the night, and then to the conference centre, where the meeting was about to start.

This time I was better prepared. I had asked one of our Finnish hosts to prepare a few sentences of introduction in Finnish, which I would read phonetically, as a gesture of goodwill to our audience. As I was the first speaker, it set the tone of the talks, and we sensed that our audience of around 200 (where did so many people come from in such an isolated area?) was warming to us. It wasn't exactly a rehearsal for the main meeting, to be held in Helsinki the next day, but when we discussed it afterwards, we agreed that we had sharpened our performance.

That evening we didn't go back to our hotel. Instead, we were invited to Professor Nurmi's home, in the countryside just outside the city. Arriving in a large, modern, glass-walled bungalow at around midnight, my overwhelming first thought was about the silence. When the land is carpeted in such deep snow, it deadens any sound. We could hear our companions breathing and the crunch of our boots in the snow, but nothing else. The sky above us was blacker than any I had ever seen, with steady, untwinkling stars in their trillions. From time to time, the northern lights put on their best show, as multicoloured curtains of light danced, glittered, brightened and faded above us. All round us in the air tiny bright specks were dancing:

Professor Nurmi explained that they were ionised particles, like the Brownian movement we learned about in physics at school. Think of the dancing spots of light you see on a TV screen when you switch on an unused channel, minimise them into points of brilliant light, space them out a little, think of them in constant random movement, and you have something of the shimmering show in which we were enveloped.

Several of us wanted to stay outside for a while, to take in all this beauty, but the cold was beginning to bite, and we were ushered inside to warm up. Of course, part of the heating process involved the ubiquitous frozen vodka. The good Professor Nurmi's wife had prepared a feast for us, and invited several lady friends around to even up the numbers, as five of the six speakers were men. We were beginning to warm up and loosen up socially as well as physically, when the prof invited the men to the sauna.

Saunas in homes in Finland aren't the wishy-washy luke-warm rooms we have here in health spas. They are places where men are men, stark naked, with birch twigs (ours were more like branches) and temperatures above the boiling point of water. It is only because the air in a sauna is bone dry so that we can lose heat by sweating that we survive in them for more than a few minutes.

We entered Professor Nurmi's sauna via a small changing room, where we divested ourselves of every last article of clothing. The sauna itself was roomy enough to accommodate all nine of us – the five speakers, the two professors, Arendt and our coach driver, who turned out to be one of Professor Nurmi's assistants. We sat there baking in the heat and whipping each other, not too gently, until the professor invited us to step outside.

248

OUTSIDE?

The temperature inside the sauna was over 100 degrees Celsius – it is hard to imagine, but I read the thermometer with my own eyes. The temperature outside was 31 degrees below zero – I had read that, too, before my vision became blurred. Overtiredness and ice-cold vodka apparently have a habit of doing that to your eyes. The way out of the sauna was through a side door that I hadn't noticed while sitting there: it didn't lead back into the house. The nine of us walked straight out into a huge bank of snow.

Amazingly, it felt good. I expected to feel so cold that it would be painful, but it wasn't. Maybe my skin's temperature sensors had switched off in despair at what I had subjected them to: the snow on the skin felt marvellous. We left steaming body-shaped holes in it as we frolicked around, dancing and jumping, hooting and hollering. Part of our odd behaviour may have had some origin in the vodka, but most of it came from the feeling of absolute freedom to run around in this pure air in the dead of night, with only the stars and the northern lights to look down upon us.

Except that they were not the only spectators. One glass wall of the house looked directly on to the yard in which we were dancing about like dervishes. Behind it were several couches and chairs, drawn up to look outwards. In them were the ten or so ladies, watching, even scrutinising us with keen interest. None of them was exactly ogling, as beetroot-red men in the buff at 30 degrees below are not showing themselves, how shall we say, to their best advantage. The Finns took this discovery in their strides: the Brits less so. Our strides, in fact, became definitely shorter and our bodies more bent as we tried to hide our embarrassment. We filed back into the changing room and dressed. The ladies welcomed us back as if we had never undressed, but I gathered afterwards that they had been scoring us. The points system was decided in Finnish and with much laughter, so I never learned on what basis it was decided or where I stood, but it appeared none of us reached Olympic medal standard. We Brits assumed that it was a Finnish custom and left it at that.

Several more liquid refreshments later, someone noticed the time. It was 3.45 am, and we had to get back to the hotel, pack and be at the airport for six o'clock for the early flight to Helsinki. As no one in the house was fit to drive, two taxis were called. They took some time arriving, so that there was no point in going to bed. I packed, went to the hotel lobby and waited there, half-asleep in a chair, for the twenty minutes that remained before the airport bus arrived. I slept fitfully on the plane, and, with the others, was taken straight to the conference hall in Helsinki University for the meeting.

The first speaker, me, was scheduled to start at 8.30. Each of us was to speak for fifteen minutes, leaving five for questions. There would be a coffee break, then lunch, after which the audience would be free to join in a 'round table' session at which they could present any of their own work for discussion. My plane home would leave at around five o'clock.

Walking into the hall, I was startled to see around 500 seats and a huge stage on which the speakers were to sit, facing the audience. In one corner of the room was a glass-fronted box for an interpreter, and in the middle of the front row were three seats with headphones placed on them. I didn't see any on the rest of the seats.

The six of us, plus Professor Nurmi, who had flown with us from Oulu, walked to our places on the stage, as the audience gradually filled their seats. I looked around at my companions. They were, with one exception, ashen-faced and red-eyed. I hoped they weren't feeling as bad as I was. There were hundreds of little men with road drills trying to burst from my skull. The exception was Wendy, who was as immaculate as ever, crisply coiffured, in a slim black trouser suit and white blouse, fresh as a daisy. She grinned at me: I found it difficult to smile back.

All the seats were occupied, and there were even a few standing at the back, ten minutes before our talk was due to begin. At the last minute, three large men in identical grey suits, white starched shirts and red ties settled into the seats at the front of the audience and put the headphones on. The interpreter was already in her booth, chatting into a microphone. The men listened intently.

As Professor Nurmi stood up to open the meeting, I took out of my pocket the piece of paper on which I had written my few Finnish sentences. I glanced at the writing, and to my horror found that I couldn't read it. I must still be dehydrated from the excesses of the night before, I thought. I should have drunk more water with it – the eternal cry of man the morning after. I swallowed all the water from the glass in front of me, sat back, gathered together my thoughts, and tried to listen to our chairman.

He started in Finnish, welcoming all the delegates in the hall, then obviously made reference to our little band of speakers. The audience laughed at one point, then settled as he turned to English.

'You will see we have special guests here today, from the city to the east of us in the Gulf of Finland. We would like to w elcome them as true Finns have always welcomed their neighbours from the east.' At that there was loud applause, and the three men in the front row beamed and looked around.

'I'll pose you a little conundrum,' the Prof continued. 'There is a football pitch with a figure at each corner flag. One is Santa Claus, one Peter Pan, one a clever Russian and the last is a stupid Russian. Who do you think ran to kick the ball on the centre spot?'

It was an old joke, and I knew the answer before he gave it, but I was still astonished that he had told it.

'Of course,' he said, 'it was the stupid Russian, because the other three are fictional characters.'

At this there was a roar of applause from all around the room. The three with the earphones smiled again and one even stood up and gave a little bow. The applause moved up a few decibels at this, then died away as the man sat down.

Prof Nurmi then asked me to speak.

I stood up, swayed a little (I was feeling a little dizzy), then made a brave attempt at my three sentences in Finnish. It was now my turn for the rapturous applause. Carrying on in English, I asked for my first slide, and struggled through my talk. The men with the road drills gradually faded away as the water started to work, and I sat down to yet another barrage of clapping. It was surely over the top, but it made me happy.

The other speakers stumbled through their speeches, and they were met with similar warmth and appreciation.

At the coffee break all became clear.

In his short Finnish introduction, the professor had explained that we had all had 'typical Finnish hospitality' the previous evening in Oulu, and it could hardly be expected that we would be on top form. So he had asked the audience of 500 doctors from all over Scandinavia to be kind to us, as we were almost certainly still half-drunk and badly sleep-deprived. Hence the extra applause. The audience hadn't understood a single word of my feeble attempt at Finnish, but they understood I had made an effort, and that was praiseworthy.

As for the gentlemen from Leningrad, of course they hadn't been told the joke. The interpreter, a Finn, had given them a prepared spiel about the wonders of Marxism and dialectical materialism, and the contribution they had made to the modern world.

Talking later, at the airport, to Arendt and Wendy about the curious reference to the welcome for 'our neighbours from the east' that had evoked such a positive reaction, Arendt explained. During the Second World War, Finland had been sandwiched between Russia and Germany. Both countries had armies on Finnish soil, Germany in the south and Russia in the east. Professor Nurmi had been a Finnish army commander, fighting on two fronts. His expertly planned strategic withdrawal from both fronts led the Russians and Germans directly into each other, and the battle that ensued left Finland free of both of them. Finland's emergence after the war as a fully independent country largely stemmed from that action. There wasn't a man in the room, apart from the three Russians, who did not understand that. Many were there purely because he was the chairman of the meeting.

As for the joke about the football pitch, the professor could be completely sure that not one of the 500 doctors in the audience would ever have told it to the three men from Leningrad. I felt quite sorry for them, but only for a few moments.

Bother in Brazil...

By 1983, I had stopped giving lectures and devoted all my time to listening to others giving them. I was more comfortable reporting conferences than speaking at them, and to be frank, it was more profitable. My constant attendance at meetings, however, had attracted the attention of people with more than reporting in mind. It all started with me standing under a flagpole in Baden Baden, just ten miles from Vienna.

It was the annual meeting of the European Society of Gynaecology, and I had been asked to report on three of the sessions by two journals and the ever-friendly Willem. He was already several steps up the ladder on which I had inadvertently set him six years before, when I had recommended him for the Paris job, and he was always pleased to commission me.

The evening before the conference began, Willem and I went for a walk around the town. We were staying at the same hotel and decided to have a look at the conference centre before retiring fairly early, to be fresh for the next day's work. The centre was a modern building set on one side of the central square. It had a semicircular array of flagpoles outside it, on which were the flags of all the nations of the speakers and delegates. A third of the way around the circle, three men were standing at the foot of one pole, looking up at it. I recognised two of them. One was Fergal Moran, professor of gynaecology at the University of Galway. The other was John O'Connor, who held the same chair in Dublin. I had worked with both during my Huizens days, and was glad to see them. In their company Willem and I were bound to have a good time. I didn't know the other man, but I could see why the three of them were staring up at the flag at the top of the pole.

It was green, white and gold, a proud sight at any time for a man with Irish blood in his veins. There was just one flaw. It was half the size of all the other flags. Willem and I strolled across to them. They were not happy Irish bunnies. It was not possible, they were saying, to leave things like this. But how could they change it? It was eight o'clock in the evening, and it would be impossible to find another flag before the morning.

John mentioned that his brother-in-law's cousin worked in the Irish embassy in Vienna: did we think that he might be able to help? We all agreed that it would be a good idea to phone him. There were no mobiles then, so we had to find a public telephone – there were plenty in the conference hall – and the number of the embassy. Willem, with his fluent German and knowledge of how the phones worked, offered to help. Within minutes, everyone in the Irish embassy had heard that the flag at the Baden Baden conference hall was too small. They set about finding a bigger one. Could we take the tram into Vienna central, where we could pick it up? And would we like the odd Guinness or two to raise our spirits?

I'm not a real fan of Guinness myself, but Irish hospitality beckoned and I wasn't going to refuse it. Thus it was that the five of us took the next tram into the city, got off outside the embassy and claimed a better flag. About two hours later, we poured ourselves (I think that is the most appropriate verb) from the return tram outside the conference hall and made for the flagpole.

The rope for the flag was tied around a hook about ten feet from the ground, so we had to devise a way of reaching it, untying it, lowering it, then replacing it with the flag we had brought with us. We three bigger men stood around the base of the pole, arms around shoulders, and Fergal and John, more slightly built, climbed onto them. Holding each other steady, not easy in the Guinness-filled circumstances and the fairly brisk wind, our two acrobats began to lower the flag.

At that point, the *polizei* arrived in their car, blue light flashing, and screeched to a stop beside us. We froze, but Fergal gallantly, in the face of the fuzz, didn't stop lowering the flag.

'What are you doing?' one of them asked.

'We are taking down this flag,' Fergal replied, unapologetically. 'It is too small. We wish to replace it with one that is more appropriate.' Actually, he said more than that, but I have left out the adjectives.

'It is Irish, isn't it?' said the policeman. 'And you are all Irishmen?'

'To be sure,' said Willem in his best Belgo-Irish accent. He had heard the three words several times that evening and was convinced that they were a typical Irish phrase. In fact, I think it was the only Irish phrase he knew. I suppose it was, in the circumstances, appropriate. It certainly didn't sound odd, except for the tad of Flemish intonation that an average Austrian policeman wouldn't hear.

'Certainly,' I said, not completely untruthfully, as one of my grandfathers was born in the Emerald Isle.

'Absolutely,' replied the others.

The policeman laughed.

'Let us help you then,' he said. He and his two mates, also laughing, fell out of the car and shored up our rather shaky pyramid. The flag was down in minutes, and the new one raised. Eight of us stood back and saluted the new flag. It was a moment of pride for all of us, and indeed for any other Irish delegate at the conference. For the new flag was fully twice as big as all the others in the semicircle. It stayed there throughout the three days of the conference, and it fluttered far better than the others, we thought, in the breeze.

I got to know the third man later. Tim Conway wasn't Irish at all, but British. He was the research director of a large, now global, British pharmaceutical company. He was curious about my background and what I was doing at the conference. Fergal, John and Willem enlightened him with tales, highly exaggerated, about my skills. At the end of the conference, he took me aside and asked if I could do two small jobs for him. I wasn't in the business of saying no.

'The first job is a bit different,' he said, 'but I'm sure you will find the second routine. They do require you to travel a bit.'

'Where?' I asked.

'How do you feel about Rio and Miami? Oh, and Buenos Aires?'

This was 1983. The Falklands War had been waged only a year before. We Brits were still not guaranteed a welcome in Argentina. A few months previously, we had heard the story of Professor Keith Warsley, a British surgeon with many international honours. He had been invited to speak at a meeting in Montevideo, but due to severe fog, his plane had been diverted to Buenos Aires, where everyone was made to disembark. Seeing his British passport, the Argentine customs arrested him, declared him *persona non grata* and put him on the next plane out – which was to Santiago de Chile.

As Keith had not paid for the trip, the airline demanded money when he arrived. Doctors on freebie trips don't carry cash, and his credit card wasn't acceptable, so he was arrested again. It was late on a Friday night, and the British consul, it was rumoured, was away for the weekend, skiing in the Andes, as people do in Chile. Keith had to wait until the Monday morning before he got help, was released and sent back across the Andes to Rio, missing out Montevideo completely, because the flights to Uruguay from Santiago all stopped in Buenos Aires. He missed his meeting, and worse, the Uruguayans had no idea why he hadn't arrived. They had phoned his home, naturally upsetting his family, who also had no idea where he was. The tabloid press in Britain got hold of the story and spread rumours that he had been kidnapped and even been 'disappeared' (the current word for political murder) by the evil Argies.

To add to his worries, he had to pay over a thousand pounds for the extra plane flights. There was also the final indignity of the bill from the Chilean prison. His board and lodging costs of some two hundred pounds – afterwards he would say that it was the worst value for a weekend's full board in history– were put on his credit card, now mysteriously acceptable again, before he finally arrived home.

I didn't want to risk a similar experience, but Tim reassured me.

'We will arrange a business visa for you beforehand, so that you will be expected and made welcome. Our company is an important money earner for the Argentine, and the new government is keen to re-establish contacts. It has changed a lot since the Keith Warsley incident.'

I let his judgment prevail and listened to what he wanted me to do. I had to visit the company's head offices and laboratories in both the Argentine and Brazil. Ostensibly, I would be there as a journalist to gather material for the company magazine. The company liked to feature in its magazine the work it was doing all over the world and it was time to put Brazil and the Argentine into the limelight. They would welcome me warmly and let me interview anyone I wished to get a good story. I would spend a weekend in Buenos Aires and three midweek days in Rio before flying home. People would look after me throughout.

But there was an underlying purpose to my visit that would need a lot of tact. Tim was worried about the state of their research in Latin America. Brazil and Argentina had laws stating that no drug could be licensed without research having first been completed in their countries, even if they had been licensed elsewhere. European and American research counted for nothing if companies had not also committed part of their research budgets to their local hospitals. So Tim's company had had to plough millions into medical research teams in Rio and Buenos Aires to establish its prescription drugs in South America.

Problem was, Tim suspected that someone was fiddling the books. Some of the trial results were just too perfect, and the doctors in both countries seemed to be completing patient forms faster than seemed possible. As payment was on the basis of numbers of patients finishing the trials, there was plenty of scope for, say, 'imaginary' forms being added to the genuine ones. It was difficult to tell the imaginary from the real from across the Atlantic.

Why should he ask me? Couldn't one of his staff do the job? Tim explained that if the staff in Argentina and Brazil knew that one of the headquarters mandarins was visiting, they would have time to put things in order. I, as an outside journalist without an axe to grind, wouldn't be seen as a threat. They might lay themselves open to an astute outside observer who was innocently producing an article about them, and as I had directed research teams in my role at Huizens, I fitted the bill perfectly.

Thus it was that I found myself, two weeks later, on a KLM flight from Amsterdam to Rio, then on to Buenos Aires. British Airways had not yet restarted its flights to the Argentine: the war might be over, but we were not yet friends, so KLM was the carrier of choice. To my great pleasure, when I checked in I was told that I had been upgraded into first class. In the executive lounge, I found a small group of other Brits waiting to board. Three of them were booked for the same hotel as I was, so we agreed that we would spend some time together at the weekend. As we got to talking about our trips, it was clear that they were slightly apprehensive, like me, about the welcome we might receive. The Dutch executive lounge personnel were interested, too. It turned out that we were the first British passport-holders since the end of the war to fly by KLM into Buenos Aires: they wondered how we would get on.

I boarded the plane, to find I was the only passenger in the first-class 'bubble' on the top deck. I had two elegant and pleasant stewardesses to look after my every whim for the eleven hours to Rio, and another two on the onward journey to the

Argentine. If I were to be incarcerated in some Argentine jail, I thought, this was the best possible preparation for it.

I needn't have worried. As the sole first-class passenger, I was off first, and was the first to encounter the dreaded Argentine immigration officers. The man before me looked fierce and grim. He took my passport and opened it at the page with my photograph and details. He looked up at me, and his face broke into a massive, welcoming grin.

'You were born in Glasgow, Scotland, and live in Ayrshire?' he asked.

'Yes,' I said, warming to his smile.

'Then you are very welcome to my country, Sir,' he said. 'My great-grandfather came from Ayrshire. From a small town called Girvan. Do you know it?'

'It is ten miles from my home,' I said. That was when I noticed his name badge for the first time. I was speaking to Enrico MacDonald.

'Please carry on, Sir,' he said. 'Enjoy your stay.'

No mention of the war or of La Thatcher, and the best welcome I had ever had from an immigration officer. I couldn't believe my luck. I had only cabin baggage, so walked through the customs with no delay, and was glad to see a board with my name on it being held up by a smart young man. Luis helped me to his car, and we chatted happily all the way to the hotel. Later that evening, after seeing Luis off in the lobby, I looked around for my three British companions. They weren't there. The receptionist told me that they hadn't yet arrived.

The next morning, Luis came to collect me at 8.30. I had slept well and was fresh and ready for the fray. As we walked through the revolving door at the entrance, my three companions from Amsterdam walked in. They were unshaven, ashen, red-eyed and still in the now crumpled suits they had been wearing the night before. They looked awful. I asked Luis to stop for a moment while I spoke to them.

They explained that they had been held all night at the airport: their bags had been searched, and so had they, intimately. They hadn't liked it much. Apparently, where they had been born mattered. They were all English, from around London. The one Welshman in their group had sailed through, like me: he was booked into another hotel, so I hadn't met him. One of the immigration officers was from Patagonia, and spoke Welsh. No, they hadn't met Enrico MacDonald. To be frank, I wasn't sure that if they had, he would have accorded them the same welcome as mine.

Luis explained later that the Argentines had ambivalent attitudes to the British. They were grateful to the Irish for their railways and roads, to the Scots for their beef and to the Welsh for their development of the whole of the south of the country. They linked England only to Mrs Thatcher, and for some inexplicable reason they weren't grateful to her. Years of exposure to the stories (maybe better called propaganda) of ex-pat Irish, Scots and Welsh immigrant families had given the average Argentinean the impression that we of the minority British nations were simply waiting our chance to get out from under the brutal and bullying English yoke.

I wasn't about to disabuse them of that wildly inaccurate impression while I was their guest. I could have told them that the Welsh in particular had suffered hugely in the Malvinas war, and that the Scots had done a lot of the fighting, but I didn't. I have a conscience about that to this day.

I had a fabulous time in the Argentine. My hosts showed me through their offices, research block and factory. They gave me a photographer for my magazine article, and the staff queued up for interviews. I was able to browse through their research records and could find nothing wrong with them. I met the doctors involved in the research, and they were honest and straightforward to a man and woman. They showed me their patient forms and I sat in on one of the clinics. They were all so pleased that I had come: a visit from a British journalist was, for them, the beginnings of normality between our two nations. I walked around the centre of Buenos Aires admiring the European architecture, the central square with its statues of Victorian age pioneers and its roadside cafes, without the slightest feeling that I might be at any time in danger. I enjoyed Harrods and a host of other shops that would have been perfectly at home in any British city.

To cap the visit, the Argentine Open Golf Championship was being held that weekend. Luis had tickets for me: we spent the weekend watching great golf in wonderful weather, and the icing on my cake was meeting Roberto de Vicenzo, probably the best Argentinean golfer ever. He won the tournament and afterwards told me that he 'was playing like a faulty motor-bike – going putt, putt, putt, all the time'. I hadn't seen anything wrong with his putting. A few years earlier, he had lost the US Masters because his partner had signed for the wrong total on one of the holes on his final round card. The penalty for this cost him the tournament. I didn't remind him of it.

That last evening, before flying on to Brazil, Luis and his wife took me to a steak house beside the River Plate. It was magical; the steak was the biggest and best I had ever eaten in a restaurant (it was on a par with the Galloway steaks sold by our local butcher in Girvan – I don't want to upset him). The friendship forged that night has lasted to this day.

I hadn't foreseen any problems with Brazil, so, the next day, after yet another KLM upgrade into first class, I walked out through customs in Rio with no fears. I should have had some. This time two men were waiting for me. They were both in a uniform that I took at first to be military, but I was assured that it was normal for a chauffeur. They walked on either side of me through the arrivals lounge to their car, parked on a side road and guarded by a third man in a slightly different uniform. There was a bulge in his jacket to the right side of his waist, which I hoped was simply one of the new brick-sized walkie-talkie phones I had heard about.

I was bundled into the car, and my two companions, leaving behind the guy with the bulge, drove me out of the airport at high speed towards downtown Rio. On the way one of them told me that I was on no account to wind down the window beside me at any point in the journey. The doors were centrally locked and to remain so until we reached my hotel. Scary stuff, I thought. There had been nothing like this in the Argentine.

It was midday, and the Rio streets were crowded with people and traffic. It took us an hour to reach my hotel, where there were armed guards at the steel gates. Our driver showed an identity card to one of them, and the gates slid open, much like the gates of a prison in an American B film. My host from the company was waiting in the lobby for me. He introduced himself as Dr Charles Watts. He helped me check in, then told me he had ordered lunch, which we would have before going to the company headquarters, where he had arranged, he said, an appropriate welcome.

His hospitality was fulsome. The table was groaning with food and a bottle of wine for the two of us. When I accepted only a glass, he finished most of the rest of it himself. I hoped he wasn't driving. The Argentines had offered only mineral water with lunch, although they were generous with their Mendoza wine in the evening after the work had been finished.

After lunch, I went up to my room on the fourteenth floor to wash and change. I strolled out to the balcony overlooking the Ipanema beach and watched the rich and beautiful play on the sands. Immediately below me a young woman was waiting to cross the road to reach the beach. She was wearing only a bikini, a light blouse over it and sandals. As I looked down at her, two young men on a moped swerved across the road straight to her side: the pillion passenger pulled a necklace from her throat and sped off. It was over in a flash, leaving the woman lying in the gutter, crying and holding what looked like a broken upper arm. One of the hotel guards rushed towards her, helped her up and ushered her into the safety of the lobby. No one bothered to chase the robbers.

When we met in the lobby, I asked Dr Watts about the incident.

'It happens every day here,' he told me. 'That's why you came in a bulletproof car with two guards from the airport. It's like a war zone for anyone who looks wealthy. And that means you or me. So don't go out on your own at any time.'

Our car rolled up just outside the hotel gates, and we walked the two yards or so to it. We were driven about six miles, to the outskirts of the city, where the company's corporate headquarters had been built only three years before. It stood on what must have been a beautiful site, on a hillside overlooking mountains and, in the distance, a jungle-covered, wild, rolling landscape. It was no longer beautiful. All around the modern building, covering the whole hillside, was a *favela*. There were shacks and apologies for houses that couldn't even be described as shacks right up to the building's walls. The road up to the main entrance had been kept clear, but within a few feet of it was poverty deeper than any I had ever seen, even in Africa.

People were living in homes built from cardboard boxes and old wooden crates, with corrugated iron for roofs, if they had one at all. Between them were dirt tracks, in the centre of which ran ditches filled with human detritus. Everywhere there were wires carrying electricity that looked makeshift and highly illegal: there were even places where they had caught fire, with blackened ruins for yards around them. From all this chaos women and children stared at us as we passed, with dull, uninterested faces, indifferent to us and apparently to the others around them. None of the children were playing, for there was nowhere for them to play except in the gutters and pathways. It was a place of abjection and hopelessness. I remembered the smiley people in Kenya, and wondered what made the difference. It wasn't just the Kenyan sun: there was just as much here.

We swept past a small group of men outside the gate, to whom Dr Watts gave a brief wave. They raised their hands in a desultory way as a return greeting. Then we were inside a courtyard, behind a high wall, in front of a state-of-the-art office and factory complex. There were lawns and flowerbeds, with gardeners diligently tending to them. There was a heady scent of tropical flowers, to which I couldn't put a name, and underneath it the vestiges of a chemical smell that I knew only too well from numerous factory visits in the past. The first didn't quite mask the second, although I was sure that was its purpose.

A man came to the door of the car and opened it. We got out

and our driver handed him the keys, and the man drove it away to a secure garage around one side. We walked up an imposing outside staircase through the front door into a startlingly bright, clean, clinical hallway. How different it was from Huizens and the old chocolate factory.

The difference went much deeper than simple appearance. There wasn't the buzz, the friendly meetings of people in the corridors or side rooms. Employees passed Dr Watts and me (we had dropped our minders) without a smile or a nod, not responding to my efforts at both. Dr Watts' expression didn't alter: he didn't even offer any small talk as we walked on. I could feel the tension in every department as we passed by them. The chief executive's office door, at the end of a long corridor, was twice the size of the ones we had passed. It opened as we approached it: the secretary who greeted us led us into a huge room that ran from the front to the back of the building, with windows on three sides. I guessed they must be bulletproof, as each one overlooked the *favela*. Venetian blinds hid it from view.

The chief executive was sitting in a massive leather armchair, behind a similarly oversized leather-topped desk. He was a small round man, who didn't rise as we entered, but waved an arm to us to sit down in the seats on the other side of the table. I guessed that he liked the feeling of power. Now that we were seated he towered over us: his seat was at least a foot higher than ours. I wondered, as I couldn't see them, if his short legs were dangling in space, not able to reach the floor.

He didn't introduce himself to me, which I thought rather rude, but his nameplate in gold on ebony stood to attention on the desk. Fernando Lopes. He leaned forward in his seat and came straight to the point.

'Why are you really here, Doctor Smith?' he asked me. 'I have done my homework. I have your CV in front of me. You are not just a journalist, are you? You have worked in our industry. Are you, what is it you say in English, a snooper?'

I brought myself together quickly. I decided to lay on the flattery.

'My industry days are behind me,' I replied, hoping that I sounded convincing. 'I make my living reporting meetings and interviewing important people for companies. The British end of the company think you are one of them, and have asked me to write about you and your workforce here in Brazil for their international magazine. I'm sure you will enjoy the result.'

I was tempted to ask him if there was anything about which I should be snooping, but didn't want to antagonise him, so I left it at that.

Mr Lopes didn't smile, but seemed satisfied with my answer.

'Dr Watts will show you around. We have a list of people for you to interview, and a timetable for you. I hope you find it suits you. We have a photographer who will go with you. Now I am very busy: I hope you will excuse me.' With another wave of the hand I was dismissed.

'A bit brisk, our Mr Lopes, isn't he?' I asked Dr Watts as we walked back down the long corridor.

'We didn't really want him as our CEO,' Watts replied. 'It is law in Brazil that all companies have a Brazilian at the head, even if they are foreign owned. He is the one they chose for us – it was have him or not get our licence to manufacture here. He makes all the local decisions.'

'Like choosing the staff?'

'That's the one thing he can't control. As soon as we started to build on this hillside, the *favela* arrived, followed in days by its bosses. They made it clear that if we didn't employ people from the *favela*, we would be burned down. We have had a hard time training them, and even though we are paying them well, many of them still resent us. No one is happy here.'

'Including you?' I asked.

'Including me.'

Over the next few days, I met the chosen interviewees. It was hard to find something good to put in the magazine, but I somehow managed. It was even harder when I met the doctors in charge of the research. In the Argentine, they had been happy to open their files, to show me their patient forms and results. We had pored over their analyses and compared them with those in other countries, openly and freely. The files here were closed to me. As I was just a journalist, I couldn't insist on seeing them: it would have been intrusive.

I had to make a report on this, but didn't know what to write. I had no reason to suspect that anything was wrong, and certainly didn't want to come to a negative conclusion unless I had proof. Yet I couldn't see how such an unhappy team could produce the wonderful results that had been sent to Britain. I spent the evenings as Dr Watts' dinner partner. He lived alone, his wife having decided to live in the States for most of the year, so he was happy to eat and drink with me. Late on the last evening, he was a little more expansive than usual.

'You wanted to know why it's so different here from the Argentine? Numbers. The Argentine has a population of 35 million, all educated at least to secondary-school level. We have 135 million, only 20 million of whom have been to school at all. The other 115 million have to do what they can – which is why we have the *favela* around us. The Brits want results from the research: we produce them. I don't know whether they are kosher or not, but I'm not going to accuse these guys of fiddling. It would make me a target, and I just want to live my life out in peace.'

I left Rio the next day. On the way to the airport, I saw a robbery in broad daylight in the main street. Two men, one with a gun, held up a man as he opened his car door, took his keys, his briefcase and his car, leaving him standing on the pavement, grateful, I suppose, that they had left him his life. My driver, who had seen the incident too, made no comment.

I was happy to get on the plane home. Tim met me at Heathrow, and I handed him my notes. The magazine gave a glowing report of my experiences in the Argentine and in Brazil. The research report gave Buenos Aires a clean bill of health. The Rio report described my grave doubts. The Argentine office has continued to flourish. Within two years, the Brazil office closed: the company decided to leave the marketing of its drugs to the new Brazilian government agency set up to deal with corruption and blackmail. It worked well enough. Luis and I still exchange Christmas cards. I didn't hear directly from Dr Watts again: Tim told me that about a year later he had gone home to the States, where he took up cattle ranching. Fernando Lopes became a politician, but not a very successful one. About five years later, he was found dead in his apartment, apparently shot by an intruder.

I hear from colleagues in Brazil today that things have changed very much for the better, that the *favelas* are turning into suburbs with proper facilities, and that the country's economy is improving. I hope that some of the improvement has trickled down to the people I saw. I haven't been back.

...AND IN MIAMI

I was only partly looking forward to the Miami job, scheduled for ten days after my arrival back from Brazil. For the previous three years, Mairi and I had been a team travelling together, and working away from home on my own was putting pressures on us. The trips to Finland, Baden Baden, then South America had been unusual in that she wasn't included, and now that the children were away at university and art school, she was lonely and unhappy. She was particularly anxious, having lost her brother in her teens and her parents in her twenties, and feared that on one of my trips she might lose me. After my deception about the trip to Omagh, she didn't fully trust me when I tried to reassure her that I would be well looked after.

Miami, however, was to be another of my solo trips. At least, I told her, it would be far easier than Rio, and I would be well looked after in the States. She wasn't totally mollified, so that she was looking strained as I left for Glasgow Airport on the first stage of my journey.

The Miami brief was a routine one. The meeting was part of the annual Congress of the American Heart Association. Tim was on its committee as one of their statutory foreign experts, and had been charged with finding someone who could interview their six main speakers on video. The film would be used worldwide to promote the work of the AHA. They didn't want it to be overtly American, so a Brit would do nicely. My voice, part West Midlands and part Scottish, appeared to suit them. I would have a team working with me on the day, and the studio and facilities would be provided.

It sounded exciting, and I was looking forward to it, but, as a countryman of mine once wrote, *the best-laid plans of mice and men...*

The first glitch was a delay of five hours at Heathrow, when our British Airways plane to Miami went out of service. The BA ground staff gave us free vouchers for food and drinks while we waited. I calculated that if there were no further delays, I would still manage to arrive at the conference hotel in time for dinner, where I was to meet the great men before interviewing them the next day.

Everything went smoothly until we reached 35,000 feet above Boston. Most of the passengers were watching the film, when there was a break in the sound track.

We all heard the words 'Stewards to door seven please', from the captain.

Door seven was one row in front of me. It was an exit door, and struggling to open it, with both hands on the big release handle and his trainer-clad feet planted at the side to give him more purchase, was a middle-sized, stocky, fortyish man in a check shirt, sweater and jeans. He either thought it was the toilet, or wanted to commit suicide, taking us all along with him. I gave him the benefit of the doubt that he had had too much of the BA hospitality before boarding and merely wished to rid himself of extra fluids. I wasn't concerned, as several stewards were converging on him, and I was sure that the door couldn't possibly be opened in flight.

What followed must have taken only a minute or so, but it seemed like an eternity. Asked to sit down by the first steward, he turned and lashed out. He caught the unfortunate man on the chin, and he dropped like a stone. Stewards number two and three held back for a minute to tend to their colleague, and a large man in a grey suit stepped forward. He was from the first-class cabin, and looked mean and angry. He grabbed the passenger by the shoulders, who responded by kneeing him in the groin. It was an eye-watering moment for every man watching, as grey suit, doubled up, joined the steward on the floor.

It took a serene stewardess to bring calm. She asked the man what he was doing. He softened, and while he was trying to explain (I heard him say 'pish', which placed him squarely in my part of the world), the other stewards jumped on him, together. They wrestled him to the floor, beside the two casualties, forced his arms behind his back and handcuffed him. At that, the man promptly fell asleep. They carried him back to a seat across the aisle from me and strapped him in. There he was constantly watched for the next three hours as the plane carried on towards Miami.

On landing, the plane didn't stop at a sleeve. We stayed for a few minutes on a side runway, waiting for a boarding party. Three very large men in grey suits, just like the one who had been knocked out, charged in and grabbed the man. They weren't too gentle with him as they frog-marched him down the aisle and off the plane. Only then did we go to a sleeve and slowly walk off. As we were waiting to pass through passport control, I saw the men again. Their prisoner must have fallen downstairs, for he now had several bruises on his cheeks, and there was a small trickle of clotted blood below one nostril.

It took ages to get through all the checks: by the time I was in a taxi I was seven hours late, and the dinner would be well under way. I had been told that the taxi would take only ten minutes, so I settled back and hoped that would be the end of my troubles. They had only just begun.

Thirty minutes later, I was still in the taxi. The driver didn't speak much English and didn't seem to know where he was going. When we passed the airport perimeter for the second time, I was worried and angry. I leaned forward to tell him the precise instructions for getting to the hotel, then noticed two things that disturbed me further. The first was that he bore no resemblance to the photograph of the man on the dashboard – the one who was supposed to have the licence for driving the taxi. The second was the handgun lying beside him on the front seat.

He shrugged his shoulders. I felt perhaps he thought he had got me angry enough and had decided to go to my destination, which shouldn't have been a bother to any cab driver. It was a well-known country club famous for its annual golf tournament: even I had heard of it in Britain.

We eventually drove up to the front entrance, where the meter was showing $60. I had been told it would cost twelve. I threw a twenty-dollar bill at him and said that was all he was getting. He lifted the gun and pointed it at me. I got out of the cab, with my case, as fast as I could, and ran up the steps to the hotel. The driver started to follow me, but thought the better of it. He turned back and drove off, in a hurry. Maybe the two police guards at the entrance put him off. I suspected he was an 'illegal' and couldn't risk being confronted for his identity.

Things didn't get better at reception. The dinner was over,

and people were dispersing for the night. It was midnight Florida time, and five in the morning for me. All I wanted to do was to find a bed.

There wasn't one. The receptionist told me my room had been given away; I was so late they had thought I wasn't coming. The rest of the guests from my plane had arrived an hour before, so I had been crossed off the list. I explained, as coolly as I could, what had happened to me. That still didn't get me a bed, but the hotel could find me one at their sister hotel ten miles away, in east Miami. I wasn't going to argue. I gave in, and the receptionist ordered a taxi to take me there. I asked her to make sure the driver was safe, and to arrange for someone to pick me up for the start of the meeting the following morning.

Of course, the morning taxi didn't arrive. After waiting for it beyond the appointed time, I had to organise one myself, and arrived at the conference hotel two or three minutes late. I walked into the foyer, to find police everywhere. I was impatient to get to the meeting, but I first had to pick up my pass at reception. It wasn't there. I asked the lady there where it was. She shuffled through the small pile on the desk, but couldn't find it.

'We have no record of you,' she said. 'I'm sorry, you can't go in.'

I must admit to you that at this point I lost the plot. My friends, I'm sure, will agree that I'm a mild-tempered man who docsn't break easily. I'm gentle, kind, wanting to understand the other person's viewpoint at all times. I would be a lousy politician. My personality is more Paddington Bear than Grizzly Bear. However, that morning the switch from the first to the second was fast and complete.

I started shouting at the poor woman. I related at full belt all that had happened to me over the previous twelve hours and how this was a terrible welcome for a guest to the land of the free. She stood her ground and signalled to one of the policemen.

The cop was walking towards me, pacifier in hand (I think that's the US word for a truncheon, but I may be wrong; it certainly wasn't a baby's dummy), when a man who had been quietly standing beside me, listening, spoke.

'You are Dr Smith?' he asked. 'Our interviewer for the video?'

'Yes,' I replied. The policeman stopped walking and started to listen.

'I'm so glad you are here,' he said. 'We thought we had lost you. Hold on a minute, and I will put things right.'

He turned to the receptionist.

'Please bring me the manager, at once,' he told her, quietly.

'But —' she started.

'No buts,' said the man. 'I am the president of the American Heart Association. If you don't bring me the manager this minute, I will make sure that your chain of hotels never holds another conference.'

Which is why, ten minutes later, I was ushered into the honeymoon suite. It would be mine for the rest of my stay. It was by far the biggest hotel room I have ever seen, with the biggest heart-shaped bed, in the centre. Off to one side was the bathroom with a bath the size of a swimming pool, also heart-shaped. The chairs, the window frames, the television, the rugs, the key fobs and all the toiletries were heart-shaped. To cap it all, they were all scarlet. I opened the curtains to look out of the window, to try to get my eyes accustomed to other colours, to find the panes were rose-tinted.

The porter who had shown me to the room watched me with the hint of a smile. He coughed.

'Would you like a little extra furniture, Sir?' he asked.

I looked around. There was enough furniture for a football team.

'No, thanks,' I replied, mystified that anyone could want more. 'There is more than enough here. All I need is a writing desk, and I can use the one over there. Thanks.'

'You from Britain, sir?' he asked.

'Yes.'

'That explains it,' he replied, and without waiting for a tip, he left the room. That mystified me further.

I quickly packed my few things away, and took the stairs down to the conference hall. I had only missed one of my key speakers, a man from Lisbon. I decided to base my questions to him on the abstract of his talk in the programme, then settled down to listen to the four others. By lunchtime, I had heard them all, had planned what I would ask them, and had forgotten my travails of the previous day. I was keen to get on with the interviews.

The Lisbon professor was first. We shook hands, and he sat down, making himself comfortable in the easy chair for the guests. I sat in the hard upright chair opposite him, keen and ready to go. I had a synopsis of his speech in front of me.

The continuity man gave me the nod, and the camera started rolling.

I started: 'I'm glad to welcome Professor Da Silva, from the University of Lisbon.'

My interviewee interrupted me. 'I'm sorry, I'm not Professor Da Silva,' he said. 'I am' – at that point someone in the background coughed and I didn't hear him clearly.

He continued: 'I have made out some cards on which is my name. That should make it easier for you. At the last moment, Professor Da Silva was unable to come and I gave his talk instead. I am one of his co-workers.'

I looked at the card. He had printed it out for me in block capitals. It read: PROFESSOR FARTEGAS. Underneath was written: THE UNIVERSITY OF OPORTO.

I looked at it once, then again. I tried pronouncing it in my mind, and couldn't believe what I was hearing.

'So this is how you wish me to introduce you?' I asked him.

He nodded.

I swallowed, hard, then started again.

'I'm glad to welcome Professor Fartegas, of the Univ–'

He stopped me again. Luckily, he had a good command of English. He was convulsed in laughter, thankfully, because he could have taken my mistake the wrong way.

'My name is not 'Fartygas': it is Francisco Artegas.'

I looked at the card again. There was a full stop between the 'F' and the 'A'. I hadn't noticed it.

Francisco and I got on very well after that. I resolved to make sure to pronounce the rest of the names perfectly. I didn't have too much trouble; it isn't difficult to read names like Wilson, McDermott, Laurence and Ho.

The last speaker came from Japan. I had heard him that morning, and he had been difficult to follow. His name would present no problem. It was Fukuoke, pronounced, as far as I could hear from the other doctors when they were talking about his work, *Fyoo-kyoo-oh-keh*. He was a prominent member of the famous and dignified heart team at Watanabe University. We settled into our chairs, and the camera swung to face the good professor: 'Our last speaker today is Professor Fyoo kyoo oh keh, of Watanabe.'

For the second time that morning I was interrupted.

'Excuse me, my name is not *fyoo-kyoo-oh-keh*. It is *fuh-kyoo-okay*.' He was smiling at me, as if I were a schoolboy in an elementary Japanese lesson. He raised the pitch slightly, at the −*ay* end of his name, making it into a question and all the more − how shall I say − interesting.

I wasn't smiling back. I couldn't believe what I had heard. A brief image of the charming Japanese professor driving along the Miami highway, infringing some minor rule and being stopped by the state's finest flitted through my mind.

I started again: 'I would like to welcome our last speaker, Professor Fuh Kyoo Okay, of Watanabe University, to the studio.'

I caught sight of the cameraman and soundman in the mirror. They were trying desperately not to laugh, but hardly managing it. We had to do three takes before the professor was satisfied, each one sounding worse than the last.

After the screening was over, he told me that it was his first visit to the United States, and he was enjoying himself immensely. People seemed to be very friendly, he said, but he was curious about the way Americans always laughed when he met them. Was this the correct cultural thing to do? In Japan, he said, people are usually very serious when they meet. It is only later that we start to laugh together, he added. He liked the American way: it broke down barriers faster, he said.

I told him that it must be that people liked him at first sight: this wasn't a routine reaction to strangers. But it might be a good idea to talk about how he pronounced his name with his English coach.

The work was over by six o'clock. I had made another introduction to Professor Fukuoke's talk after he had left, making his name sound a little less odd to Western ears. The film crew promised to send an original to him, and the altered one to everyone else.

I had initially planned to stay another day and see a little of Miami before I left, but the events of the previous evening had given me a jaundiced view of the place. On leaving the room we had used for a studio, I had walked across to reception, where I asked if there were any seats on that night's BA plane to London. There were, and I could change my flight at no extra charge. I went to my room, packed, brought my case down to reception, checked out and asked for a taxi – one whose driver I could trust. I needn't have worried. The hotel chauffeur was at my disposal. And the manager, who had left a written apology for me, had paid the bill. Which gave me a great feeling until I turned to pick up my case. It had gone.

'Disturbed' doesn't adequately describe my reaction to finding that someone had taken my case. 'Berserk' is more accurate. Seeing my distress, a porter asked if he could help. I explained about the case.

'Oh, we thought it was one of the pile for Chicago,' he said. 'It has gone to the airport.'

I phoned the number on my BA card for the Miami airport office. A very pleasant voice answered; soothing, calming, seductive. It would be no trouble to rescue my case from the American Airways baggage and have it in the cabin for me. The owner of the voice looked forward to seeing me in the executive lounge. Did I have a favourite cocktail that she could have waiting for me on arrival?

As I put down the phone, I noticed the police again. They

were milling around ushering people, mostly delegates to our meeting, into a large room at the side of the foyer. One of them approached me.

'Did you stay in this hotel last night, sir?' he asked me.

'No,' I said, then described exactly when I had arrived and where I had been sent.

'That's fine, sir, then you can go.'

At that moment, the AHA president who had been so good to me the night before walked up to me. Noticing that I was leaving, he shook my hand, then said that it would be a long night for the rest of them.

Why was that? At around three in the morning, someone had broken into a guest's room, beaten him up and robbed him, leaving him for dead. The victim was recovering in a Miami hospital, but everyone who had stayed in the hotel the previous night was to be interviewed. I only escaped because I had been refused a room.

In the plane waiting for take-off, I saw familiar faces in the adjacent seats. It took me a few seconds to realise that they were the stewards and stewardess from the previous day's fracas. They weren't in uniform. They were astonished to see me. They hadn't heard of anyone before staying only one day in the US. I was just as surprised to see them: didn't they rest for a day before working their way back?

BA hadn't wanted them to stay in Miami. They had appeared in court that morning as witnesses to the attempted air piracy charge that the poor drunken Scotsman was facing. It was a federal charge, because the grey suit had been an off-duty CIA man on the way home from a tour of duty in Britain. It looked as if he was going to be found guilty, and then face fifteen to 40 years in jail. BA wanted the crew out of the country fast, to avoid further involvement in the jailing of one of their passengers. He had been a sailor travelling to join his ship, poor guy.

I wondered about him. Was he really so drunk, or was he ill? He had fallen asleep suddenly, as soon as he had been restrained, and he stayed asleep for the rest of the flight. He was still groggy when the plain-clothes men took him away, and he was being half carried by them when being taken through the airport. Maybe it really was a fall that had bruised his face.

'What was he like in the court?' I asked the stewardess.

'We didn't think he knew what was going on around him. He seemed bemused, unaware of the serious trouble he was in,' she said. 'He couldn't remember anything about the flight.'

That didn't sound like a normal hangover. Hungover, you may have the mother and father of all headaches, but your brain can still function. He would have known, if not in perfect detail, at least where he was and why he was in such trouble. There's a form of epilepsy in which people act bizarrely, for a short period – out of character – then fall deeply asleep. For around 24 hours after the attack they are drowsy and confused. The sailor fitted that bill exactly. I explained my thoughts to the stewardess, and she said she would pass them on to BA. If the company could help him, she was sure it would. If he did turn out to have temporal-lobe epilepsy – an electroencephalogram (EEG) would provide the answer – he might not have to face years in a Florida jail.

They enjoyed the story of the rest of my day, including the odd bit about the room needing extra furniture. Two months later, the hotel was in the British news. It had been a regular meeting place for organised crime, and a whole family of racketeers had been arrested there for running drugs and providing call girls. The beaten-up guest was a gangster who, after the beating, had responded by giving the American equivalent of our Queen's Evidence and spilled the beans on the mob. The television report showed my room, the heart-shaped bed being 'furnished' with four young ladies. They weren't playing bridge.

BACK TO NORMALITY

Returning home a day early hadn't been an entirely good idea. My phone call home from the States to tell Mairi about cutting short my trip had alarmed the family. Why would I give up the chance to have a day exploring what Miami offered, and maybe a game of golf, just to come home early? It wasn't like me. Mairi and the children sensed that something had gone badly wrong in Miami, and decided to meet me, en masse, at Glasgow Airport. We had a family discussion, at which they stressed that I should take fewer risks and avoid travelling on my own in future. I suppose I didn't look good. I hadn't slept for two nights, and looking back on the two days, I realised that I hadn't eaten either.

Happily, I wasn't booked for another conference for a month, and while I was away, the family had decided to de-stress me. They had booked four days for the four of us in Tobermory on the Isle of Mull, away from work, medical or journalistic. Mairi's family connections had led to us spending many summer holidays there when the children were small, and the islanders knew us well. Our days were filled with invitations to fish or walk or sail, and we spent the evenings at the

Mishnish, the local watering hole on the quayside, or in the comfortable lounge of the Western Isles, the imposing castle of a hotel high on the hill above the town. As luck would have it, both Alasdair and Catriona were on a break from their respective studies, so we rolled the years back and forgot all about travels and travails.

We drove to Calgary Bay on the north-west coast and walked on the sands: we sailed across to the Treshnish islands, and then over to Staffa, where we settled down in the grass within feet of the puffins and marvelled at them. We walked into Fingal's cave and imagined Mendelssohn there, composing the music in his head as he listened to the waves and the wind. We wandered the shore of the west coast of the island opposite Ulva at low tide, snatching up scallops, oysters and razor shells before they could burrow into the sand. They made good eating later. Alasdair and a friend fished for trout in one of the lochs, and brought back more than enough for a feast in the cabin we had hired. A good-sized brown trout straight out of a loch into a pan must be the tastiest fish dish of all; washed down with a little whisky half and half with water, or a glass of wine, it puts everything right. Afterwards, we walked down to the Mishnish where live music, laughter, great hospitality and friendship surrounded us. Those few days were balm for us all.

On the third evening, just before dinner, the doctor in Salen phoned me. Could I stand in for her? She needed a few days off for family reasons, and had heard I was on the island. There wouldn't be much work, she said – she had seen all her 'chronics' in the last few days, so there would be no planned home visits, the tourist season was almost over and it would only be for three days at the most. She needed someone at short notice. Seeing as I was already on the island, I could start tomorrow.

I looked at the family. They knew the look. Our two students had to be back at university and college on the following day anyway, so I wouldn't be spoiling their short holiday. They shrugged their shoulders. Mairi shrugged hers too. I knew she wanted to go home, but three more days of the island life did appeal. So, against her better judgment, we moved to Salen after breakfast the next morning.

Dr Summerville was delighted to see me, and was off on the ferry to the mainland within an hour, leaving me with her practice to look after. It wasn't a hardship. Annie, her receptionist and Liz, the practice nurse, were professional and capable, and could probably, between them, have run the practice without me, but of course that would have been illegal. The doctor had left me a few notes on patients who might be a problem, but there was no one, as far as she knew, who needed urgent day-to-day attention.

There were two extra notes. One was about an aircraft that had gone missing a few days before. The only airstrip on the island is just south of Salen village, where the river Forsa meets the sea. The homely Glen Forsa Hotel served as the airport 'terminal', although none of its users would apply such a grand description to it. The small aircraft that used its grass runway transported estate owners and their guests to Glasgow, and the occasional flying farmer or fisherman. The rest of us took the ferry to Oban from Craignure a few miles down the road.

The previous day, a light aircraft had taken off from Glen Forsa with only the pilot aboard. It had turned south, then west, and simply disappeared. There had been no trace of the plane and no radio mayday message. Everyone on Mull had been asked to look out for wreckage, but it was thought more likely that it had been lost at sea than on land. Dr Summerville's note simply said to look out for anything unusual while I drove about: if the plane had crashed on land, it would almost certainly have been on her patch.

You might think that a crashed plane would be easily seen on an island, but it is densely forested, and tracks are few and well spaced out. A plane could nose-dive through the canopy, which would hide it from anyone searching from above. There was little chance of anyone stumbling on it by chance. It was the end of August: the early summer visitors who walked through the forests had gone, and as this was the height of the midge season, few would brave them now. Any of the year-round hill climbers would be on the bare and midge-free slopes of Ben More, the highest mountain on Mull, to the south and west, so they wouldn't come across the plane if it were in a woodland grave.

The second note was about a new landowner who had arrived in the district to claim his inheritance. Dr Summerville's concern wasn't his status in society, but the manner in which he treated her and her staff. He had only been on the island for a month, but was already a 'heart-sink' patient. All doctors know about 'heart-sinks', and I think the feeling these patients induce when they walk into a room can be guessed at.

Please don't take this description the wrong way. There are many patients who need a lot of help, very often, and whom we may see every few weeks with many complaints. They take up a lot of our time, but they are not 'heart-sinks'. 'Heart-sinks' are the ones that order us around, always seem to be angry about something and take their anger out on us and our staff. They also don't subscribe to the rules we try to make so that our jobs flow more easily and more effectively. They want to see us on their terms, rather than ours, whether or not their problems are as urgent as those of the rest of our patients.

From Dr Summerville's note this man was a double-rated 'heart-sink'. He wouldn't attend the surgery like everyone else: his new status in society meant that when he needed personal attention, it was at a time and a place convenient for him. Other people were less important, regardless of their needs. In her note, Dr Summerville asked me not to be at his beck and call, and to try to discipline him, if at all possible, to come to the surgery at the proper time if he had problems.

His name was Lord Drumfinn. He had bought or inherited, no one on Mull was sure which, Drumfinn Castle, the family seat of his clan, which was reputed to have been founded by Fingal himself, the ancient giant of the cave on Staffa. This bemused the Mull residents, as they didn't know of a clan Finn. They were MacLeans to a man, and Finn didn't sound right to them. Still, they welcomed him as a newcomer who might spend some money doing up the old place, and they offered him the correct respect accorded to one who might employ them and spread a little money around.

Mairi and I settled into Dr Summerville's comfortable home that evening after a surgery of two patients. She had left us groceries and milk and a welcome note asking us to make ourselves at home: she had set a fire before leaving, and Mairi and I were sitting by the blazing logs watching the television after dinner, when the phone rang.

The woman's voice at the other end was anxious and high pitched. I recognised it at once. It was Molly Gould's. She was the wife of Professor Harry Gould, a good friend for many years. Professor of mechanical engineering at Glasgow University, his 'flash' desalination process still provides the Middle East with its drinking water to this day. He could have lived like a millionaire, but he had other priorities, and they were all on Mull. The island fulfilled all Harry's needs. He had a house in Tobermory where he and Molly spent all the time they could, when university and research duties allowed.

'Tom, I'm glad I've caught you,' Molly said. 'Harry went out to the Ba this afternoon and he hasn't come back. I expected him half an hour ago, and he is never late. What do you think I should do? Who is there near the Ba who could find him for me?'

I'd better explain here about Mull. It's an island of three parts, with three medical practices. At the north end is Tobermory, whose doctor looks after the town and the small surrounding villages and crofts. In the middle is Salen, sitting at the eastern end of an isthmus on the Sound of Mull, facing the mainland. The road through the isthmus from Salen to Gruline, on the west coast on Loch Na Keal, is only two miles long. The Ba, famous for being the shortest salmon river in Scotland, runs alongside it for the last mile, emptying into the loch. The Salen practice looks after the middle portion of the island, east and west, down to Craignure, with its pier for the Oban ferry. To the south-west of Craignure is the 37-mile-long peninsula, the Ross of Mull, leading to the Isle of Iona. In the middle of the Ross is Bunessan, the village in which the doctors in the third practice serve the people of the Ross and Iona. The three practices work well together: it is an ideal system for both patients and doctors.

I knew that Harry's other passion, apart from Molly, of course, was his fishing. He knew every inch of the mile-long Ba, where the fish were, what fly to use on what type of night and at which time of year to catch them. If he had gone out that afternoon, he must have known that there was a good sea trout run: the best time to catch them was in the early evening.

'Don't worry, Molly,' I told her. 'I'll go myself. I know his car, and it will be parked near where he is fishing. It's easily seen from the road. I'll phone from the box at Gruline when I find him.'

She thanked me, I told Mairi what had happened, then went out to my car.

I was at Harry's car within ten minutes of the call, and pulling him out of the river within another two minutes. I had found him, in the semi-darkness, crawling about on all fours in a shallow area formed by a bank of gravel washed down by the last rains. He couldn't stand up. When I tried to bring him to his feet, he lurched to one side.

'Hi Tom,' he had said when he saw me. 'Glad you came. I'm too dizzy to stand. I think I've overdone the tobacco.'

He made a good diagnostician for a mechanical engineer, I thought. Scotland has great scenery and wonderful scope for fishing, but you have to pay the price for it. In the west highlands and islands that price is the ferocious midge. Harry had taken his favourite repellent with him; tonight it had worked well, but at another price. Midges don't like the reek of pipe tobacco and stay away, but only as long as the person is smoking it. As soon as the smoke dies down, they swing into attack. Nowhere on the body is safe. They go for your face, hair, neck, ears, backs of your hands, and if they get inside your clothing, they are agonisingly itchy. Harry had had to smoke a full pouch of tobacco over the four hours he was standing in the river to keep them at bay.

That is well over the toxic dose of nicotine and carbon monoxide for a human. Their blood levels in Harry might even have killed a midge daring to bite him. They nearly killed Harry.

The first symptom of nicotine toxicity is dizziness. If you keep on smoking after that, you become so dizzy that you have to lie down and shut your eyes to try to dispel the feeling that the world is spinning ever faster around you.

Lying down and shutting your eyes in the middle of a fast-flowing river in the approaching darkness is not to be recommended, which is why Harry had to settle for being on all fours and sticking to the only part of the river in which, in that posture, his head would be above water. His fast-approaching problem was that the Ba is tidal, and his gravel bed would be six feet deeper within an hour or so. He had long arms and legs, but not as long as that.

I bundled Harry into my car and phoned Molly from the phone box nearby. I told her that Harry was safe and I was taking him back to the Salen doctor's house to get him warm and dry and to give him an injection of stemetil to stop the dizziness. We would find a way of getting him home later that night, and someone would deliver his own car the next morning.

About two hours later, Harry was fit to go home, and one of his neighbours from Tobermory collected him. Mairi had two beautiful sea trout to clean and put in the fridge, and Harry promised to come back the next evening with Molly to enjoy them with us.

The next morning started badly. A Mrs MacLean called in to say that she was bringing her husband Archie into the surgery, as he had had a 'wee accident' with his tractor. Could I see him fairly urgently, as he was champing at the bit? He was doing his silage, you see, and he had to get the rest of it done today. The forecast was for a dry spell for the next three days, and it was crucial that I get him back on his feet before the rains came and ruined the crop.

I was used to calls like this and was expecting that Archie would have a minor injury that Liz and I could sort out together. A few minutes later, Mrs MacLean arrived with the casualty. She had brought him the five miles from their farm on the west coast in the back of their pick-up. He hadn't been able to bend himself enough to get into the car. He was still in his farm clothes – at least what was left of them. The right trouser leg was torn from ankle to mid-thigh, revealing a mud-laden leg. There were strange mud marks over his right hip, stretching across the front of his old tweed jacket to his left shoulder. He was stiff, so that Liz and I had considerable difficulty shifting him off the back of the pick-up into a wheelchair and into the surgery.

As we did so, Archie told me his story. He had been out early with his tractor and trailer in the silage field, when something had gone wrong with the link between the two. He climbed off the tractor to sort it out, leaving the engine running and in neutral. Just as he stepped down, his dog, which had been riding behind him, suddenly sprang forward – Archie thought he might have seen a hare – and knocked against the gear lever. It had been faulty for weeks, and Archie had meant to sort it, but had never found the time. Now in gear, the tractor leapt forward. Archie was just in front of the main wheel, and it simply rolled over him.

'It was lucky we were in a boggy part of the field,' Archie said, 'otherwise I might have broken something.'

I wasn't so sure about that.

The strange mud marks on his clothes exactly matched red marks on the skin underneath, produced by the tread of the tractor tyre. I couldn't believe he hadn't broken a few ribs or suffered some internal organ injury. He definitely had crushed thigh and stomach muscles, and that worried me.

'Can you fix me up so I can get back to the silage?' Archie asked. 'All I need is to get rid of this stiffness. What about a wee bit of massage, or some ointment?'

'No way,' I told him. 'At the least you have crushed muscles. In the next 24 hours you are at high risk of going into shock as the chemicals from the damage are released from the muscles into your circulation. You may have internal injuries, too, that you don't know about yet. You will have to go to Oban on the next ferry and go to hospital for a day for observation. I can't let you stay here. What could we do on the island if you go into shock tonight, after the last boat has gone?'

'But I'm OK,' he protested. 'I got up immediately and ran after the tractor to stop it going over the cliff at the end of my field. If I hadn't done that, it would have been in the sea. And I don't think it crushed me too badly, because the ground was so soft. Do you know those Tom and Jerry cartoons on the television, Doctor?'

'Yes.'

'Well, it was like that in the field. When I got up, I left a perfect outline of myself in the mud – it was about a foot deep. Have a look at it later, if you like.'

Medical emergencies on an island are never simple, I thought.

'It's not your condition now that I'm worried about,' I repeated. 'It's tonight. I can't take the risk of keeping you here.'

I thought he was going to protest again, but Liz waded in on my behalf.

'Right, Uncle Archie,' she told him, like a schoolmistress would scold a naughty child, 'you are going, and that's that.'

'Uncle?' I asked.

'She is my niece,' said Archie, 'and she terrifies me. It's fine Doctor, I'll go.'

Liz grinned at me.

'Result,' she said.

Annie phoned the hospital for me, and an ambulance met the ferry in Oban. The surgeon phoned me about Archie an hour later. Amazingly, there were no broken bones, but he did have soft-tissue crush injuries and would need to stay. If he had a peaceful night, he would be home on the midday ferry tomorrow. I doubted whether he would manage the silage, but I needn't have worried. His dutiful niece rang round the MacLean clan that evening, and three volunteer, though amateur, silage men knocked on Mrs MacLean's door before breakfast.

I was disturbed before breakfast, too. Lady Drumfinn called from the castle. Her husband, Lord Drumfinn, had developed a severe headache and was feeling sick: could I come at once? When I asked if she could bring him down to the surgery, she said, 'Certainly not. He is far too sick to get out of his bed.' There was a strong hint that she was outraged that I should ask such a thing. I needed to come at once: she thought it might be a developing stroke.

I thought of the warning note left by Dr Summerville, but remembering the story of the boy who cried wolf once too often – it is a parable hammered into every medical student during training. So I gathered my things and, leaving my breakfast untouched on the table, started on the journey to the castle. Mairi was not amused. She had had to clear away uneaten breakfasts many times in the past and had thought that these times had gone.

The castle was at the end of a half-mile of rough road. At

one time it must have been imposing, an impressive show of a Victorian factory owner's vast profits. Now the road needed surfacing, the gardens weeding, the roof slating, the windows painting, the walls patching. I walked up to the massive wooden front door and yanked at the brass bell pull at its side. A man sitting in a chair by the window to the right of the door must have seen me, but he didn't budge. I waited a few seconds and yanked again. I could hear a loud clanging from far inside, presumably the direct result of my efforts. Still the door didn't open and the man remained in his seat. After a third yank, I heard a key turn in a lock and a bolt being withdrawn, and the door slowly opened.

A tall, bald, thin, almost cadaverous man in a classic butler's uniform stood in front of me. He was wiping wet hands with a cloth, and was sweating and breathless. I supposed he had run a long way from some task in the kitchen. It didn't seem right for a butler, if that was who he was.

'You will be the doctor, sir?' he asked.

'Yes,' I replied. With a stethoscope and bag in my hand, I wondered how he would have reacted if I had said 'No, I'm the plumber'. Of course, I would never have been so rude.

'His Lordship is in the drawing room,' he replied. 'Please follow me.'

I walked after him into the room on the right, where I came face to face with the man sitting in the window seat. He didn't look ill. There was a glass on a small table beside his chair. It was filled with a red liquid, through which there was swirls of black. I guessed it was a Bloody Mary laced with Worcester sauce. A hangover cure.

Lord Drumfinn didn't get up, didn't smile, didn't offer to shake my hand, didn't introduce himself or expect me to do so either. He waved his right hand imperiously at the poor butler-cum-kitchen-hand, who flashed me what I thought was an apologetic trace of a smile, and left the room.

'I have a hell of a headache,' he said, 'and I want you to examine me, to make sure it isn't high blood pressure. I've had trouble with it before.'

I choked back my natural response and smiled at him.

'I'm Doctor Smith. I thought you might at least like to know my name before we begin,' I said. Then I walked over to his chair and bent over him to take his pulse. The smell of stale whisky was overpowering. He was dehydrated, his pulse was bounding, his eyes red, and the hand I wasn't holding was shaking in his lap. His blood pressure was a little low, in accord with his dehydration and his hangover.

I stood up and looked at him. He had been rude and insensitive, but I was determined not to be rude back. I decided to be cool and collected.

'As far as I can tell, Lord Drumfinn,' I said, 'all you are suffering from is the drink you had last night. I'm not going to examine you until you are completely sober, and only then in the surgery, so I'll see you there this afternoon at two o'clock. It's far more efficient to see you there than here, where I don't have the equipment to assess you fully.'

I turned to go out, and he leapt from his chair, grabbed me by the elbow and spun me round to face him. It was expertly done. I had felt that grip before.

'I won't see you there, Smith. If I want to see you, I'll see you here, and you will come at a time of my choosing.'

I looked at him closely. I didn't recognise him, but I did recognise his accent, his grip and his attitude. Johannesburg.

'Take it or leave it, Drumfinn. Until you give me my title I won't give you yours. And I won't be back here unless there is a real medical emergency. Like everyone else, if you need me, you come to me. I have more important things to do than be your private medical attendant.'

I didn't wait for the butler to see me out.

I was raging all the way back to the surgery, but I was also intrigued. I had to know who this man really was. I had looked after titled patients before, every one pleasant, polite, respectful, and they had waited their turn in the Collintrae surgery along with everyone else. This man's behaviour was boorish, but what kind of boor was he?

The rest of that day passed without incident. Naturally, Lord Drumfinn didn't turn up at two. Mrs MacLean let me know that Archie was home after an uneventful night in the hospital. Liz and I went to see him, to make sure he would stay off work for a few days. We found him standing in a field, leaning on a ram's-horn-handled crook, whistling at his collie in a Herculean effort to pen five obstinate blackface sheep. He was still stiff and in pain, but irrepressible.

'Hi, Doc,' he said, smiling. 'The dog trials are on Saturday: we'll be OK for them, won't we?'

How could I say no? Then I saw it. The outline of a man immediately in front of me in the grass. It was like Tom and Jerry. Archie had been pushed about a foot deep into the soft earth. There were the tractor wheel tracks going over his outline, then carrying on down a slope towards a stake-and-wire fence about 100 yards away. The ground was muddier in that lower part of the field, so I could see the holes in it made by a man's boots. The two parallel tracks, of tyres and boots, ended just two yards from the fence. Beyond the fence was a sheer drop of about 300 feet into the sea far below.

Archie had left his tractor chasing pretty late. Two seconds more and he and his tractor, but not his dog (a much wiser animal) would have been in Loch Na Keal. He didn't seem in the least the worse for the near miss.

That evening the sea trout were delicious, as were the fresh vegetables brought from Molly's garden, the raspberries and the oatmeal of the cranachan, and the glass of Isle of Mull whisky from the Tobermory distillery. The four of us, sitting around the fire after our meal, pondered on the self-sufficiency of the islands, and how fortunate we were to be here.

I turned the conversation to Lord Drumfinn.

'He is no more a lord than I am,' Harry said, laughing. 'I'm at least a fourth-generation Muilleach, and I've never heard of clan Finn. As far as I know, the family name for the Drumfinn estate was Matheson, and the last one died three years ago, somewhere abroad. The lawyers have taken a long time chasing up his heirs. We wondered if this guy just assumed that all estate owners were lords. He might not know any better, being South African. Anyway, who cares? If he wants to call himself a lord, let him. As long as he pays his bills, and he doesn't cause offence.'

'Well, he does cause offence,' I said, 'and he is expecting to get the equivalent of private medical care for free. He is using his title, spurious or genuine, to put himself above us hoi polloi.'

I told Harry and Molly about my morning. Harry was intrigued. He was especially interested in the elbow-pinching.

'I'd like to know his background,' he said. 'Do you know his family name? It must be in the records.'

'He is simply down as Drumfinn on the card I was given, and his records haven't yet come through from his previous doctor, but I'm sure I can find out.'

'I can probably do that better than you,' Harry said. 'I have connections.'

Two days later, Mairi and I drove home. We were sorry to leave Mull, but were delighted to be back in the Stinchar Valley.

The next day, Harry phoned.

'Drumfinn,' he said. 'Real name Hendrik van Matthiessen. South African national; occupation in South Africa policeman, but not your normal bobby. Claims he is the distant cousin several generations back of the last Matheson. Bought an old lord of the manor title at an auction. Need to know more?'

Yes, as a matter of fact I did. The name rang a bell. James M of L had left me a copy of the letter, seven years before, from the South African authorities in which they said they didn't want me back. I'm not a very tidy person, but Mairi, business trained, files everything away meticulously. We found it in minutes and read the signature at the bottom. H v Matthiessen. I had made the connection: I wondered if he had, but decided that he hadn't. How could he possibly link a low-life country bumpkin doctor like me with a man he had decided was a danger to South Africa?

I wondered what he was doing, hiding himself away on Mull, as far away from South Africa as he could get, and under a different name. And where he was totally out of place and out of sympathy, too, with the locals.

I decided to phone the one man I knew who might be interested in him. Billy the banker. We had kept in touch through the years with Christmas cards and the odd phone call. This one was longer than usual. Billy said he would look into it. He asked me how I knew Drumfinn's Afrikaans name: I told him about

Harry Gould. He laughed and asked me to pass on his good wishes. It is a small world, I thought. And an intriguing one, in the real sense of the word.

A month later, Dr Summerville telephoned. Lord Drumfinn had been arrested. No one knew why, but there were rumours that he might be deported to South Africa. I never heard the full story, but a year later, the British tabloids carried a story of a South African pretender to a British peerage who had been sentenced to 42 years in jail in Johannesburg. The trial had been held in secret, and involved blackmail, extortion and even possibly murder, all involving the government of the time. It was all rumour and innuendo, but if the story is correct, he is still in jail. Drumfinn castle is now a luxury hotel, but when we go to Mull, we still prefer the Mishnish and the Western Isles.

Oh, and the missing plane? Two years after our stint in Salen, a party of birdwatchers was scanning the treetops for eagles in the forest about four miles from the Glen Forsa airstrip. They found more than they expected. Stuck high in the branches of one of the trees was the body of the pilot. There was no trace of the plane. It was assumed that he had decided to jump out and let the plane continue over the sea until it ran out of fuel. He had no parachute.

Real life is like that. We will never know why the poor pilot decided to jump. Or why 'Drumfinn' did what he did, or even what he did. Agatha Christie would have tied up all the ends, but this isn't detective fiction, so I have to leave them loose.

EPILOGUE

With the story of my three days locum on the Isle of Mull, *Going Loco* ends. That was the autumn of 1984. I was 45 then, and my future life, I thought, would be divided fairly equally between writing and locum work. My days of charging around the world in medical research would be over, and I could settle into a fairly comfortable rural life, enjoying my beloved Stinchar Valley.

I kept in touch with James M of L until he retired: the company that took over Huizens honoured him by naming its British headquarters Montrose House. He deserved it. I'm still friendly with Willem, whose career skyrocketed into the stratosphere of big business. Laden with honours, he is happily retired into the English countryside. He spends much of his time and his pension with the World Health Organisation, fighting the tropical diseases that are still killing millions in Africa, South America and the Far East. Years ago, I put him in touch with Tennyson.

Tennyson still struggles with authority: given well-deserved promotion and responsibility when Nelson Mandela became president, he fell foul of President Tabo Mbeki's crazy attitude to HIV and AIDS. He is keeping his head down, but we still manage to correspond. I'm sure that Willem, and maybe Billy the banker too, should take some credit that Tennyson is still alive. Mr van Matthiessen is 25 years through his 42-year sentence: the change of government in South Africa didn't help him. Naturally, we don't correspond.

You might have thought that the next 25 years would have been quieter and less eventful, with little of interest to write about. It wasn't like that at all.

The conference reporting work expanded: Mairi and I continued to travel the world producing newspapers, articles, audio-visuals and booklets on meetings. As an independent doctor with a pharmaceutical background, I became an overseer of clinical trials and assessor of reports. There were good times and bad. Mairi and I divided cities into 'been-tos' and 'go-back-tos'. Jerusalem, New Orleans and Geneva (surprisingly) were definite 'been-tos', and Boston, Sydney, Budapest and Barcelona were sure-fire 'go-back-tos'. Very good days in Minneapolis and Cincinnati made up for hairy days in Los Angeles and Houston. Cairo and Istanbul were fantastic; Mexico City daunting and dangerous. Moscow I don't know about: when I applied for a visa to attend a meeting there, it was refused. Somewhere in the Kremlin are three photographs of me taken in 1988, with '*NIET*' stamped across them. I don't know why the Soviets didn't like me.

I still work a few days a month in a practice in the west of Scotland, and combine it with weekly newspaper columns. As a member of the Medical Journalists' Association, I chew the fat regularly with old friends and colleagues who have enjoyed similar double careers in medicine and writing. My MJA contacts led me to the *Guardian*, for whom I now write the Saturday

Magazine's Doctor Doctor column. *Guardian* readers are an eclectic lot, and my weekly emails from them are an education and an eye-opener. They are very special.

Manu retired last year after more than twenty years of practice in rural Worcestershire. His adoring patients gave him a wonderful and well-deserved send-off. We see each other every few months, and once a year we take a long holiday together. Next month it's Australia, Indonesia, Singapore and Thailand. One day we will visit his beloved India.

Medicine has changed in the training of student doctors and in its techniques and in management, but the fundamental relationship between caring doctors and their patients remains. Our new generation of younger doctors are every bit as good as we 'auld yins', and they have the added bonus of many more facilities and much more effective treatments. I'm impressed and delighted with them. I wonder, when they reach my stage in life, what they will find to write about.

ALSO BY DOCTOR TOM:

A SEASIDE PRACTICE
Tales of a Scottish Country Doctor

£8.99   978-1-906021-79-5

"It's all in a day's work for the James Herriot of human beings…"
Glasgow Evening Times

"An entertaining and insightful read…" *Daily Express*

"Characters and cases unfold in this delightful book that reads like *All Creatures Great and Small*" *The Glaswegian*

"Dr Tom Smith is an engaging storyteller who invites the reader to sit back in a comfortable chair and slip into a slower, more innocent world" *The Glasgow Herald*

When he arrives to take up his first posting as a GP in Collintrae, a small fishing village on the West coast of Scotland, young Tom Smith isn't quite sure what to expect. Certainly, nothing in his medical training could have prepared him for what he finds – a baker with nine lives, Mad Maggie in the River Muck, and a gaggle of giggling nuns, to name but a few of the extraordinary cases that he comes up against in his first few years there.

Heartwarming, gloriously eccentric, Dr Tom's stories will touch everyone with their easy comic charm. They capture the beauty of the Scottish lowlands, the joys and sorrows of its inhabitants, and the richly rewarding experiences of life as a Scottish country doctor. Whoever thought that a job could be so wildly unpredictable…